Danish Studies in Classical Archaeology
ACTA HYPERBOREA
1

© Collegium Hyperboreum and Museum Tusculanum Press

COLLEGIUM HYPERBOREUM
c/o Institute of Classical and Prehistoric Archaeology,
Vandkunsten 5, DK – 1467 Copenhagen K.

Published in 1988 by
MUSEUM TUSCULANUM PRESS
Njalsgade 94, DK – 2300 Copenhagen S

Printed in Denmark by
Special-Trykkeriet Viborg a-s

ISBN 87-7289-061-4
ISSN 0904-2067

Cover: Decoration on base of Protocorinthian clay box.
About 700 B.C.

Danish Studies in Classical Archaeology
ACTA HYPERBOREA

1

East and West

Cultural Relations in the Ancient World

Edited
by
Tobias Fischer-Hansen

Museum Tusculanum Press · Copenhagen 1988

CONTENTS

TOBIAS FISCHER-HANSEN, Preface 7

ERIK HALLAGER, The Roundel in the Minoan Administrative System. A Summary 9

LONE WRIEDT SØRENSEN, Greek Pottery from the Geometric to the Archaic Period found on Cyprus 12

LENE ANDERSEN, Greek Epic and Greek Mythology and their Links with The Near East. 33

JOHN LUND, Prolegomena to a Study of the Phoenician/Punic Colonization of Tunisia 44

FINN O. HVIDBERG-HANSEN, The Pyrgi Texts seen in an East-West Perspective 58

HELLE SALSKOV ROBERTS, Some Observations on Etruscan Bowls with Supports in the shape of Caryatids or Adorned by Reliefs . 69

ANNETTE RATHJE, Manners and Customs in Central Italy in the Orientalizing Period: Influence from the Near East 81

JETTE CHRISTIANSEN, Some Early Etruscan Revetment Plaques in the Ny Carlsberg Glyptotek 91

MARIE-LOUISE THOMSEN, The Wisdom of the Chaldaeans. Mesopotamien Magic as Conceived by Classical Authors 93

ELISABETH NEDERGAARD, The Four Sons of Phraates IV in Rome... 102

SANNE HOUBY-NIELSEN, Augustus and the Hellenistic Kings. A Note on the Augustan Propaganda 116

GUNHILD PLOUG, East Syrian Art of 1st Century B.C.-2nd Century A.D. 129

BENTE KIILERICH, Graeco-Roman Influence on Gandhāra Sculpture 140

ANNE KROMANN, Western Features in the Kushan Coinage 151

ADAM BÜLOW-JACOBSEN, Mons Claudianus. Roman Granite-quarry and Station on the Road to the Red Sea. 159

ABBREVATIONS 166

PREFACE
by TOBIAS FISCHER-HANSEN

The first volume of the ACTA HYPERBOREA contains the papers of a seminar held at the University of Copenhagen, 22-24th April 1987, dealing with the reciprocity of contacts and influences between the eastern and western world in the Greco-Roman periods; old and new archaeological, and other, evidence of exchange and interplay between the Mediterranean cultures.

The choice of this subject should be seen in light of the fact that a number of Danish scholars have been and are today engaged in this field of research. It was appropriate that the seminar took place on the 75th anniversary of the publication of the first monumental and detailed analysis of the oriental influence on western art: – Frederik Poulsen, Der Orient und die frühgriechische Kunst (1912). The view of Herbert Hoffmann,[1] that to trace Greek decorative motifs in Near Eastern art is no longer fashionable, is not borne out by these *Acta*. However, the evidence of East-West contacts is obviously now more often seen in a wider cultural context.

Danish scholars have a long tradition for research into the relations between the Near East and the Greek and Etrusco-Italic world, based also on excavations in the Levant[2] and in Greece, where Rhodes is of paramount importance in this connection.[3]

Aspects of the western cultural influence on the East was the subject of a number of papers, serving also the purpose of showing the dialectics of the subject. The Hellenistic and Roman periods are here of great importance, and the pronounced place this period has in Danish re-

---

1. *Hephaistos* 1, 1979, 64.
2. Cfr. P. J. Riis, 200 Years of Danish Scholarship in the Study of Oriental Influence in the Greek – Roman World. Talk given at the seminar, now published in *Meddelelser fra Klassisk Arkæologisk Forening* (Copenhagen) 9, 1988, 3-17 (in Danish). For Hama: *Hamā* II,1-IV,3. Copenhagen 1948-1987; P. J. Riis, *Ḥamā. Danske arkæologers udgravninger i Syrien 1930-38*. Copenhagen 1987, with full bibliography 173-174. For Tell Sukas: *Sūkās* I-VIII. Copenhagen 1971-1986.
3. *Lindos*, I-IV,1. Copenhagen 1931-1984; S. Trolle, An Egyptian Head from Camirus, Rhodes, *ActaArch* 49, 1978, 139-150; M.-L. Buhl, Eleven Scarabs and one Fragment of a Faience Figurine Acquired at Lindos, *ActaArch* 56, 1985, 197-200. K. F. Kinch, *Fouilles de Vroulia*. Berlin 1914.

search has to some extent its background in the Palmyrene collections of the Ny Carlsberg Glyptotek.

The subject of the seminar was found well suited to an interdisciplinary approach, and although most of the papers were given by Classical archaeologists, several themes were treated by Classical and Semitic philologists, historians, and Near Eastern archaeologists. It is obvious that not all periods are covered. The seminar itself, however, was more richly faceted, as some of the papers read there are not published here.[4]

The initiative in arranging the seminar was taken by Pia Guldager, John Lund, Marjatta Nielsen, Annette Rathje, Jan Zahle and the editor. I would like to thank my colleagues for their help. The Danish Research Council for the Humanities generously gave a grant towards the cost of the seminar. The publication of the papers was made possible by grants from The University of Copenhagen, Ny Carlsbergfondet, Bikubefonden, and G. E. C. Gads Fond. The maps in the publication were drawn by Poul Christensen of the Institute of Classical Archaeology, Copenhagen. For this support, and for the positive interest of all participants the editor and the members of the organizing committee tender their warm thanks.

University of Copenhagen
Institute of Classical Archaeology
Vandkunsten 5
DK-1467 Copenhagen K

---

[4]. Tobias Fischer-Hansen, Mycenaean and Related Ivory Carvings. Traditions of Craftmanship in East and West. Jan Zahle, The Hellenization of Lycia during the 6th-4th Centuries B.C. (To be published in *Lycia* II. Copenhagen 1988 (forthcoming)). Marjatta Nielsen, The Orient and Etruria in the Classical and Hellenistic Periods. Anne Marie Nielsen, The Hellenistic Ruler-Portrait between East and West. Dan Potts, Points of Contact between Eastern Arabia and the Greco-Roman World. Hans Erik Mathiesen, Parthian Sculpture in Iran. An Outline. (To be published in *Studies in Ancient History Presented to Rudi Thomsen*. Århus 1988). Karin Weinholt, The Aniconic Proscription and Figurative Art. Some Outlines from Talmudic Judaism in the Encounter between East and West.

THE ROUNDEL IN THE MINOAN ADMINISTRATIVE SYSTEM*
by ERIK HALLAGER

A roundel is a small clay disc with one or more seal impressions along the edge and more frequently than not inscribed with symbols or regular signs in Linear A on one or two sides. (*Plate* 1a). Such roundels are independent documents within the Minoan administrative system. They vary in size from 1.8 cms to 7.6 cms in diameter and the number of impressions found along the edge varies from 1 to 15. The space for impressions of seals along the edge of the roundel is better utilized the larger the roundel is. This connection between size and number of seal impressions is not fortuitous and one must conclude that the administrators knew before the roundel was made, how many times the seal was going to be impressed.

The inscriptions on the roundels – when they can be understood – are ideograms, which are with one certain exception never followed by numerals and it is therefore surmised that the number of seal impressions is quantifying the ideogram. (HALLAGER 1988).

From a number of analyses it can be demonstrated that two "parties" are involved in the transactions expressed by the roundels, where the one part is the administration and the other part an "individual" who may also be an administrator (HALLAGER 1987c). It is always the "individual" who sets his seal on the edge of the roundel,[1] and it may thus be conjectured that the "individual" with each stamp of his seal recognizes the receipt of one unit of what is mentioned on the roundel. In other words the roundels may have functioned as receipts for commodities or services delivered from the administration to "individuals". There exist no exact parallels to the Minoan Roundel, but one does find in the Ur III Dynasty from the end of the 3rd Millennium B.C. a large amount of simple sealed documents which are different types of receipts and

---

* This paper was originally presented at the BSA Centenary Conference in Manchester, 1986 and it will be fully published in the proceedings from that conference, see HALLAGER 1987b.

1. On four exceptional roundels from Knossos are also found seal impressions of the administration, see HALLAGER 1987a.

which roughly go after the following formula: "He receives at a certain date a fixed number of items, seal of receiver" (*Plate* 1b) and the tablet is (when sealed) invariably sealed by the one who receives the items in his hands.² The Minoan Roundels may possibly reflect some of the receipt-types found in the Ur III bureaucracy (HALLAGER 1987b). If so the main difference between the two types of documents is physical: where the Mesopotamians wrote the actual number of items on the tablets, the Minoans who received goods wrote the number themselves by impressing their seal the agreed number of times along the edge of the roundel.

This possible parallel to a Near Eastern administration does not mean that one can equate the two administrations. It is, however, known that Minoan Crete had close contacts to the countries around the Eastern Mediterranean and that the island belonged to the large family of bureaucracies which had an extensive use of sealings in their administration. It may therefore be considered a possibility that some basic ideas had been adopted in Minoan Crete, where they were developed individually – as is, for example, the case with script – and where a detail like receipts may have developed into the unique document of the roundel.

Østersøgade 4
DK-8200 Århus N

---

2. The quotation is from STEINKELLER 1977, 42. For a more detailed description of sealed receipt-types with examples, HALLO 1958, 69-108.

BIBLIOGRAPHY

CMS	*Corpus der Minoischen und Mykenischen Siegel*
GORILA, 1-5	L. GODART & J.-P. OLIVIER, *Recueil des inscriptions en Linéaire* A, 1-5 (Études Crétoises XXI, 1-5), Paris 1976-1985.
HALLAGER 1987a	E. HALLAGER, "The Knossos Roundels", *BSA* 82, 55-70.
HALLAGER 1987b	E. HALLAGER, "The Roundel in the Minoan Administrative System" in *Problems in Geek Prehistory. Proceedings of the BSA Centenary Conference, Manchester 1986*. Eds. L. French and K. Wardle. Bristol. Forthcoming.
HALLAGER 1987c	E. HALLAGER, "On the Track of Minoan Bureaucrats and their "Clients", in ΕΙΛΑΠΙΝΗ ΤΟΜΟΣ ΤΙΜΗΤΙΚΟΣ ΓΙΑ ΤΟΝ ΚΑΘΗΓΗΤΗ ΝΙΚΟΛΑΟ ΠΛΑΤΩΝΑ. Heraklion, 347-353.
HALLAGER 1988	E. HALLAGER, "The Use of Seals on the Minoan Roundel" in *Fragen und Probleme der Bronzezeitlichen ägäischen Glyptik. 3. Internationale Marburger Symposium*, (*CMS*, Beiheft 3). Marburg. Forthcoming.
HALLO 1958	W. W. HALLO, "Contributions to Neo-Sumerian", *HUCA* XXIX, 69-108.
STEINKELLER 1977	P. STEINKELLER, "Seal Practice in the Ur III Period", in *Seals and Sealings in the Ancient Near East*. Eds. McG Gibson & R. D. Biggs. Malibu.

GREEK POTTERY FOUND IN CYPRUS
by LONE WRIEDT SØRENSEN

In order to establish reliable evidence for the existence of contacts between two geographically separated cultures at a given time it is necessary, in the absence of other evidence, to analyse the occurrance of finds which have travelled between the two places.

The simplest way to perform an analysis of this kind is to count the number of finds originating in one particular culture, which have been found in the geographical sphere of another, and to hypothezise that there has been regular contact between the two cultures if the number seems sufficiently large.

The purpose of the present paper is to examine the relation between Cyprus and Greece in the first half of the first millennium B.C. by using such a type of analysis, and in particular to examine the number of ceramic finds of Greek origin in Cyprus (*fig.* 1).[1]

At least three kinds of information relevant to the present study are inherent in Greek pottery. Firstly, the dating of the pottery in question can often indicate the approximate time of the contact between two areas. Secondly, the assignment of the pottery to local production centers in the Greek area may provide information about a region or regions of Greece with which Cyprus had contact at a specific time. Finally, the range of shapes of particular classes of wares can serve as supporting evidence for contact, since the presence of a large variety of pottery forms from a certain period and place excludes, to some extent, the possibility that a concentration of ceramic finds could be merely a coincidence reflecting abnormal find conditions or a single contact occasion. A high count of certain vessel shapes may, on the other hand, provide us with information about preferences on the consumer's market and/or help to establish a picture both of the production at the Greek ceramic centers and the pattern of distribution in various parts of the Mediterranean world.

---

*J.N. Coldstream's article, The Geometic and Archaic Periods in *Archaeology in Cyprus* 1960-1985. Nicosia 1984 was not available in Denmark when this paper was written.

1. Transport amphoras are not included in this study since specific problems are connected with them.

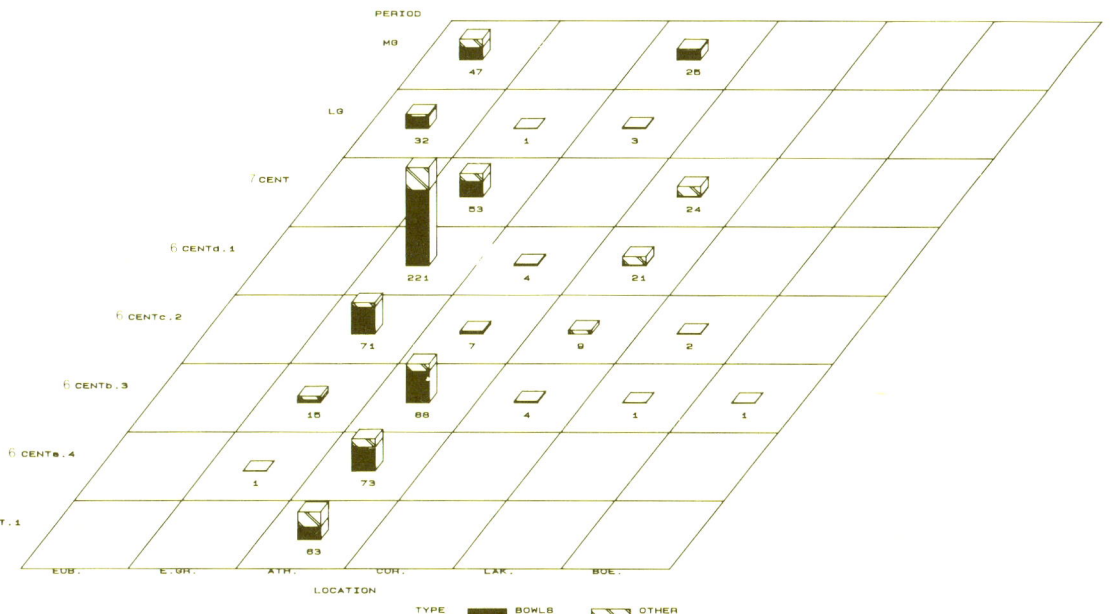

Fig. 1. Block chart of sums of Greek vessels found in Cyprus during the first part of the first millennium B.C. The black parts of the columns indicate the amount of bowls and cups and the outlined part of the columns indicate other pottery forms.

Recent publications concerned with finds from various localities in Cyprus or from specific periods greatly facilitate the quest for obtaining an overall impression of the pattern of Greek ceramics in an island with a mixed population and a central position between the Near East and the Greek world.

In support of this analysis comparisons are made with finds of Greek pottery from Tell Sukas, Ras el-Bassit and Al Mina on the Syrian coast close to Cyprus, in so far as it is possible from the published material.[2]

In the following the Greek ceramic finds from Cyprus have been divided into chronological periods and sub-periods. The number of finds from each period is listed in tables indicating the actual numbers of a specific shape belonging to a specific ware class. In some instances this way of representing the finds may appear to be too rigid and to desregard chronological uncertainties of dating of one or several vessels within the range of, for instance, one quarter of a century. Nonetheless, it is believed that in this way the general pattern of the Greek ceramic finds from the island is easier to comprehend.[3]

The Middle Geometric Period: 850-750 B.C.

EUBOEA:		ATTICA:	
skyphos	: 22	skyphos	: 21
Atticizing skyphos	: 6	krater	: 3
plate	: 17	oinochoe	: 1
krater	: 1		
oinochoe	: 1		

The breakdown of the Mycenaean world brought an end to the close contact between Cyprus and the Greek mainland, and apart from a few Protogeometric cups and a skyphos, Greek pottery has not been documented in the island before the Middle Geometric period.[4] Judging from the ceramic finds Cyprus seems by then to have established contact with two places in Greece, Athens and Euboea, and the Greek skyphos represents the predominant shape here – as elsewhere in the

---

2. GJERSTAD 1977, PERRAULT 1986. PLOUG 1973, COURBIN 1986.
3. BOARDMAN 1979, 36.
4. COLDSTREAM 1981, 20 note 9.

Fig. 2. Examples of Greek bowls and cups found in Cyprus. a: Euboian Geometric skyphos. b: Attic Geometric skyphos. c: East Greek bird bowl. d: East Greek rosette bowl. e: Ionian cup. f: Attic Little Master cup. (Drawing by Poul Christensen).

eastern Mediterranean. The greater part of the Attic Middle Geometric skyphoi from Cyprus are decorated with meander-hooks or meanders flanked by vertical lines and stars[5] (fig. 2b), while only two pieces are decorated with chevrons,[6] and a single skyphos decorated with groups of vertical strokes on the inside of the rim is likewise thought to be Attic.[7] Another series of six skyphoi from Amathus decorated with chevrons, multiple zigzags or a narrow band of gear pattern also corresponds to the Attic Middle Geometric shape, but may according to Coldstream rather be Atticizing products from the Euboean North Cycladic area.[8] A third group of skyphoi carry the characteristic concentric circles or pendant semi-circles decoration (fig. 2a). Coldstream has proposed that three of these, two from the Phoenician sanctuary of Astarte at Kition and one without exact provenance, which are related to the so-called Sub Protogeometric I-II skyphoi from Lefkandi are the earliest representatives within this group. The others with pendant semicircles are comparable to Sub Protogeometric III skyphoi at Lefkandi where they are dated to 850-750 B.C.[9]

The plate likewise decorated with pendant semicircles has turned out to be another important shape within this group. Parallels at Lefkandi have been dated to the same period as the Sub Protogeometric III skyphoi, but recently a similar plate was found in a Sub Protogeometric I context at the same locality.[10] It has, however, been suggested that both shapes may appear in contexts of the later 8th century in the Levant and therefore a reliable date is lacking.[11]

Compared to the bowls other shapes are represented only by small numbers. Three kraters and an oinochoe are of Attic origin, while another oinochoe and a krater were probably manufactured in Euboea.[12]

---

5. GJERSTAD 1977 no 28-45.
6. GJERSTAD 1977 no 46-47.
7. GJERSTAD 1977 no 51, COLDSTREAM 1979, 257.
8. COLDSTREAM op. cit. GJERSTAD 1977 no 52-53, AUPERT 1978 fig. 31, KARAGEORGHIS 1980 fig. 25, idem 1981a fig. 106, idem 1982a fig. 44.
9. GJERSTAD 1977 no 4-17, COLDSTREAM 1981 no 2-4, AUPERT 1978 fig. 33. KARAGEORGHIS 1980 fig. 7, idem 1981a fig. 123, idem 1982a fig. 26, idem 1985 fig. 59.
10. GJERSTAD 1977 no 18-27, AUPERT 1978 fig. 34, POPHAM et al. 1980, pl. 30, 20-21, POPHAM et al. 1982, 232 fig. 6 pl. 28f.
11. COURBIN 1983, 202.
12. GJERSTAD 1977 no 48-50, COLDSTREAM 1981 no 1, AUPERT 1978 fig. 30 and 32.

Late Geometric: 750-700 B.C.

EUBOEA:
- skyphos : 24
- kotyle : 3
- krater : 3
- oinochoe : 2

ATTICA:
- plate : 1
- krater : 1
- oinochoe : 1

RHODES:
- kotyle : 1

During the Late Geometric period the amount of Greek pottery found in Cyprus decreases. The Euboean-North Cycladic products clearly predominate, and the skyphos remains the most important shape. Some of the skyphoi in question are decorated only with linear motifs[13] while others show birds and floral designs, products imitated by the local potters.[14]

Other shapes include three kraters and two oinochoai.[15] A new shape, the kotyle is also represented. Three may have been produced in the same area while one decorated with vertical lines and wavy lines in a reserved panel between the handles has parallels in Rhodes.[16]

The recorded amount of Attic pottery now amounts to three pieces: an amphora, an oinochoe and a plate hardly indicating intensive contact between Athens and Cyprus.[17]

Discussion

The presence of Euboean Middle to Late Geometric pottery in Cyprus is not surprising. The larger part of the Attic Middle Geometric pottery, however, was found together in one of the tombs at Salamis. Gjerstad interprets this find as evidence of an Attic princess having been married to a member of the royal family at Salamis, while Desborough

---

13. GJERSTAD 1977 no 57-58, THALMAN 1977 no 2-4. The following may also be Euboean imports: KARAGEORGHIS 1981a fig. 105, VANDENABEELE 1985 fig. 121-123. For parallels cf. POPHAM et al. 1980 pl. 36,3.

14. GJERSTAD 1977 no 59-65, 78-80. CALVET/YON, 1977 no 30. The sherds from Amathus tomb 2, GJERSTAD 1977 no 66-77 are here estimated to belong to two skyphoi. COLDSTREAM 1979, 261 pl. XXX, 3.

15. GJERSTAD 1977 no 90-92. THALMAN 1977 no 1. KARAGEORGHIS 1981a fig. 125.

16. GJERSTAD 1977 no 85-87. KARAGEORGHIS 1986 fig. 46. These may belong to the early 7th century cf COLDSTREAM 1968, 283. See also ANDRIOMENOU 1984, 37f.

17. GJERSTAD 1977 no 54-55. COLDSTREAM 1981 no 8.

and later Coldstream explain the presence of these vessels as evidence of gift exchange.[18] Concerning the much less impressive finds from Kition, Coldstream has suggested that the single Attic oinochoe found there may have reached Cyprus by way of Euboea, where an increasing number of Attic pottery of this period has been found.[19] Since the Salamis tomb in question also contained two skyphoi and 10 plates decorated with pendant semicircles from Euboea, the presence of the Attic pottery in the tomb may be explained in a similar way, in which case it is not *per se* evidence of a direct and more intensive contact between Attica and Cyprus as stated by some.[20] It should also be noticed that the remaining seven plates with a similar decoration were found together in a disturbed tomb at Amathus and thus represent another example of a batch of foreign pots probably from one shipment having ended up in the possession of a single individual either as items in a gift exchange system or as trade items.

We may also observe that the so-called Eteo-Cypriots at Amathus, who according to several scholars retained their indigenous Cypriot culture, were not opposed to Greek products since most of the Greek pottery recovered so far on the island was found here or at Salamis and Kition on the east coast.[21] The Greek finds from Amathus would thus also seem to contradict the suggestion that Greek skyphoi represent personal belongings of Greeks settled in the Levant, at least during the period in question.[22] Furthermore it should be noticed that Greek pottery is absent from the comparatively large tomb material from Lapethos, Ktima, Skales and Kaloriziki.

A brief comparison with the situation at some of the Levantine coastal cities closest to Cyprus where Greek pottery from various periods has been found reveals the following picture. Apart from a single Late Protogeometric amphora from Bassit, Middle Geometric skyphoi represent the earliest Greek finds here as well as at Sukas and at Al

---

18. GJERSTAD 1979, 93. DESBOROUGH 1979, 122. COLDSTREAM 1979, 257, COLDSTREAM 1983, 206.
19. COLDSTREAM 1981, 19.
20. BOARDMAN 1980, 44.
21. KARAGEORGHIS 1982, 114.
22. RIIS 1970, 129. RIIS 1982, 243. COLDSTREAM 1977, 95 and 1982, 21.

Mina.²³ The Euboean concentric circles or pendant circles skyphoi are found at all three localities, while Atticizing skyphoi also present in Cyprus only appear at Al Mina. None of the finds are considered Attic with any degree of certainty and chemical analyses point towards Euboea as the place of production, at least where the analyzed sherds are concerned.²⁴ At Sukas fragments of one skyphos and two kraters are considered Late Geometric, and according to the excavator the second part of the 8th B.C. century witnessed a slight increase in the number of Greek finds, especially Euboean skyphoi at Bassit. The number of Greek finds from Al Mina also grows and again Euboean skyphoi predominate.²⁵ It is generally agreed that from about the middle of the 9th B.C. century the political situation in the Levant was favorable for enterprise with the Greek world, and Cyprus is no exception to this.²⁶ Although it should not be forgotten that we are dealing with rather small numbers, the slight increase of finds at Al Mina, and perhaps at Bassit, in the later 8th century seems to represent a reversed picture of that seen in Cyprus. However, the decreasing tendency in the numbers of Greek finds in Cyprus should perhaps not be taken too seriously considering the fact that the large Middle Geometric find in one of the Salamis tombs may distort the general picture somewhat. To judge by the ceramic evidence known so far contact between this part of the Mediterranean world and the Greeks seems to have focused on the Euboean area and to speak of a burst of Attic activity in the Levant even during the early part of the 8th century is perhaps not altogether convincing.²⁷

23. PLOUG 1973, 11 and 92, RIIS 1982, 243. COLDSTREAM 1968, 312. COURBIN 1986, 190.
24. POPHAM et al. 1983, 289, JONES 1986, 690f.
25. COLDSTREAM 1977, 94.
26. COLDSTREAM 1977, 92. RIIS 1982, 255.
27. COLDSTREAM 1977, 94, BOARDMAN 1980, 44.

The 7th century B.C.

EAST GREECE:
- bird bowl : 20
- band bowl : 4
- Ionian cup : 10
- Aryballos : 1
- Wild Goat bowl : 1
- Wild Goat plate : 1
- Wild Goat krater : 1
- Wild Goat amphora : 3
- Wild Goat dinos : 1
- Wild Goat oinochoe : 10
- Wild Goat lid : 1

CORINTH:
- skyphos : 1
- kotyle : 1
- oinochoe : 1
- aryballos : 14
- alabastron : 6
- olpe : 1

The evidence of Greek pottery in Cyprus from the early part of the 7th century B.C. is scant. However, about the middle of the century East Greek pottery represented by the so-called bird bowls (fig. 2c) begins to appear in Cyprus, and during the last quarter of the century their number is tripled, and they are accompanied by bowls decorated with bands, Ionian cups, and vessels belonging to the Wild Goat style, mainly oinochoai.[28]

During the first part of the century the number of Corinthian vessels is restricted to one Middle Protocorinthian aryballos and one skyphos, but in the second part of the century the amount of Corinthian pottery likewise increases comprising one Transitional oinochoe and fourteen Early Corinthian aryballoi, six alabastra, one skyphos and one kotyle.[29] Salamis and Amathus are the most important find places.

Discussion

When Greek pottery reappears in Cyprus in significant numbers during the latter part of the 7th century various kinds of bowls and cups again predominate amongst the finds. This situation seems to be repeated at Sukas, Bassit and Al Mina where East Greek products likewise prevail.

---

28. GJERSTAD 1977 no 105-106, 122-124, 151, 163, 342, THALMAN 1977 no 6-15, 22-25, 46-50, 100-116, 150-151, 155, CALVET/YON 1977 no 35-40, 48-49, 53, 57, 64-65, KARAGEORGHIS 1977 no 12, KARAGEORGHIS 1981a fig. 97.

29. GJERSTAD 1977 no 343-358. CALVET/YON 1977 no 18-25.

It should be noticed, though, that bird bowls, evidently popular in Cyprus and at Al Mina and at least present at Bassit, were not encountered at Sukas.³⁰ At Al Mina on the other hand, Wild Goat style has an early occurrence and according to Boardman Corinthian pottery is well represented especially in the early 7th century while both ware classes are mostly of a late 7th century date at the other localities.³¹ It comes as no surprise that the aryballos is the leading Corinthian shape, and the lack of bowls of Wild Goat style was to be expected since this shape was evidently not common as such in this ware class.³²

The unstable political situation in North Syria may explain the small amount of Greek pottery found at Sukas and Bassit. In Cyprus the slight evidence of contact with the Greek world could be the result of Assyrian supremacy, but although the Cypriot kings submitted to Sargon II in 707 B.C. and were forced to pay tribute to him, the Assyrians apparently did not interfere with matters in the island where the material culture was still in bloom. In Greece, on the other hand, the Lelantine war may have brought an end to the contact between Euboea and the East Mediterranean, and some time seems to have lapsed before new ceramic production centers were discovered or new traders discovered the Levantine market possibilities.³³

30. PLOUG 1973, 17 and 92, CALVET/YON 1978, 43f. COURBIN 1986, 198.
31. BOARDMAN 1980, 49, but see also ROBERTSON 1940, 16.
32. COOK 1972, 120.
33. KARAGEORGHIS 1982, 129. COLDSTREAM 1977, 200. BOARDMAN 1980, 48.

600-575 B.C

EAST GREECE:			CORINTH:		
bird bowl	:	4	kotyle	:	2
rosette bowl	:	24	oinochoe	:	2
band bowl	:	40	aryballos	:	13
Ionian cup	:	88	alabastron	:	2
»one handlers«	:	7	pyxis	:	2
Wild Goat bowl	:	1			
Wild Goat plate	:	5	ATTICA:		
Wild Goat krater/ amphora	:	13	cup	:	1
			amphora	:	1
Wild Goat oinochoe	:	20	krater	:	1
Wild Goat lid	:	3	lekythos	:	1
Chian chalice	:	2			
Chian phiale	:	1			
Vroulia cup	:	3			
Vroulia amphora	:	1			
Vroulia oinochoe	:	9			

During the first quarter of the 6th century B.C. Greek pottery is much better represented in Cyprus. The number of East Greek products has increased considerably. Bird bowls and rosette bowls (*fig.* 2d) amount to four and 24 pieces respectively[34] while bowls merely decorated with bands are more numerous.[35] Ionian cups represent another large group. The Samian series is present,[36] but the larger number so far registered has been attributed to Hayes' Rhodian types.[37] Two groups should be noticed. One is comparable to Tell Sukas group 9 which may be a variant of type V,[38] the other group is related to the so-called one-

---

34. GJERSTAD 1977 no 108-113. CALVET/YON 1977 no 41-44. THALMAN 1977 no 16-21.

35. GJERSTAD 1977 no 114-115, CALVET/YON 1977 no 45-47. THALMAN 1977 no 26-33.

36. GJERSTAD 1977 no 88-89. CALVET/YON 1977 no 66-72, 74. According to THALMAN 1977, 70 about 10 pieces should be of the Samian type, but they are not specified. KARAGEORGHIS 1981a fig. 96.

37. GJERSTAD 1977 no 130-149, CALVET/YON 1977 no 73, 75-98. THALMAN 1977 no 51-55, 66-74, COLDSTREAM 1981 no 12. KARAGEORGHIS 1977a fig. 14-15. Idem 1982a fig. 55. Since type VIII and IX are generally dated to the first half of the 6th century the total number of these types are here divided equally between the two first quarters of the century. The finds from Vouni, GJERSTAD 1977 p. 33, are excluded from this analysis because the information is insufficient.

38. GJERSTAD 1977 no 125-129. THALMAN 1977 no 56-65. COLDSTREAM 1981 no 14. PLOUG 1973, 32.

handlers at Sukas, and the finds from Cyprus thus prove that this kind of bowl may be provided with string-holes, or one or two handles.[39] It has been suggested, though, that at least the finds from Kition may be of local make, and a date to the first quarter of the 6th century B.C. is by no means secured either. On the basis of the finds from Ras Shamra Stucky has inferred that the one-handlers may not necessarily be East Greek and that the type continued being made until much later.[40]

Furthermore the Wild Goat style is also much better represented. Not surprisingly the oinochoe is still the leading shape, but in Cyprus the krater is also well represented compared to other shapes such as dishes and plates generally considered common within this style.[41] A few products of Chian style, which together with oinochoai, cups and an amphora of the Vroulia style probably also belong to the early 6th century and complete the list of East Greek finds.[42]

The picture of Corinthian pottery is almost unaltered. The aryballos is still the dominant shape while other shapes are represented by only one piece each.[43] Together with four Attic black figure vessels these finds hardly point towards an intensive contact between Cyprus and the Greek mainland.[44]

575-550 B.C.

EAST GREECE:
- rosette bowl : 4
- eye bowl : 1
- Ionian cup : 48
- Rhodian plate : 4
- Wild Goat bowl : 8
- Wild Goat amphora : 1
- Wild Goat oinochoe : 1
- Fikellura oinochoe : 1
- Black figure : 3

CORINTH:
- aryballos : 6
- pyxis : 2
- hydria : 1

ATTICA:
- bowl/cup : 3
- amphora : 2
- lekanis : 2

LACONIA:
- cup : 2

---

39. GJERSTAD 1977 no 116-120. COLDSTREAM 1981 no 15-16. PLOUG 1973, 38.
40. STUCKY 1983, 125.
41. GJERSTAD 1977 no 161-162, 166. CALVET/YON 1977 no 54-55, 58-60. THALMAN 1977 no 117-157.
42. GJERSTAD 1977 no 103, 122-124, 157-158. THALMAN 1977 no 158-170.
43. GJERSTAD 1977 no 359-368, CALVET/YON 1977 no 26-29, THALMAN 1977 no 176-183.
44. GJERSTAD 1977 no 513, CALVET/YON 1977 no 8, THALMAN 1977 no 185, KARAGEORGHIS 1978 fig. 42.

During the second quarter of the 6th century various Ionian cups (*fig. 2e*) are clearly the most popular foreign ceramic article in Cyprus.[45]

Other products from the East Greek area include some Rosette bowls and an Eye-bowl,[46] Rhodian plates,[47] a Fikellura oinochoe and some fragments of other East Greek black figure closed shapes may also belong here.[48] The number of vessels belonging to the Wild Goat style is now strongly reduced.[49]

Products from the Greek mainland are still on an unimpressive scale including seven Attic pieces of various shapes,[50] two Laconian cups[51] that together with a reduced number of Corinthian vessels, mostly aryballoi hardly changes the picture noticed during the first quarter of the century.[52]

Discussion

The pattern of Greek pottery found in Cyprus during the first part of the 6th century B.C. evidently contrasts with that at Al Mina whereas the situation at Sukas and probably also at Bassit seems to parallel that in Cyprus, although the number of finds at Sukas evidently is small in the very beginning of the century.[53] At Sukas the number of Ionian cups and vessels of Wild Goat style likewise dominate, and as in Cyprus Attic black figure pottery has a low representation, and no specific shape seems to be preferred. Corinthian pottery is still present, but the amount hardly indicates that this fabric was particularly favoured by those living on the tell as it has been suggested.[54]

The lack of finds at Al Mina may be connected with the policy of the Babylonian overlords or may indicate that the period witnessed an interest in direct communication with central Syria as suggested by

---

45. Cf. note 37 and GJERSTAD 1977 no 152. THALMAN 1977 no 75-77. COLDSTREAM 1981 no 13.
46. THALMAN 1977 no 34-37. GJERSTAD 1977 no 107.
47. CALVET/YON 1977 no 50-52. THALMAN 1977 no 89.
48. GJERSTAD 1977 no 164. CALVET/YON 1977 no 61-63.
49. GJERSTAD 1977 no 175. CALVET/YON 1977 no 56. THALMAN 1977 no 38-45.
50. GJERSTAD 1977 no 506. CALVET/YON 1977 no 9-10. THALMAN 1977 no 186-189, 224.
51. THALMAN 1977 no 184. COLDSTREAM 1981 no 16.
52. GJERSTAD 1977 no 369-376, 381.
53. BOARDMAN 1980, 52, PLOUG 1973, 95, COURBIN 1986, 201. PERREAULT 1986, 154 Tab. 1.
54. PLOUG 1973, 96.

Boardman.[55] At any rate the situation at Sukas and Bassit differs very much from that at Al Mina. The destruction of Sukas which has been connected with an attack by the Egyptian pharaoh Apries in 588 B.C. and Amasis' conquest of Cyprus in 570 B.C. did apparently not bring the influx of Greek pottery to a stop at these places. The continued contact between Cyprus and the Greeks is also underlined by the large number of figurines of Cypriot style found especially in sanctuaries in Samos and Rhodes.[56] Amathus is furthermore supposed to have been a transit port for Greeks sailing to Egypt.[57] This may be partly true, but at least during the early 6th century a somewhat different pattern of Greek pottery may be observed here as well as in the Cyrenaica since early Attic black figure pottery was evidently much more common here. It has been suggested that Athens established her earliest overseas ceramic market in Egypt in order to avoid causing any troubles with Corinth over the western market.[58] If those in charge of shipping Attic pottery made regular stops at the Cypriot harbour towns, a somewhat larger amount of Attic black figure pottery would have been expected to be found here than is so far the case.

550-525 B.C.

EAST GREECE:
- Ionian cup : 6
- Fikellura amphora : 6
- Clazomenian amphora : 1
- Clazomenian plate : 1
- Chian kantharos : 1

CORINTH:
- kotyle : 2
- oinochoe : 1
- pyxis : 1

ATTICA:
- bowl/cup : 71
- krater : 2
- amphora : 5
- oinochoe : 7
- lekythos : 2
- olpe : 1

LACONIA:
- bowl : 1

BOEOTIA:
- bowl : 1

---

55. BOARDMAN 1980, 52.
56. SØRENSEN 1978, 111f.
57. KARAGEORGHIS 1982, 139. For East Greek trade with Cyprus and Naucratis cf. ROEBUCK 1959, 66.
58. VENIT 1984, 153.

The pattern observed in Cyprus during the first part of the 6th century changes radically towards the middle of the century. The Attic black figure style now plays the leading part, and contrary to what was seen during the first part of the century bowls and cups, especially Little Master cups clearly dominate the Attic finds.[59] What may be called jugs and bottles are represented by 10 pieces while only seven belong to large shapes such as amphorai and kraters.[60]

Other products from the Greek mainland are limited to four pieces from Corinth, and two bowls from Boeotia and Laconia may also date to this time.[61]

East Greek products are strongly reduced. Some Ionian cups are still found together with a few Clazomenian pieces and some amphorai belonging to the Fikellura style.[62]

525-500 B.C.
EAST GREECE:
    Fikellura amphora : 1
ATTICA:
    black figure:
    bowl/cup : 46
    krater : 1
    amphora : 7
    lekythos : 8
    olpe : 1
    pelike : 1
    oinochoe : 1
    red figure:
    bowl/cup : 8
    alabastron : 1

---

59. GJERSTAD 1977 no 385-387, 401-428, 434-450, 471. CALVET/YON 1977 no 14-15. THALMAN 1977 no 190-204, 217-218. KARAGEORGHIS 1977 fig. 101, idem 1979 fig. 44, idem 1980 fig. 79, idem 1982 fig. 45.

60. GJERSTAD 1977 no 489-495, 497-500, 502, 514-515. CALVET/YON no 11-12, THALMAN no 233.

61. GJERSTAD 1977 no 377-380, 384. KARAGEORGHIS 1977 no 16. BOARDMAN & HAYES no 1008. BOARDMAN & HAYES 1973 no 2117.

62. GJERSTAD 1977 no 121, 153, 155, 174, 176, 178-179. THALMAN 1977 no 78-80, 171-173.

During the last quarter of the century the amount of Attic pottery is reduced, but the bowl/cup shapes remain the most popular shape.[63] Amphorai and lekythoi are represented by six and eight pieces respectively while only one krater, pelike and olpe have been found so far.[64] The new red figure style hardly manifests itself amongst the finds. Except for an alabastron we are dealing with cups all found at Marion on the north coast.[65]

500-475 B.C.
ATTICA:
- black figure:
  - bowl/cup : 29
  - lekythos : 25
  - oinochoe : 2
  - olpe : 1
  - alabastron : 1
  - lid : 1
- red figure:
  - krater : 1
  - amphora : 1
  - lekythos : 1
  - head vase : 1

In the first quarter of the 5th century the number of Attic vessels found in Cyprus amounts to about the same as what was seen at the end of the 6th century. Black figure bowls and cups still have a high representation, but the lekythos has now become another important shape[66] while other shapes with black figure decoration together with vessels in red figure style are few.[67]

---

63. GJERSTAD 1977 no 429-433, 451-469, 472-479. THALMAN 1977 no 205-216, 222-223. ROBERTSON 1981 no 15. KARAGEORGHIS 1978 fig. 16.
64. GJERSTAD 1977 no 496, 501, 503-505, 512, 516-522. CALVET/YON 1977 no 12-13. THALMAN 1977 no 225, 232, 234.
65. GJERSTAD 1977 no 548-555, 558.
66. GJERSTAD 1977 no 388-400, 430-432, 480-488, 523-547. ROBERTSON 1981 no 8-9, 12.
67. GJERSTAD 1977 no 511, 556-557, 559, CALVET/YON 1977 no 16-17 THALMAN 1977 no 227-230. KARAGEORGHIS 1981 a fig. 75.

Discussion

Comparing the pattern seen in Cyprus with that at places on the Syrian coast-line the following trends are to be observed. At Sukas a similar decrease of East Greek products and an increase of Attic bowls and cups may be observed during the third quarter of the 6th century. At Bassit the situation seems to be the same, while the finds from Al Mina continue to be very few.[68]

Of course it is to be expected that some time would lapse in between the beginning of the Attic black figure production and its introduction to other areas, but in the Levantine area it took about half a century for this ceramic product to become an established commodity, and when this finally happened it seems to coincide with the production of the so-called Little Master cups which now substitute the Ionian cups so popular during the previous quarter of the century while other shapes appear to have had little importance. The impression obtained from the finds from both Cyprus and the localities on the Syrian coast is indeed that the production of the Little Master cups actually opened up the market for Attic pottery in this part of the Mediterranean. During the last quarter of the century the Attic finds from Sukas increase slightly and at Bassit the amount of Attic pottery grows considerably. This growth continues into the beginning of the 5th century here as well as at Sukas, and a veritable boom of Attic black figure products can now be seen at Al Mina. The interest in bowls and cups continues and as in Cyprus the lekythos represents another important shape whereas red figure products remain remarkably few.[69]

In the East as well as in the Nile valley the lack of interest in the Attic oinochoe, which was important at Greek symposia, has been explained from the point of view that they were quite simply not used at Eastern banquets where wine was served in other types of vessels.[70] This explanation seems not entirely convincing, at least where Cyprus is concerned, and it is quite possible that wine was poured from metal jugs whenever it could be afforded or from decorated jugs of local make. The popularity of the lekythos is not restricted to the Eastern market and the number of specimens found in Cyprus and the coastral cities of

---

68. PLOUG 1973, 97, PERREAULT 1986, 154. COURBIN 1986, 201.
69. PERRAULT 1986, 154 tab. 1. MAFFRE 1971.
70. VRIES 1977, 545.

Syria may need no other explanation than the fact that they were mass products cheap to buy.[71]

As was the case early in the 6th century B.C. the political situation in the later part of the same century and the beginning of the 5th century B.C. seems to have had no immediate impact on the Greek ceramic "import" to Cyprus, Sukas and Bassit. As it was quite possibly the case with Al Mina, the Persians rather seem to have been in favour of a continued contact with the Greeks.[72] This appears to be in contrast with the situation in Egypt, if it is correct that the Persians tried to direct Egyptian trade to the East to weaken Egypt's dependence on Athens.[73] It has been pointed out, however, that the decreasing tendency in the amount of Attic pottery found in Egypt started earlier than the Persian conquest and that the situation under the Persians rather continued an already established pattern which nontheless differs entirely from what is to be observed in the Levantine area.[74]

Conclusion

The analysis performed above has shown that except for the Geometric period the general pattern of Greek ceramic finds in Cyprus during the first half of the first millennium compares with what is seen at Tell Sukas and Ras el-Bassit rather than at Al Mina. This would seem to support the impression of Al Mina as a locality with conditions that differed from the other places on the Syrian coast. However, the finds from Cyprus, Sukas and Bassit show various differences of which the total lack of bird bowls at Sukas is the most remarkable. This may of course merely reflect the taste of the inhabitants, but it may on the other hand indicate differences concerning points of contact in the Greek world or other variables, such as different tradesmen calling upon different harbors. A much more meticulous study of the Greek finds in this area might lead to a more precise conception of subjects such as these.

Another interesting result of the present analysis is the observation that throughout the period concerned the bowl or cup was always

---

71. BOARDMAN 1974, 146.
72. BOARDMAN 1980, 52, cf. also MAIER 1985, 37.
73. VENIT 1984, 153 note 85.
74. VENIT 1984, 153.

found in larger numbers than any other type of vessel. An explanation for this is not immediately available, since it is not known with certainty whether the bowl was at all times in the period concerned a popular item for production or for exportation and hence produced for that purpose. Neither is it known with certainty why in particular the bowl is such an apparently popular item for import to Cyprus and the cities on the Syrian coast. In Cyprus for instance there was a vast production of bowls, and therefore it seems unlikely that import of bowls from Greece is a consequence of a market which could not be fully supplied by the local producers.[75] Greek pottery may, of course, have been popular because of its often superior quality and foreign bowls and cups which were used at banquets or symposia may have underlined the owner's status in society. However, the larger part of both Greek and local finds in Cyprus come from tombs. It may therefore be inferred that the preference for certain shapes reflects local burial customs, and that it does not represent a true picture of the actual import of Greek pottery, let alone a differentiated production pattern as to shapes in the local pottery workshops.

After all it is perhaps not too surprising that bowls are found in such large numbers compared to other pottery shapes. A survey into present days domestic cupboards will clearly reveal that the number of bowls and cups of many shapes and for many purposes predominates among the forms of pottery, glass and china. Water and various juices in which water is the main component is a prerequisite for the existence of man and shapes serving these purposes are those that we might expect to find most abundantly in the search for remnants of past cultures.

The present analysis has shown, that although it is important to examine the presence of many pottery ware forms in the search of contacts between cultures, it seems to be fully justified to use the number of bowls and cups as a good item for such an analysis.

University of Copenhagen
Institute of Classical Archaeology
Vandkunsten 5
DK-1467 Copenhagen K

---

75. SØRENSEN 1987, 129f.

BIBLIOGRAPHY

ANDRIOMENOU 1984	A. ANDRIOMENOU, Skyphoi de l'etalier de Chalcis (Fin de Xe-fin de VIIIe s. av. J.C.), *BCH* 108, 37-69.
AUPERT 1978	P. AUPERT, Traveaux de l'ecole française à Amathonte en 1977, *BCH* 102, 781-815.
BOARDMAN & HAYES 1966	J. BOARDMAN, J. HAYES, Excavations at Tocra. The Archaic Deposits I. BSA suppl. 4. London.
BOARDMAN & HAYES 1973	J. BOARDMAN, J. HAYES, Excavations at Tocra. The Archaic Deposits II and later Deposits. BSA suppl. 10. London.
BOARDMAN 1974	J. BOARDMAN, *Athenian Black Figure Vases.* London.
BOARDMAN 1979	J. BOARDMAN, The Athenian Pottery Trade. *Expedition* 21 no 4, 33.
BOARDMAN 1980	J. BOARDMAN, *The Greeks Overseas.* London.
CALVET & YON 1977	Y. CALVET, M. YON, Céramique trouvée à Salamine. In GJERSTAD 1977, 9-21.
CALVET & YON 1978	Y. CALVET, M. YON, Salamine de Chypre et le commerce ionien in Les ceramiques de la Grece de l'est et leur diffusion en Occident. *Centre Jean Berard. Bibliotheque de l'institut Francais de Naple.* (Naples). Deuxieme serie vol. IV, 43-51.
COLDSTREAM 1969	J. N. COLDSTREAM, *Greek Ceometric Pottery.* London.
COLDSTREAM 1977	J. N. COLDSTREAM, *Geometric Greece.* London.
COLDSTREAM 1979	J. N. COLDSTREAM, Geometric Skyphoi in Cyprus, *RDAC*, 255-269.
COLDSTREAM 1981	J. N. COLDSTREAM, The Greek Geometric and Plain Archaic Imports. In KARAGEORGHIS 1981, 17-22.
COLDSTREAM 1982	J. N. COLDSTREAM, Some Problems of Eighth-Century Pottery in the West seen from the Greek Angle. In *Cahiers du Centre Jean Berard III.* (Naples). *La ceramique grecque ou de tradition greque au VIIIe siecle en Italie centrale et meridionale*, 21-37.
COLDSTREAM 1982a	J. N. COLDSTREAM, Greeks and Phoenicians in the Aegean, *MBeiträge* 8, 261-275.
COLDSTREAM 1983	J. N. COLDSTREAM, Gift Exchange in the Eighth Century B.C., *OpAth* 4, XXX, 201.
COOK 1972	R. M. COOK, *Greek Painted pottery.* London.
COURBIN 1983	P. COURBIN, Une assiette cycladique a Ras el-Bassit. In *Archeologie au Levant. Recueil a mémoire de R. Saidah.* (Lyon & Paris). Collection de la Maison de l'Orient Mediterraneen 12, série archeologique 9, 192-204.
COURBIN 1986	P. COURBIN, Bassit, *Syria* LXIII, 175-219.
DESBOROUGH 1979	V. R. d'A. DESBOROUGH, A Postscript to an Appendix. In DIKAIOS, 119-122.
DIKAIOS 1979	*Studies Presented in the Memory of P. Dikaios.* Nicosia.
GJERSTAD 1977	E. GJERSTAD, Pottery From Various Parts of Cyprus. In Greek Geometric and Archaic Pottery found in Cyprus, *OpAth* 4, XXVI, 23-59.
GJERSTAD 1979	E. GJERSTAD, A Cypro-Greek Royal Marriage in the Eighth Century B.C. In DIKAIOS 1979, 89-93.
JONES 1986	R. E. JONES, Greek and Cypriot Pottery. A Review of Scientific Studies. *BSA Fitsh Laboratory. Occasional Paper 1.* Athens.
KARAGEORGHIS 1977	V. KARAGEORGHIS, Pottery from Kition. In GJERSTAD 1977, 61-63.
KARAGEORGHIS 1977a	V. KARAGEORGHIS, Chronique des Fouilles a Chypre en 1976, *BCH* 101, 707-779.

KARAGEORGHIS 1978	V. KARAGEORGHIS, Chronique des Fouilles a Chypre en 1977, *BCH* 102, 879-938.
KARAGEORGHIS 1980	V. KARAGEORGHIS, Chronique des Fouilles a Chypre en 1979, *BCH* 104, 761-803.
KARAGEORGHIS 1981	V. KARAGEORGHIS, *Excavations at Kition IV. The Non-Cypriote Pottery.* Nicosia.
KARAGEORGHIS 1981a	V. KARAGEORGHIS, Chronique des Fouilles a Chypre en 1980, *BCH* 105, 967-1024.
KARAGEORGHIS 1982	V. KARAGEORGHIS, *Cyprus from the Stone Age to the Romans.* London.
KARAGEORGHIS 1982a	V. KARAGEORGHIS, Chronique des Fouilles a Chypre en 1981, *BCH* 106, 685-744.
KARAGEORGHIS 1986	V. KARAGEORGHIS, Chronique des Fouilles a Chypre en 1985, *BCH* 110, 823-880.
MAFFRE 1971	J.-J. MAFFRE, Vases grecs de la collection Zenon Pierides, *BCH* 95, 627-702.
MAIER 1985	F. G. MAIER, Factoids in ancient history: the case of fifth-century Cyprus, *JHS* 105, 32-39.
PERREAULT 1986	J. PERREAULT, Céramique et Échange Les importations attiques au Proche Orient du VIe au miliau di Ve siècle avant J.-C. Les données archeologiques, *BCH* 110, 145-175.
PLOUG 1973	G. PLOUG, Sukas II. The Aegean, Corinthian and East Greek Pottery and Terracottas. Copenhagen.
POPHAM et al. 1980	M. R. POPHAM, L. H. SACKETT, P. G. THEMELIS, Lefkandi I. The Iron Age. *BSA suppl. II.* London.
POPHAM et al. 1982	M. R. POPHMAN, E. TOULOUPA, L. H. SACKETT, Further Excavations of the Toumba cemetary at Lefkandi, *BSA* 77, 213-248.
POPHAM et al. 1983	M. R. POPHAM, A. M. POLLARD, H. HATCHER, Euboean Exports to Al Mina, Cyprus, and Crete: A Reassessment, *BSA* 78, 281-290.
RIIS 1970	P. J. RIIS, *Sukas I. The North-East Sanctury and the First Settling of Greeks in Syria and Palestine.* Copenhagen.
RIIS 1982	P. J. RIIS, Griechen in Phönizien. *MBeiträge* 8, 243-260.
ROBERTSON 1940	M. ROBERTSON, The Excavations at Al Mina Sueidaia IV. The Early Greek Vases, *BSA* 60-62, 2-21.
ROBERTSON 1981	M. ROBERTSON, The Attic Black Figure and Red Figure Pottery. In KARAGEORGHIS 1981, 67-73.
ROEBUCK 1959	C. ROEBUCK, *Ionian Trade and Colonization.* New York.
STUCKY 1983	R. A. STUCKY, *Ras Shamra. Leukos Limen. Die Nachugaritische Besiedlung von Ras Shamra.* Paris.
SØRENSEN 1978	L. WRIEDT SØRENSEN, Early Archaic Limestone Statuettes in Cypriot Style, *RDAC*, 111-121.
SØRENSEN 1987	L. WRIEDT SØRENSEN, Cypriote Iron Age Pottery. An Experiment Employing simple Quantitative Analysis, *SIMA* LXXVII, 129-135.
THALMAN 1977	J. P. THALMAN, Ceramique trouvee a Amathonte. In GJERSTAD 1977, 65-86.
VANDENABEELE 1985	F. VANDENABEELE, Une depot de ceramique archaique chypriote dans un silo a Amathonte, *BCH* 109, 629-655.
VENIT 1984	M. S. VENIT, Early Attic Black Figure Vases in Egypt, *JARCE* XXI, 141-154.
VRIES 1977	K. de VRIES, Attic Pottery in the Achaemenid Empire, *AJA* 81, 544-548.

THE GREEK EPIC AND GREEK MYTHOLOGY AND THEIR LINKS WITH THE NEAR EAST

by LENE ANDERSEN

The Greek myths link the epic of which they often, via the narrative, form part to religion and the religious concepts they reflect. The debt to the Orient of this complex: Greek epic – Greek myth – Greek religion is becoming more and more widely acknowledged.

More than 2000 years ago Herodotus told us that much of what is considered ancient and venerable in religion and art has come to Greece from abroad, from fabled Egypt. Not until the discovery- and subsequent study of a vast amount of textual material from Mesopotamia, Phoenicia, Asia Minor, and Egypt has the idea gradually given way that the Greek myths sprang into being as perfectly self-contained units, born directly of the Greek spirit – the Greek myths that have played such an overwhelming role in later European art and literature.

There is a parallel here to the Old Testament which is deeply indebted to the tradition of the Near East for its world picture and its narrative material.[1] Thus the foundation stones of Western European culture in relation to its Greek as well as its Jewish heritage are not as monolithic as formerly assumed, but complex and pieced together of many elements by influence, adaptation and assimilation.

In dealing with questions of cultural interaction one is faced with the problem of how to distinguish between the type and degree of similarity which clearly indicate relationship and interdependence and those which are rooted in our common inheritance, and those which are merely accidental. If one wants to set up a "genealogical table" for material of this kind one must decide how many "missing links" one can accept for the table to be other than just arbitrary.

This type of question, unfortunately, will invariably be easier asked than answered. Much depends, in the first place, on the theoretical

---

1. Important texts in English translation collected in PRITCHARD 1950, and THOMAS 1958. The *Enuma Elish* and the *Gilgamesh* translated into Danish by RAVN 1953.

approach to the subject.[2] The structural theory of myths, for instance, will be inclined to deny kinship and refer noted resemblance to the intellectual equipment common to all mankind which generates given types of myths at different times and in different places independent of each other, whereas the historically orientated theories of myths tend to discover and to trace concrete relations.

Secondly, whatever theoretical approach one chooses a large part of this field will always lie open to individual interpretation of the relative importance of the similarities in question.

In the following I will point out a number of distinctive features of the Greek epic – mostly from the poetry of Hesiod – which either immediately or after close analysis turn out to be adaptations from some source; and I will attempt to show that the sources of these features are most probably to be found in the Near East. The features that will be discussed are myths and mythological and religious concepts plus a few examples of literary forms.

Hesiod of Boioetia[3] (about 700 B.C.) is counted among the Greek epic writers on account of the language and metrical form of his poems despite the fact that his works are only in part narrative. The two works of his that have come down to us: the *Theogony* and *Works and Days*[4] both show kinship with Oriental ideas and myths, but in different ways.

The *Theogony* which is the first attempt in Greek at a systematized mythology has as one of its organizing elements the so-called succession myth which tells how Zeus assumed power displacing his father Kronos who in his turn had displaced his father Uranos. To this succession myth there is a number of analogies in Hurrian/Hittite, Phoenician and Babylonian myths. These have been often treated and various theories have been launched about the relationship between the diverse manifestations of this myth.[5] Not intending on this occasion to go over

---

2. Survey of theories of myths in ANDERSEN 1978.
3. Translated into Danish in ANDERSEN 1973. The whole body of work treated in ANDERSEN 1977.
4. Edited with introduction, commentary, and bibliography by WEST 1966 and 1978.
5. Texts in PRITCHARD 1950, THOMAS 1958, and CLEMEN 1939. Of the vast body of literature about this problem WEST 1966, 18-31, with copious references, and WALCOT 1966, chapts. I-II deserve special mention. My own suggestion to a solution of the problem in ANDERSEN 1976 and 1977, chapt. 4.

this familiar ground, I just want to point to the succession myth in the Theogony as one of the best examples of an adopted myth. Although the final conclusion has not been reached as to the time and place of the Greek assimilation of it, we are dealing with a myth which is so widespread and so complex, so rich in motifs that it is safe to assume that at some stage it must be derived from parallel myths of the Near East.

With the *Works and Days*, Hesiod's second poem, the case is different. In this work one detects a number of mutually independent features which each of them in different ways point to the Near East; many of the religious conceptions, the myths and the literary form of the poem show a marked affinity with those of the tradition of the Near East, but when it comes to the pinning down of their actual origin it turns out to be far more difficult than in the case of the succession myth of the *Theogony*. In some cases the common base is far too general for any specific source to emerge; in other cases the Greek poem turns out to be older than the oriental parallel which means, of course, that this cannot in its presently known form be the direct source. But although one must give up finding concrete models we still have here a number of cases in which the Greek version shows itself to be adapted and assimilated. Relating this to the accumulation of oriental parallels one cannot doubt the strong influence which must have taken place, and mainly from the East.

In the following I shall attempt to concretize the abovesaid, first by a series of examples from the *Works and Days*, followed by some examples of the handling by the Greek epic poets of a certain type of religion, well-known in the Near East, namely the religious practice related to fertility- and vegetation gods. The genre of the *Works and Days* has been the subject of fierce debate,[6] because the poem in its entirety is unlike any other poem. The "works" of the title refers to the instruction given in how to cultivate the land which takes up the greater part of the poem, followed by similar instruction in navigation; and the "days" of the title refers to the last part of the poem which is a *hemerology* i.e. an enumeration of the days in the month which are suitable or unsuitable for doing this or that. However there is more to the poem than the title indicates. It opens with a short introductory narrative in which we

---

6. Survey in ANDERSEN 1977, chapt. 7.

are told of a dispute between the poet and his brother over the succession to property which apparently sets the whole poem in motion; there are myths, a fable, and a series of gnomic sayings, and there are moral and practical prescriptions which are not particularly related to the needs of the farmer.

After a brief hymn to Zeus the poem itself starts with an explosive attack on the brother who is accused of having cheated Hesiod at the division of their patrimony. The brother is represented as an idler who always looks for the easiest way out, and, if necessary, trading on others. This is the background of the subsequent instruction in how to provide ones daily bread in a much more desirable way, namely as an industrious farmer. But first the poet feels obliged to tell his audience why man must work for his living. For this purpose he employs two myths: the *Pandora* myth and the *Five Races* myth. In v. 42-105 he relates how man has been afflicted with toil as a punishment because of the deceit of *Prometheus* when at the expense of the gods he secured the fire for mankind. Zeus carries out the punishment by means of a woman *Pandora* and her notorious *pithos* (in the later tradition termed Pandora's *box*). As she lifts the lid of her pithos catastrophy pours over mankind – disasters, diseases and sufferings among which is counted labour (never particularly highly esteemed by the ancient Greeks). There are many blemishes and irregularities in this tale, but the message is clear: man has forfeited his blissful state on earth which of its own accord brought forth everything. Man's lot has become one of suffering and toil through the agency of a foolish woman. The likeness to the account of the Fall of Man in *Genesis* is obvious, but it is only a superficial likeness: In the Greek myth there is a series of intermediate links and complications which have not been related here; these, however, indicate that there is no close correlation between the Hebrew and the Greek story as it stands. They do have one element in common though, the mythologem: Man has lost the golden Paradise by a disastrous action of the first woman.

Whether this story be taken as part of our common heritage, or has emerged independently as a general misogynic invention must be a matter for private speculation. There are other aspects of the Pandora myth which point in other directions which we shall see later.

In v. 106-201 Hesiod once again explains the origin of evil by means of a myth: The *Five Races myth*. To begin with there was the golden race of men who lived a life of eternal youth in a blissful paradise without toil and sorrow. After these came the silver race who enjoyed the same blessings, but who were curiously degenerate and far inferior to the golden race. The silver race was followed by the "brazen race", described as savage and brute. (The description of this race seems to reveal a vague and distorted memory of an *archaeological* bronze age). Then follows the race of the heroes. They are "better and more just" – here is actually an advance and improvement, only temporary however. This is the race of heroes which we know from the battles of Thebes and Troy. Finally we have the hideous iron-age in which injustice rules and in which decency – personified in the gods *Aidos* and *Nemesis* – leaves the human scene.

In this sequence can be detected one of the most obvious examples of adaptation: The race of the Heroes, representing the great age of Greek legend must, of course, be included in the Tale of the Ages of the World, but it fits in remarkably badly; it ruins the intention of the narrative by signifying advance and it is not like the other races characterized by a metal. Do we know any such myth of the ages of the world which shows a gradual decline, characterized by metals of increasingly inferior worth? We do, in fact. In Zoroastrian teaching,[7] unfortunately, quoted only from two books of the *Avesta*, now lost, we hear about four ages of the world, each of a thousand years, revealed to the prophet in a dream in which Ahura Mazda shows the prophet a tree with four golden branches, four silver- four brazen and four iron ones, and tells him that these are the future four ages of the world. The *Book of Daniel* 2.3ff. is a further parallel. Here again the story is told in the form of a dream: The image in Nebuchadnezzar's dream has a golden head, breast and arms of silver, belly and loins of copper and legs and feet of iron mixed with clay. Here are five stages, corresponding to five successive realms of the world. As in Hesiod we have five steps, but they proceed without any irregularities. None of these tales, however, can be the actual model for Hesiod since he is older than both the

---

7. SINCLAIR 1932, 16; WEST 1978, 174 f. Here is also treated a somewhat more distant parallel, an Indian notion of four ages of the world (yuga) of decreasing quality, not characterized by metals, however, but by the various marriage rituals. These Indian texts are somewhat younger than Hesiod.

others, but they may easily originate in some older, oriental version of this mythological pattern.

After these myths follow several long, moralizing passages on injustice and laziness, the two faults that characterize Hesiod's brother. This section starts with a short fable about a hawk and a nightingale symbolizing injustice and abuse of power. The animal fable is certainly a wide-spread literary form but it is particularly strongly represented in the Near East where it is well-known as far back as the Sumerians who often employ this form for moralizing purposes or to open people's eyes to the hard facts of life.[8]

This whole introductory section belongs to the genre termed Wisdom literature which is to be found in the literatures of many nations but which is, again, extremely richly represented in Egypt and the Near East.[9] The most well-known examples are probably the, in this context, rather recent ones of the *Book of Proverbs* from the Old Testament and the *Book of Wisdom* and the *Book of Jesus Sirak* from the Apocrypha. The oldest known example, however, is Sumerian from about 2500 B.C. and this already employs one of the most frequently used formulas: father giving moral instruction to son. We also find the genre in Babylonian ethics, and from Egypt we know numerous examples which are roughly of the same age as the Sumerian one. Among these are some in which the basis or explanation of the subsequent moralizing is dissatisfaction with the addressee.[10] One text, known as *The Words of Ahiquar*[11] has a framework which resembles that of Hesiod. It is a story about an uncle, vizier to king Senacherib, who gives advice to his offending nephew. The poem is known in several languages but the oldest surviving text, an Aramaic one, is from the 5th century B.C. and thus cannot be the model for Hesiod. But given the age and the dissemination in the Near East of the genre it is tempting to see in this a subcategory of the Wisdom literature.

One can point out passages with a clear affinity to Wisdom literature

---

8. NØJGAARD 1964, 433-46; WALCOT 1966, 90; ANDERSEN 1977, 93 f.
9. Good documentation in PRITCHARD 1950. Sumerian texts in ALSTER 1974 and 1975; Babylonian texts in LAMBERT 1960; further references in WALCOT 1966, chapt. IV and WEST 1978, 3-25.
10. WEST 1978, 11.
11. PRITCHARD 1950, 427-30; THOMAS 1958, 270.

in the Homeric poems too,[12] and the genre is continued in Theognis and Phokylides. Whether it has been taken over by the Greeks directly from the Near East can obviously not be proved, but it is very tempting to see an oriental inspiration in the Greek use of the genre considering how extremely common it was everywhere in the Near East.

The concluding section of Hesiod's poem about good and bad days is possibly indepted to Babylonian hemerologies or to Egyptian calendars of lucky and unlucky days. Herodotus drops a remark (2.82) to the effect that the Egyptians associate certain gods with certain days and months, and that they had "discovered", as he terms it, what events would befall people born on this or that day.

In this rather sketchy survey I have attempted to show how surprisingly many parallels to the Near East we find in Hesiod's works. We have had to content ourselves with noticing a series of parallels and similarities, not being able to prove any specific correlation between the Greek and the oriental manifestations in question, but we note several obvious examples of Greek adaptation; in other words, they are the ones who assimilate transmitted material.

We have already noted one example, viz. the *Five Races myth* from the *Works and Days*. The presence of the Race of Heroes reveals that we are dealing with borrowed material. Hesiod's version is celarly secondary, although we cannot trace the original form of the myth we can be fairly certain that it must have run along the same lines as the Persian myth of the stages of the world.

In the following I will give a few examples of a phenomenon which the Greek epic tradition regularly attempts to interpret away and thus revealing itself as secondary in relation to an older tradition – here I am thinking of the mythological material associated with vegetation- and fertility gods.

From Egypt and the Near East we know a whole range of typologically related gods – mother goddesses, earth-goddesses or mother/earth goddesses accompanied by a male vegetation deity, regarded as lover or son – or both – of the goddess. Examples are Isis and Osiris, Cybele or Magna Mater and Attis, Atargatis (Dea Syria) and Hadad and several

---

12. Moral advice in, for instance, Nestor's speech in the first book of the Iliad, and in Phoinix' speech in the ninth book; practical didactics in Nestor's advice to his son Antilochos in *Iliad* 23, v. 306-48.

others. The vegetation deity by the side of the mother-goddess can also be female as in the case of Kore and Demeter.

It is furthermore a widely held assumption that a similar type of cult existed in the Aegean region before the Doric invasion, just as Cretan images of (supposed) goddesses, surrounded by wild animals or with youths at their side are interpreted in the same way. In strong support of this latter we have, from historical times, tales of Cretan Zeus, a figure vastly different from the Hellenic sky- and weather god; he was the dying god (who was presumably reborn every year). They tell about the childhood of Zeus, rationalizing the notion of some vegetation cult: The *Kuretes,* a typical band of vegetation deities dance and sing noisily round the new-born god in order to hide his cries from his father Kronos who wants to kill him.

The first mythological harmonizing between these two gods we find in the *Theogony* of Hesiod who adds something to the above-mentioned succession myth of the three generations of ruling gods: Uranos – Kronos – Zeus. In Hesiod's tale Kronos swallows his children as they are born, but when Zeus is about to enter this world his mother and grandmother bring him in safety to Crete where he grows up, while Kronos is deceived with a stone swaddled as a baby. This motif, the hidden and threatened god-child, has no oriental counterpart and probably owes its existence to the need of the Greeks to create a connecting link between two essentially different gods. The Cretan god must have played an important part *before* the assimilation of the succession myth, since it was felt to be urgent to incorporate him in the mythology around the supreme god. So Hesiod or his predecessor harmonized the tales, installing the Cretan deity among the Olympians, toning down at the same time the element of fertility cult.

In the fourth book of the *Odyssey* Menelaos is telling Telemachos about his meeting with the sea-god Proteus who reveals to him the fate of his friends, and also predicts Menelaos' own fate. In v. 561-69 he learns the astonishing news that he will not die but will go to the islands of the blessed because he is married to Helen and thus the son-in-law of Zeus! This notion of eternal life and bliss is totally alien to the epic in general, and its association with the person of Helen is a surprising feature of the Homeric poems. Outside the poems, however, Helen is actually the object of a cult and not only in her mythological homeland of Laconia, but as far away as Rhodes where she is worshipped as a vegetation deity under the name of *Dendritis* (her of the tree);[13] this again reminds us of the importance of tree-worship in Minoan religion. If Helen belongs to the group of vegetation deities who have disappeared, either because they are dead, have left in anger, or have been stolen away from home with disastrous results for mankind, the enormous effort to get her back takes on a totally different significance from the one we know from the Greek epic. But it also shows how, apart from this one glimpse into another religious world, the role of Helen has been completely rationalized in the Homeric poems, so that she has even become the prototype of the beautiful but wanton woman whose erotic escapades create infinite woe.

In the case of Pandora we see her pictured as a femme fatale, the cause of endless disaster, not only, like Helen, of a great war, but, like Eve, of the whole miserable state of mankind. This mythological feature may have ancient roots, but it is still secondary and is an indication of a rationalizing process. Pandora is almost certainly originally a fertility goddess of which her name bears witness. The most plausible interpretation of this is: "she who gives all". Hesiod goes to great lengths to explain that she is thus named because *all (pantes)* the gods have given her *gifts (dōra)* at her creation. But this passive interpretation seems far-fetched and inconsistent with the linguistic interpretation which seems most natural i.e. the active sense of "she who gives all". "Pandora" is well-known as another name for the *Earth (Gaia)*[14] in which connection the word must undoubtedly be taken in its active and positive sense. There can hardly be any doubt that Pandora is an original fertility-goddess, re-interpreted and rationalized by Hesiod or his predecessor. If this is correct it must be reasonable to ask: »From where comes the *pithos*? In Hesiod's tale it is just there. There are two possiblities: 1) The pithos may be the "stage property" to the well-known folk-tale motif of someone peeping into casks or chests or behind locked doors with disastrous consequences to the curious. Or 2) the pithos may be an organic part of the Pandora figure. If this is the case I boldly suggest that, originally, it contained good things and not catastrophies. Pandora, the "giver of all", understood as the giver of all evil would be

---

13. FARNELL II 1896, 675; NILSSON 1932, 73-75, 170-74.
14. E.g. Aristophanes, *The Birds* v. 971 with scholia; Homer *Epigram* 7, v. 1.

inconceivable in an original fertility myth whatever later rationalizing and interpretation may have put into the name. We know from the sources of many examples in Hittite and Syrian mythology of the great mother-goddess being depicted with a vessel in her hand, and it must also here be mentioned that the name Cybele (Hittite Kubaba) has been interpreted as "the goddess with the vessel".[15] Information of this kind leaves open several possibilities of interpretation. One possible interpretation of the vessel is as a kind of cornucopia, symbol of the giving of gifts by the fertility deity.

Anyway it seems clear that these vegetation- and fertility cults, widespread in the Near Eastern and Aegean regions, probably as some kind of religious koinē, have left their traces in the epic, but in a negative way i.e. they have been explained away, but no more so than they still allow us to form a certain opinion of what went before.

Summary

In the present century the debt to the Near East of Greek myths and mythological concepts is widely acknowledged. The eldest epic writers bear witness to this; in Hesiod, particularly, it is often possible to point to traces of alterations and adaptation. The present paper examines a number of elements in Hesiod's poem *Works and Days* and shows that the mythological material as well as the litarary forms have parallels in the Near East; furthermore, it draws attention to several instances in Homer and Hesiod of re-interpretation and rationalizing of myths and religious concepts which in their basic form must have been connected with the types of fertility- and vegetation deities, well-known throughout the Near East.[16]

University of Copenhagen
Institute of Classical Philology
Njalsgade 94
DK-2300 Copenhagen S

---

15. FINK 1958, 23 ff. (Kubaba, Hittite predecessor of Phrygian Cybele: GURNEY 1952, 138).

16. This paper has been translated by Hanne Carlsen.

BIBLIOGRAPHY

ALSTER 1974	B. ALSTER, *The Instructions og Šuruppak*. Copenhagen.
ALSTER 1975	B. ALSTER, *Studies in Sumerian Proverbs*. Copenhagen.
ANDERSEN 1973	L. ANDERSEN, *Hesiod: Theogonien, Værker og dage, Skjoldet*. Ovs. med Indl. og noter. København.
ANDERSEN 1976	L. ANDERSEN: »Nogle forudsætninger for Hesiods Theogoni«. *MusTusc* 27, pp. 3-19.
ANDERSEN 1977	L. ANDERSEN, *Introduktion til Hesiod*. København.
ANDERSEN 1978	L. ANDERSEN, »Overvejelser over mytebegrebet«. *MusTusc* 32-33, pp. 3-14.
CLEMEN 1939	C. CLEMEN, »Die phönikische Religion nach Philo von Byblos«. *MVAG* 42,3, 1-77.
FARNELL 1896-1909	L. R. FARNELL, *The Cults of the Greek States I-V*. Oxford.
FINK 1958	G. FINK, *Pandora und Epimetheus*. Fürth.
GURNEY 1952	O. R. GURNEY, *The Hittites*. Pelican Books (1954).
LAMBERT 1960	W. G. LAMBERT, *Babylonian Wisdom Literature*. Oxford.
NILSSON 1932	M. P. NILSSON, *The Mycenaean Origin of Greek Mythology*. Berkeley, California.
NØJGAARD 1964	M. NØJGAARD, *La fable antique*. Copenhagen.
PRITCHARD 1950	J. B. PRITCHARD (ed.), *Ancient Near Eastern Texts Relating to the Old Testament*. Princeton.
RAVN 1953	O. E. RAVN, *Verdensreligionernes Hovedværker II: Babyloniske religiøse tekster*. Copenhagen.
SINCLAIR 1932	T. A. SINCLAIR, *Hesiod, Works and Days*. London.
THOMAS 1958	D. W. THOMAS (ed.), *Documents from Old Testament Times*.
WALCOT 1966	P. WALCOT, *Hesiod and the Near East*. Cardiff.
WEST 1966	M. L. WEST, *Hesiod, Theogony*. Ed. with Prolegomena and Commentary. Oxford.
WEST 1978	M. L. WEST, *Hesiod, Works and Days*. Ed. with Prolegomena and Commentary. Oxford.

PROLEGOMENA TO A STUDY OF THE PHOENICIAN/PUNIC COLONIZATION OF TUNISIA[1]

by JOHN LUND

The present paper is intended as a first step towards a comprehensive study of the Phoenician and subsequent Punic colonization of a part of north Africa corresponding to present day Tunisia (*fig.* 1). It seems natural to single out Tunisia as the study area in view of the fact that the most important Phoenician colony in the western Mediterranean, Carthage, is located here. Furthermore, it is commonly accepted that the Phoenicians played a major role in the transmission of Oriental culture from the eastern Mediterranean to the west, although the importance of the Phoenician contribution is assessed differently by the scholars. Danish archaeologists have a more than 150 years old tradition for working in Tunisia, beginning with the pioneering investigations carried out by C. T. Falbe (LIVENTHAL 1986, LUND 1986b) in the first part of the nineteenth century and continued with the excavations by the Danish National Museum in Carthage from 1975 to 1984. This tradition is now carried on by the "Project Africa Proconsularis", of which the first full scale campaign took place in 1987.

It should be stated at the outset that the point of departure for the following remarks is constituted by the archaeological material, i.e. the actual finds including inscriptions; however, literary sources can of course not be neglected, and they will be treated separately in the planned, more extensive study of the subject.

Furthermore, it may be useful to begin with a clarification of some of the terms used in this paper. The ancient Greeks called the inhabitants

---

1. I should like to thank Dr. Joseph A. Greene for kindly allowing me to mention some of the results from his survey work in the Carthaginian hinterland and Mr. Niels Levinsen for drawing fig. 1 and table 1. It should be stated at the outset that it is beyond the scope of this paper to give a full documentation of the subject; as a rule references are only given to important, recent publications, which usually contain copious bibliographical information. The "Bibliographie Analytique de l'Afrique Antique" published regularly since 1961-1962 by Jean Desanges and S. Lancel is an invaluable tool for scholars in the field. Cf. also FANTAR 1983 and ENNABLI 1983.

PHONICIAN/PUNIC COLONIZATION OF TUNISIA

Fig. 1. Map of Tunisia.

of a narrow strip of the Levantine coast more or less corresponding to present-day Lebanon "Phoenicians", and archaeologists and historians have continued to use this designation.² The culture of the descendants of the Phoenicians, who emigrated from this area and settled in the western Mediterranean is often referred to as "Punic". A study by G. Bunnens (BUNNENS 1983) has shown, that to the ancient Greek authors the inhabitants of Carthage were Phoenicians no less than the inhabitants of e.g. Sidon, and that the Roman writers did not distinguish between the western and eastern branches of the Phoenician people before the late Republic: the word "Poenus" was until then used as the designation of a Carthagenian as well as a Phoenician in our sense of the word. However, from the time of Cicero onwards "Poeni" was increasingly used as a name for "Phoenicians in the western Mediterranean". It would thus perhaps be more accurate to refer to the culture of the Carthagenians and their kinsmen as Phoenician instead of Punic. It seems best, though, to adhere to the traditional names in order to avoid unnecessary confusion.

The presence of Phoenicians and their descendants in Tunisia is well documented, but the same does not hold true for the original population of the area, who are called Libyans by Greek sources, Numidians by the Roman ones and who are now usually referred to as Berbers (HORN & RÜGER 1979, DECRET & FANTER 1981, FERCHIOU 1986). Thanks to literary sources we are relatively well informed about the situation of the Libyans in the second and third centuries B.C. (Cf. BERTHIER 1981). However, the culture of the Libyans in the earlier part of the first millennium B.C. remains a white spot on the archaeological map, and chronological uncertainty shrouds many of the monuments, which may be associated with this people. Megalithic graves, clearly a non-Phoenician/Punic type of burial,³ thus occur at a number of sites in Tunisia, and many scholars have referred the tombs in question to a relatively remote period of time.⁴ A large number of such megalithic

---

2. Cf. the recent discussion in HUSS 1985, 5-6 for a recent discussion of the ancient name of the Phoenicians. The delimitation of the exact area dominated by the Phoenician city states is a subject for discussion, cf. ELAYI 1982.
3. Megalithic tombs are not mentioned in BENICHOU-SAFAR 1982.
4. The megalithic tombs of Tunisia are now usually thought to go no further back in time than to around 1500-1400 B.C., cf. KUPER & GABRIEL 1979, 41-42. However, cf. infra note 5.

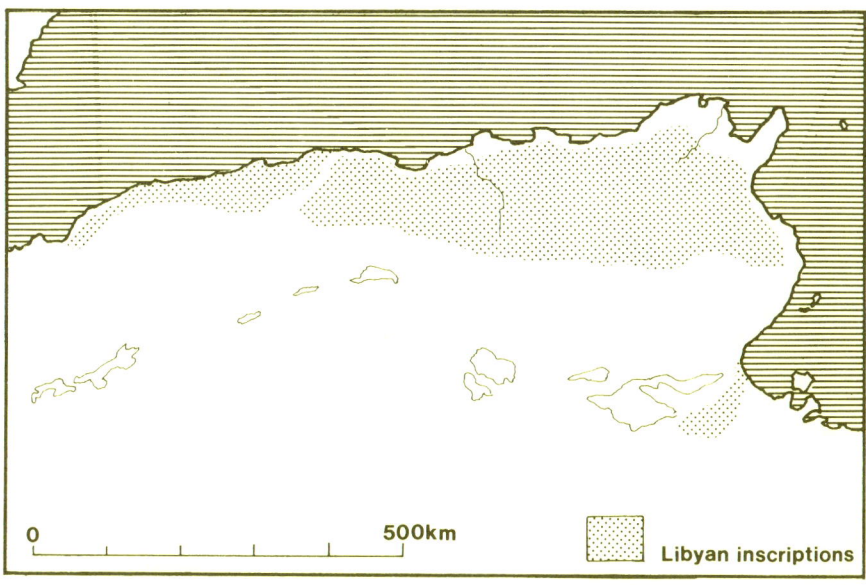

Fig. 2. Distribution of Libyan inscriptions in Algiers and Tunisia (After RÖSSLER 1979, 94 fig. 24).

graves have been excavated, e.g. at Dougga and Ellès, and they usually contain finds dating from the third to the second century B.C. or of an even later date.[5] Of course we may be dealing with re-used tombs in a number of instances (Cf. CINTAS 1961, 41), though hardly in all cases. But the fact that megalithic tombs are sometimes located in the vicinity of urban centers from the Hellenistic/Roman period, almost certainly indicates that they were (still?) being constructed in the Hellenistic and Roman periods. Libyan inscriptions constitute another, late, source informing us about the people (Cf. RÖSSLER 1979). It appears that the oldest datable inscription is located on the well known Mausoleum at Dougga, usually dated to the second century B.C. A map tracing the distribution of Libyan inscriptions thus illustrates the situation after the fall of Carthage in 146 B.C. (*fig.* 2). Nevertheless it seems likely that it

---

5. A comprehensive list of megalithic tombs in North Africa may be found in CINTAS 1961, 20-22. Obviously, many new finds have been made since then, and it is beyond the scope of this paper to attempt to update Cintas' list. Cf. e.g. POINSSOT 1983, 68: "A Thugga, comme ailleurs en Afrique, les documents archéologiques recueillis dans les dolmens ne sont jamais antérieurs au IIIe. siècle av. JC." and for Ellès 30 Ans 1986, 45-50.

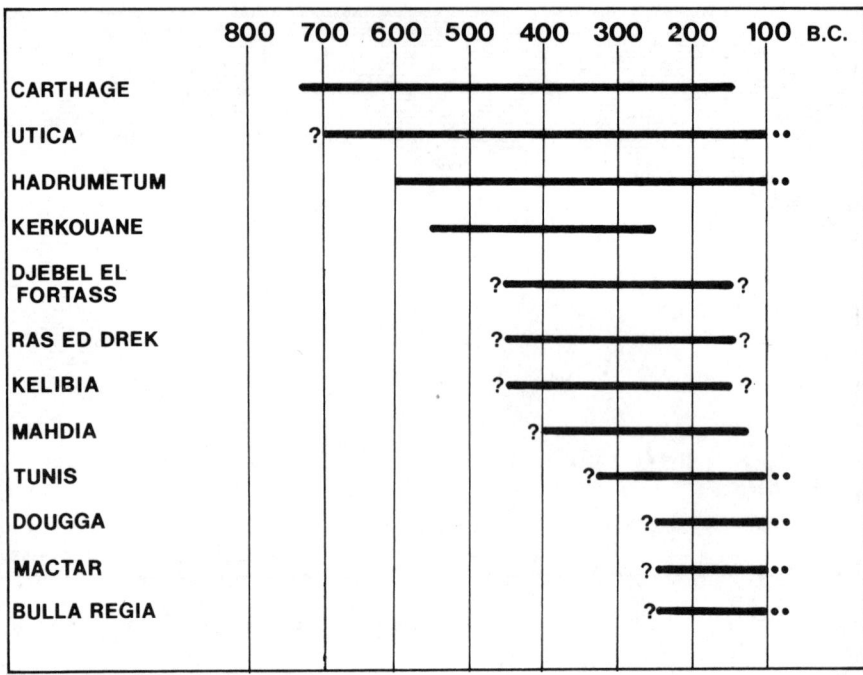

Table 1. A selection of major sites in Tunisia with indication of the datable archaeological material.

gives some idea of where Libyans were living before that date as well; indeed there is little reason to doubt that Libyans occupied all of the Tunisian territory when the Phoenicians arrived.

The Phoenician expansion in the western Mediterranean has been the subject of intensive study in recent years. Among the plethora of recent contributions a few studies may be singled out: the survey by Hans Georg Niemeyer (NIEMEYER 1984), and the "Geschichte der Karthager" by W. Huss (HUSS 1985) as well as a monograph by Guy Bunnens dealing with the subject on the background of literary traditions (BUNNENS 1979). In the case of Tunisia one may especially single out the important studies by P. Cintas (CINTAS 1970 and CINTAS 1976) and M. H. Fantar (FANTAR 1971, FANTAR 1984, FANTAR 1985 and FANTAR 1986) as well as further contributions by Tunisian archaeologists (e.g. BEN YOUNES 1981, not yet published, cf. FANTAR 1978).[6] The questions

---

6. See also the contributions by Tunisian scholars in the new journal *REPPAL* (published since 1985).

to be discussed in the following have, of course, been addressed previously both by these and other authorities, but it appears that most scholars have concentrated on the early phase of Phoenician colonization of Tunisia, whereas a general study of the process throughout the centuries up to the destruction of Carthage by the Romans in 146 B.C. based primarily on the archaeological sources has apparently rarely been attempted (however, cf. FANTAR 1971).

As a point of departure for such a study it will be necessary to gather together and evaluate all relevant published data from the archaeological investigation of Tunisia during the last two centuries. Of course, the interpretation of the material is no straightforward matter. On the basis of e.g. ceramic finds at a given site it is difficult to determine with any degree of certainty whether it was once inhabited by Phoenicians and/or their descendants, Libyans or Liby-Phoenicians (on the latter see DECRET & FANTAR 60-64). However, it will be necessary to establish criteria for a classification of the people involved, if we wish to draw any significant conclusions about the interrelationship between the peoples involved. As an end result of the investigation, it will hopefully be possible to draw a series of maps illustrating the changing distribution pattern of settlements, fortifications, sanctuaries, cemeteries etc. through the centuries.

The results of a major study along these lines cannot be discounted in advance. Nevertheless, it seems that a survey of the material can provide us with a background for formulating working hypotheses. *Table 1* comprises some of the most important archaeological sites in Tunisia and indicates the periods, for which datable archaeological material is present. It is important to stress this, because the dates provided by the archaeological material do not always coincide with the dates given by ancient authors. In the 8th and 7th centuries B.C. the documentation is virtually limited to the sites of Carthage and Utica.[7] We are in both cases dealing with coastal localities, the geographical setting of which is in accordance with the type of setting chosen elsewhere by the Phoeni-

---

7. For a well documented recent account of the literary traditions about the foundation of Carthage cf. HUSS 1985, 39-43. General surveys of the results of the investigation of Punic Carthage since 1972 have been published by S. Lancel and F. Rakob; references to these and other relevant publications can be found in LUND 1986a; cf. also RAKOB 1987 and LUND 1988. The basic bibliography of Utica is cited in FANTAR 1971, 129-133, ENNABLI 1976a and HUSS 1985, 34.

cians for their colonies and emporia in the western Mediterranean. Witness e.g. the situation in southern Spain, where H. G. Niemeyer has recently singled out two types of geographical setting of special interest to the Phoenician settlers: 1) narrow tongues of land cropping out from hills near the coast towards the mouths of rivers and 2) tiny islands located near the coastline likewise often in the vicinity of rivers (NIEMEYER 1984, 48-51). Utica exemplifies more or less the first situation, but Carthage differs from the norm in not being located near a river mouth. As underlined by H. G. Niemeyer, Carthage is also exceptional among the Phoenician settlements in having a foundation myth and the city had a larger hinterland than usually seen (NIEMEYER 1984, 57-60).

An archaeological survey in the Carthaginian countryside was conducted by Joseph A. Greene in connection with the work carried out by the Canadian expedition to Carthage. The first campaign, which took place in eight months in 1979-1980, covered an area of 900 square kilometers, and the strategy employed consisted in concentrating on previously identified sites, of which the location is indicated on the Archaeological Atlas of Tunisia from 1893. More than 112 sites were visited, dating from the 7th century B.C. to the 19th century A.D. according to the preliminary report. The 7th century B.C. sites are of a special interest in the present context. Joseph A. Greene will shortly publish the results in full, but he has kindly allowed me to refer to the relevant evidence here. In 1979/1980 two sites were located, nos. CS 019 and CS 1020, which were dated to the 7th century B.C. The 1983 survey, which was conducted within a 3 km. radius of the Byrsa hill, yielded no finds of a comparable antiquity – in fact nothing earlier than the fourth century B.C.[8] It is hardly possible to evaluate the new information properly until the material from the two sites discovered in 1979/1980 is made fully public. Can it be taken as evidence for actual Phoenician/Punic presence at the two sites in question or will the finds rather point towards a Libyan presence? It is important to remember, that if the finds, presumably sherds, are of Phoenician/Punic origin,

---

8. The information about the results of this survey was kindly put at my disposal by Joseph A. Greene in a letter dated the 17th of May 1987. Cf. also GREENE 1983, GREENE 1985 and GREENE 1988.

then it does not follow with certainty that they are evidence of colonists in the area. We may simply be dealing with fragments of pots imported to Libyan sites from the Phoenician/Punic territory. It is probable, that such questions will remain unanswered until the sites in question have been excavated, since a surface survey is unlikely to have uncovered evidence of the architectural remains connected with the finds. The emergence of the new material thus raises as many questions as it answers – a common enough situation.

At all events it seems best to conclude that the situation in Tunisia in the 8th and 7th centuries B.C. was probably more or less similar to that of the southern littoral of Spain with Phoenician settlements located on the coastline and little or no evidence for expansion into the interior of the country. Niemeyer has observed that the local sites in the hinterland of the Phoenician sites in Spain have produced no evidence for intensive acculturation and that the cultural radiation from the Phoenician colonies appears to be limited to export of wheel-made pottery.[9] Of course, our conception of the situation in Tunisia may need revision when the new survey results are made fully public.

In the 6th and 5th centuries the picture becomes somewhat more complex. Phoenician/Punic presence is now documented in Hadrumetum (= Sousse)[10] as well as at the site now called Kerkouane on the Cap Bon peninsula, where Tunisian archaeologists have uncovered a substantial part of a Punic city, which appears to have been destroyed violently around the middle of the third century B.C. never to be rebuilt (MOREL 1969, FANTAR 1984, FANTAR 1985, FANTAR 1986). Furthermore, Tunisian and Italian archaeologists have identified and investigated three fortifications on the coastline of Cap Bon, which are dated to the fifth century B.C. (BARRECA & FANTAR 1983); the date is based on stylistic comparisons between the architecture of the localities in question and better dated fortifications in Sardinia, and none of the published finds appears to predate the 4th or the 3rd centuries. At all events it seems legitimate to conclude, that the new Phoenician/Punic settlements in the 6th and 5th centuries B.C. continue to be limited to the

---

9. NIEMEYER 1984, 54-55.
10. See especially FOUCHER 1964; the basic bibliography is given by FANTAR 1971, 135-136, ENNABLI 1976a, HUSS 1985, 33.

coastal zone. However, a move towards the interior of the country may already have begun in the 5th century, as witnessed by the finding of Greeek black glazed pottery dated to the 5th-4th century B.C. at Uzita (VAN DER WERFF 1982). This site is located on the coastal plain, but not on the beach itself. Interestingly, evidence for relations between the new settlers and the original population now exists: at the fortress Djebel el-Fortass on Cap Bon, traces have been found of a Libyan settlement with tumulus graves in the vicinity of the fortification (BARRECA & FANTAR 1983, 13-14). Later: in the fourth and third centuries, we have rock-cut inscriptions on graves near Kerkouane apparently giving a Libyan name, but written with the Punic alphabet (FANTAR 1973, 269, FANTAR 1986, 414-426).

The scene changes in the 4th and 3rd centuries B.C. By then substantial evidence exists for a Punic expansion into the interior of the country. The results of the previously mentioned survey work by Joseph A. Greene in the Carthaginian hinterland is of interest in this connection. Dr. Greene has concluded that: »Thus there seems to be a few early (i.e. 7th century B.C.) sites at some distance from the city, but none in the immediate vicinity until the 4th century B.C. I would put the real surge in hinterland settlement as late as 3rd century B.C.". These conclusions are in accordance with other finds in the vicinity of Carthage: what appears to be a "rural villa" has been excavated at Gammarth (FANTAR 1985, 14-24) and a private house likewise dating from the late 3rd-first half of 2nd century B.C. have been located at the Bai des Singes (FANTAR 1985, 13-14) and in near-by Tunis no finds predating the 4th century B.C. have appeared (FANTAR 1979). Considering the fact that Tunis is the capital of Tunisia with approximately a million inhabitants and intensive building activity it seems likely that the finds are representative, scarce though they are.

A similar situation exists for the rest of Tunisia, where burial grounds from the 4th to 2nd centuries B.C. are numerous, and M. H. Fantar has stated that they occur "almost everywhere" in the country (FANTAR 1971, 142)[11]. However, it is not clear in all cases whether we are dealing

---

11. A bibliography of some of the sites can be found in HUSS 1985, 33-34. To this may be added a number of recent contributions: BEN YOUNES 1985, BEN YOUNES 1986, BEN YOUNES 1987, BEN YOUNES & MANSOUR 1987. A review of the settlement remains may be found in FANTAR 1985, 11-29.

with the burial grounds of the Libyans containing 4th century and/or Hellenistic material, or if the tombs in question contain the remains of the Punic population. It seems likely that the former is more probable with a number of the burial grounds excavated in the interior of Tunisia, e.g. at Dougga and Bulla Regia. An important new study by N. Ferchiou (FERCHIOU 1987) of the funerary evidence from two inland regions of Tunisia has resulted in the identification of about sixty monumental tombs dating from the late 3rd to the 2nd centuries B.C., of which a number are tentatively identified as those of Punic landlords, built on their estates.[12]

A recent survey of the Kasserine area in the interior of Tunisia has resulted in the identification of eighty-nine sites, and twenty-three of these are said to date to the first milennium B.C. or earlier. The finds from the sites in question have not yet been examined in detail, but it has been tentatively concluded that there is evidence of pastoral nomadism until the late 1st century A.D., where agriculturally-based settlements make their appearance (HITCHNER 1988, 12 and 39). It is reasonable to assume that the twenty-three sites are to be associated with the native, Libyan population.

B. S. J. Isserlin has recently pointed out (ISSERLIN 1983) that rural establishments are virtually unknown in the Punic world, and he expressed the wish that a surface survey project could be carried out in order to localize such settlements.[13] It is to be hoped that the "Project Africa Proconsularis" will in the not too distant future identify and excavate one of the Late Punic rural sites. Two field campaigns of this joint Tunisian/Danish venture have taken place until now: a limited exploration in 1984 mostly limited to previously known sites and a full scale campaign in 1987. The publication of the preliminary results will appear shortly.

In conclusion it may be said that even though the material reviewed here is fragmentary, the outline of the picture of the Phoenician and

---

12. This hypothesis is supported by the finding of a few Hellenistic sherds on the site itself both in 1984 and in 1987. However, the Late Punic presence appears to have been on a more limited scale than in the Early Roman period, where the number of sherds increases dramatically.

13. The evideence for rural settlements in present day Tunisia was in 1983 limited to a building at Gammarth, published by M. H. Fantar and the by then unpublished work carried out by Joseph A. Greene.

subsequent Punic colonization of Tunisia seems clear. It appears that the activities were mainly limited to the littoral area right down to the late fifth/fourth centuries B.C. In fact the sites are generally located at the beach. Furthermore it can be seen that several of the cities (Carthage, Kerkouane as well as the fortresses at Cap Bon) were surrounded by defensive walls. It may be guessed that the enemies of the new settlers were the Libyans no less than the Romans or other external enemies. An expansion towards the interior of the country does not seem to have occurred earlier than the late fifth/fourth or possibly as late as the third century B.C as argued by Joseph A. Greene. In this connection it can be recalled that the army of Agathocles, which invaded Cap Bon in 310 B.C. advanced through an extremely fertile countryside with plantations of olive trees and fields of grapes and many farms according to Diodorus Siculus (XX, 8,2-4).

It is reasonable to assume, as several authorities have previously done,[14] that the drive towards the interior of the country is to be connected with political events: the losses of territories overseas as a consequence of The first Punic war. However, this event may have accelerated a development, which had begun earlier: in the 5th and 4th centuries B.C. Interestingly, the intensive investigation of Carthage, which has been carried out during the last decades, has shown that these two centuries were characterized by an intensive building activity, where previously uninhabited areas were utilized for habitation purposes. What was the reason for the apparent boom in the Punic Metropolis in the fifth and fourth centuries and the seemingly more or less contemporaneous beginning of colonization of the interior of Tunisia? The historical sources (WARMINGTON 1964, HUSS 1985) tell us about fights between Carthagenians and Libyans in the centuries in question resulting in a widening of the Carthaginian sphere of influence. However, it may be asked whether the military expansion should not be considered as yet another symptom of the development, rather than as its true cause. Perhaps the developments in Tunisia are in some way related to the political events in the eastern Mediterranean, where Phoenicia lost its independence in the sixth century forcing the colonies to become more self-sufficient. It will be a central goal for the more

---

14. Cf. e.g. FERCHIOU 1987, 67; Joseph A. Green.

complete study of the question treated here to attempt to throw light on this complex question; perhaps no single answer can be given. It is likely that a number of causes contributed to the developments in Tunisia, and that the situation in this area cannot be viewed in isolation from that of the other regions dominated by Carthage in the western Mediteranean.

The National Museum of Denmark
The Department of Classical
and Near Eastern Antiquities
Frederiksholms Kanal 12
DK-1220 Copenhagen K

BIBLIOGRAPHY

BARRECA & FANTAR 1983	F. BARRECA & M. H. FANTAR, *Prospezione Archeologica al Capo Bon – II, Collezione di Studi Fenici,* 14. Rome.
BEN YOUNES 1981	H. BEN YOUNES, *La Présence Punique au Sahel d'après les données littéraires et archeéologiques,* unpublished.
BEN YOUNES 1985	H. BEN YOUNES, Rapport sur la Campagne de fouilles Effectuée dans la Grande Nécropole de la Région de Mahdia – Oct.-Nov. 1982, *REPPAL* 1, 23-61.
BEN YOUNES 1986	H. BEN YOUNES, La Necropole Punique d'el Hkayma, Mai 1984, *REPPAL* 2, 31-172.
BEN YOUNES 1987a	H. BEN YOUNES, Note sur les tumulus de Henchir el Mizouri (Sidi Alouane) au Sahel Tunisien, *REPPAL* 3, 33-42.
BEN YOUNES & GHAKI 1987	H. BEN YOUNES & M. GHAKI, Sahel, *REPPAL* 3, 261-273.
BENICHOU-SAFAR 1982	H. BENICHOU-SAFAR, *Les Tombes Puniques de Carthage, Topographie, Structures, Inscriptions et Rites Funéraires.* Paris.
BERTHIER 1981	A. BERTHIER, *La Numidie, Rome et le Maghreb.*
BUNNENS 1979	G. BUNNENS, *L'expansion phénicienne en Mediterranée.* Brussels/Rome.
BUNNENS 1983	G. BUNNENS, La Distinction entre Phéniciens et puniques chez les auteurs classiques, in: *CongrFenPun* 1983, I, 233-238.
CINTAS 1961	P. CINTAS, *Elements d'etude pour une Protohistoire de la Tunisie.* Paris.
CINTAS 1970	P. CINTAS, *Manuel d'archéologie punique* I.
CINTAS 1976	P. CINTAS, *Manuel d'archéologie punique* II.
CongrFenPun 1983	*Atti del I congresso Internazionale di Studi Fenici e Punici* – Roma, 5-10 Novembre 1979, I-III. Rome.
DECRET & FANTAR 1981	F. DECRET & M. H. FANTAR, *L'Afrique du Nord dans l'Antiquité.* Paris.
ELAYI 1982	J. ELAYI, Studiees in Phoenician Geography during the Persian Period, *JNES* 41, 83-110.

ENNABLI 1976a	A. ENNABLI s.v. Hadrumetum, in: *The Princeton Encyclopedia of Classical Sites*, Princeton, 372.
ENNABLI 1976b	A. ENNABLI s.v. Utica, in: *The Princeton Encyclopedia of Classical Sites*, Princeton, 949-950.
ENNABLI 1983	A. ENNABLI, North African Newsletter 3: Part 1. Tunisia 1956-1980, *AJA* 87, 197-206.
FANTAR 1970	M. H. FANTAR, Recherches Puniques en Tunisie, in: Ricerche Puniche nel Mediterraneo Centrale, Pubblicazioni del Centro di Studio per la Civiltà fenicia e punica 6, *Studi Semitici* 36, 75-89.
FANTAR 1971	M. H. FANTAR, Tunisie in: L'Espansione Fenicia nel Mediterraneo, Pubblicazioni del Centro di Studio per la Civiltà fenicia e punica 8, *Studi Semitici* 38, 99-143.
FANTAR 1973	M. H. FANTAR, Présence Punique au Cap Bon, *Kokalos* 18-19, 1972-1973, 264-277.
FANTAR 1978	M. H. FANTAR, Antiquitès Puniques, *Karthago* 18, 145-147.
FANTAR 1979	M. H. FANTAR, Présence punique et Romaine a Tunis et dans ses environs immédiats, *AntAfr* 14, 55-81.
FANTAR 1983	M. H. FANTAR, Les Études Puniques en Tunisie, in: *CongrFenPun* 1983, I, 179-186.
FANTAR 1984	M. H. FANTAR, *Kerkouane, Cité Punique du Cap Bon (Tunisie)* I. Tunis.
FANTAR 1985	M. H. FANTAR, *Kerkouane, Cité Punique du Cap Bon (Tunisie)* II *Architecture Domestique*. Tunis.
FANTAR 1986	M. H. FANTAR, *Kerkouane, Cité Punique du Cap Bon (Tunisie)* III *Sanctuaires et Cultes, Societe-Economie*. Tunis.
FERCHIOU 1986	N. FERCHIOU, Niveaux Numides decouverts a Mustis, *REPPAL* 2, 277-285.
FERCHIOU 1987	N. FERCHIOU, Le paysage funéraire pré-romain dans deux régions céréalières de Tunisie antique (Fahs-bou Arada et Tebourba-Mateur): Les tombeaux monumentaux, *AntAfr* 23, 13-69.
FOUCHER 1964	L. FOUCHER, *Hadrumetum*. Paris.
GREENE 1983	J.A. GREENE, Carthage Survey in: *Archaeological Survey in the Mediterranean Area*, eds. D.R. KELLER and D. RUPP, *British Archaeological Reports* 155, 1983.
GREENE 1985	J.A. GREENE, Canadian Carthage Survey in: *CEDAC CARTHAGE Bulletin* 6, Mars 1985, 19-21.
GREENE 1988	J.A. GREENE, Ager and 'Arsot: Rural Settlement and Agrarian History in the Carthaginian Countryside.
HITCHNER 1988	R.B. HITCHNER, The Kasserine Archaeological Survey, 1982-1986 (University of Virginia, USA – Institute National d'Archéologie et d'Art de Tunisie, *AntAfr* 24 1988, 7-24.
HORN & RÜGER 1979	H. G. HORN & C. B. RÜGER, *Die Numider, Reiter und Könige nördlich der Sahara*. Bonn.
HUSS 1985	W. HUSS, *Geschichte der Karthager (Handbuch der Altertumswissenschaft* III.8). Munich.
ISSERLIN 1983	B. S. J. ISSERLIN, Phoenician and Punic Rural Settlement and Agriculture: Some Archaeological Considerations, *CongrFenPun* 1983, I, 157-163.
KUPER & GABRIEL 1979	R. KUPER & B. GABRIEL, Zur Urgeschichte des Maghreb in: HORN & RÜGER, 41-42.
LIVENTHAL 1986	V. LIVENTHAL, C. T. Falbe – søofficer og arkæolog, *MusTusc* 56, 1984-1986, 337-361.
LUND 1986a	J. LUND, Ny viden om det puniske Karthago, *MusTusc* 56 1984-1986, 363-381.

LUND 1986b	J. LUND, The Archaeological Activities of Christian Tuxen Falbe in Carthage in 1837, *Carthage 8, Cahiers des Études Anciennes 18*, 9-24.
LUND 1988	J. LUND, Two Late Punic amphora stamps from the Danish Excavations at Carthage, *Studia Phoenicia* 6, in print.
MOREL 1969	J.-P. MOREL, Kerkouane, Ville punique du Cap Bon. Remarques archéologiques et historiques, *MEFRA* 81, 473-518.
NIEMEYER 1984	H. G. NEIMEYER, Die Phönizier und die Mittelmeerwelt im Zeitalter Homers, *JbzMusMainz* 31, 3-94.
POINSSOT 1983	C. POINSSOT, *Les Ruines de Dougga*, 2nd edition. Tunis.
RAKOB 1987	F. RAKOB, Zur Siedlungstopographie des Punischen Karthago, *RM* 94, 333-349.
RÖSSLER 1979	O. RÖSSLER, Die Numider, Herkunft-Schrift-Sprache, in HORN & RÜGER 1979, 89-97.
VAN DER WERFF 1982	J. H. VAN DER WERFF, Uzita, Matériel de fouilles d'une cité antique de Tunisie centrale – in Dutch. Quoted from a review by A. Bourgeois, *RA* 1987, 185-189.
WARMINGTON 1964	B. H. WARMINGTON, *Carthage*. Harmondsworth.
30 Ans 1986	*30 Ans au Service du Patrimoine, De la Carthage des Phéniciens à la Carthage de Bourguiba*. Tunis.

THE PYRGI TEXTS SEEN IN AN EAST-WEST PERSPECTIVE
by FINN O. HVIDBERG-HANSEN

The discovery in 1964 of three inscriptions on golden plates – two with Etruscan and one with Phoenician characters – in the temple area at Santa Severa, the ancient Pyrgi, the port of Caere (Cerveteri), has recently been called "eine der bedeutendsten epigraphischen Entdeckungen des 20. Jahrhunderts und ein Meilenstein in der etruskologischen Forschung".[1] The importance of the discovery for Etruscan studies has been rightly stressed, whereas the find is perhaps of minor importance, from an epigraphical point of view, for Semitic studies. The importance of the Phoenician or Punic inscription contributes above all to our knowledge of the Phoenician political and religious spheres in the Western Mediterranean.

The gold laminae from Pyrgi are now in the Museo archeologico di Villa Guilia in Rome. Here we also find the short Phoenician inscription on one of the silver bowls from Tomba Bernardini (Praeneste).[2] Another similar inscription was published in 1977 after being revealed by a cleaning of the silver bowl, well known since 1872, from Pontecagnano.[3]

The two bowl inscriptions just mentioned, both of them from an Etruscan archaeological context, can together with the inscription from Pyrgi be considered as indubitable traces of a Phoenian and/or Punic influence and presence in Central Italy from the 8th-7th cent. B.C. and onwards (the Phoenician graffiti dated to the end of the 8th cent. from Pithekoussai will be mentioned below).

Owing to their Egyptianizing inconography the two silver bowls constitute – as demonstrated by A. Rathje[4] and G. Markoe[5] – a separate group within the unity of the Italic silver bowls, these having their

---

1. WEEBER 1985, 30; 32.
2. *CIS* I, 164 = GUZZO AMADASI 1967, appendice, 1; p. 157-169.
3. d'AGOSTINO 1977, 51-58; GARBINI 1977, 58-62; concerning the history of the Pontecagnano bowl: VACCARO 1963, 241-247.
4. RATHJE 1980, 7-12.
5. MARKOE 1985, 141-142.

nearest parallels in the Cypro-Phoenician group of bowls. As regards the Egyptianizing style on the two Italic bowls it has its closest parallel to a silver bowl from Athienou (Golgoi), Cyprus[6], dated by E. Gjerstad to the 7th cent. B.C.[7]

Of particular interest in relation to the Egyptianizing style is the inscription on the bowl from Praeneste: "Eshmunya'ad, son of 'Ashtō/ā".[8] Important is here the name of 'Ashtō/ā, which seems to be a shortened form of the name of 'Ashtarte, known also from a Phoenician seal inscription from Sidon, published by N. Avigad, bearing the inscription: "Abinadab who has vowed to 'Asht in Sidon. May she bless him".[9] The dating of the inscription to the 7th cent. B.C. fits well with that of the Praeneste bowl to the 8th-7th cent.[10] Important is further that this form of the name of the goddess, apart from the Sidonian one, only occurs in Egyptian inscriptions from the 19th Dynasty to the Persian age, i.e. 1300-500 B.C.[11] If 'Ashtō/ā is identical with the goddess known from the Egyptian inscriptions (and it should be accentuated that the goddess in these inscriptions is of West-Semitic origin: "'Ashtarté à cheval"[12]), then we have an epigraphical relation between the 'Asht(a) in Phoenicia proper, in Egypt, and the Egyptianizing stilistic tradition on the bowls from Praeneste and Pontecagnano.

The inscription from Praeneste is considered to be Phoenician and is dated to the 7th cent. B.C.,[13] while that of the Pontecagnano bowl has been characterized as Phoenician with Aramaic elements and dated to the 8th-7th cent. or probably a little later.[14] It should be pointed out that the Aramaic elements may be related to Egypt where we find Aramaic-speaking Semites already from the 7th cent. B.C.[15]

---

6. RATHJE 1980, 11.
7. GJERSTAD 1946, 3-4.
8. GUZZO AMADASI 1967, 157-158; concerning the final *'aleph* as a vowel-letter indicating *ā* or *ō:* GIBSON 1982, 71.
9. AVIGAD 1966, 242-251.
10. GUZZO AMADASI 1967, 157.
11. WEIPPERT 1975, 17-21.
12. LECLANT 1960, 1-62.
13. GUZZO AMADASI 1967, 157, PECKHAM 1968, 124 sqq.; 173; cf. already BARTON 1919, 44.
14. GARBINI 1977, 58-62.
15. GRELOT 1972, 33-42.

The two bowl inscriptions and especially the name of 'Ashtā/ō emphasize the symbiosis of Phoenician and Egyptian elements characterising the stylistic tradition usually related to the Phoenician Cyprus with its Egyptianizing inconographic tradition. Furthermore it can be said that the Phoenician character of the two inscriptions is a solid argument for the presence of Phoenician trading and handicraft in Central Italy in the 8th-7th cent. B.C. This Phoenician presence is furthermore confirmed by three Phoenician graffiti from Pithekoussai, one of them on "un piatto importato di produzione fenicia", another on an imported Greek amphora, and the third one on a potsherd of local fabrication.[16]

In addition to this Phoenician epigraphical material comes the inscription from Pyrgi, the interpretation of which has caused an immense literature. The translation offered here is essentially based on that of G. Garbini;[17] it runs:

> To the Great Lady 'Ashtarte
> (is) this holy place
> which has made and which has given
> Thefarie Velianas, the regent of Cisra (Caere)
> in the month of the sacrifice to the Sun
> as a gift in the temple.
> And he has built a (star-shaped) sign (or: a cella)
> because 'Ashtarte has given him in hand to reign
> for three years,
> in the month of KRR,
> on the day of the burial of the deity.
> And (may) the years (granted) to the statue
> of the deity in its temple (be as many) as these stars!

Of the two Etruscan texts it is the longer which is most cognate with the Phoenician one; the differences reflect that we are dealing with a *quasi*-bilingual text. However, in spite of several obscurities, especially in the Etruscan text, the evident indentification of 'Ashtarte with Uni,

---

16. BUCHNER 1978, 130-140; IDEM 1982, 290-296. TEIXIDOR 1979, 387, considers the longest inscription to be Phoenician – contra GARBINI 1978, 143-148, who believes it to be Aramaic.

17. GARBINI 1980, 205-233, cf. also WEEBER 1985, 32.

the Etruscan Iuno, can be stated; the Etruscan *unialastres* can only be interpreted as an attempt to adapt the Etruscan dedication to 'Ashtarte in the Phoenician one. On the other hand the twice occuring *heram* in the Etruscan text can hardly – as does A. J. Pfiffig[18] – be interpreted as the name of Hera, how tempting this may be, taking in consideration the usual identification of Hera with Iuno and the fact that Hera is found in Greek 4th-3rd cent. inscriptions from Caere.[19] The word *heram* more likely means "il simulacro divino" = the Greek *herma, hermes, hermaion*.[20]

Among the various interpretations of the final passage of the Phoenician or Punic text: "and (may) the years (granted) to the statue of the deity in its temple (be as many) as these stars" the interpretation of G. Pugliese Carratelli should be mentioned; he refers to the Etruscan or Roman ritus of marking an inaugurated place by a starshaped sign, to which alludes a passage by Festus Pompeius: "Ateius Capito says, according to the augur P. Servilius, that a star means good fortune and prosperity – a star made from bronze laminae and fixed on inaugurated places". In addition Pugliese Carratelli cites Cornelius Dolabella mentioning the very same ritus.[21] If the final clause in the Semitic text just cited refers to a similar ritus, it may throw a light upon the word *taw* (line 6), which has been translated "cella"; but after all it means a cruciformed or star-shaped sign, corresponding to the very shape of the letter *taw*, especially in its archaic forms.[22]

The two Etruscan inscriptions and the Phoenician or Punic one from Pyrgi are dated from their archaeologial context to about 500 B.C., the temple B being dated to about 510 and temple A to about 460 B.C.:[23]

Keeping the Pyrgi texts in an East-West perspective, the Phoenician or Punic inscription must be considered the most important as regards the content and the paleography, these being the criteria for which it may be decided if the inscription is Phoenician or Punic.[24]

---

18. PFIFFIG 1965, 25-26.
19. COLONNA 1981, 131, with a reference to R. MENGARELLI, *StEtr* 10 (1936), 84 sq.
20. PALLOTTINO 1964, 84; BLOCH 1976, 14; RIX 1981, 84.
21. PUGLIESE CARRATELLI 1965, 303-305.
22. GARBINI 1980, 213-214.
23. COLONNA 1981, 24-29.
24. It should be clarified that "Phoenician" refers to archaeological and epigraphical discoveries from Phoenicia proper and from Cyprus, whereas "Punic" is referring to material having its provenance from Carthage or from other sites in the Western Mediteranean being dependent on the North-African metropolis, i.e. from after about 700 B.C.

The only word not translated above was the name of the month KRR which – as it can be seen from the Alalakh texts – should be vocalized *Kirar.*[25] The meaning of KRR is much debated, but most relevant is the meaning "to dance", i.e. "the month of dance". Here one can refer to the Arabic name of the month *dhul-ḥiǧǧa* and to the Hebrew name of the feast of Passover, *pesaḥ.*[26] In favour of this meaning of KRR may be argued that the corresponding word in the Etruscan text (line 10), *Churvar,* according to J. Heurgon, is a genitive plural of *Churu* which K. Olszcha in the Zagreb inscription translates "dance" = Greek *Choros.*[27]

Another meaning of KRR may be "burning" or "fire", so M. Delcor referring to Accadian *kararū,* "brilliance of the sun at midday".[28]

But in either case the name of the month KRR points to the cult of Melqart: so the ecstatic and cultic dance of the Tyrian seamen, as described by Heliodorus (*Aethiopica* IV, 16) and celebrated in connection with a sacrifice to Heracles (Melqart), has been compared with the ecstatic dance of the priests of Ba'al on the Mount of Carmel (I Reg. 18).[29] The presence in Pyrgi of the cultic dance, here related to Aphrodite-'Ashtarte, is according to M. Verzár confirmed by one of the antefixes from temple B with a representation of a dancing female.[30].

The relation between the cult of Melqart and the meaning of KRR: "fire, burning", is among other things based upon a Phoenician inscription on a stone bowl from Sidon (4th cent. B.C.) showing four cultic scenes: 1. a figure standing on a podium enveloped in flames; 2. a pyramidal object, apparently a tomb stone or stele; 3. a flaming cauldron or incense burner; 4. a figure standing on a podium under a temple pediment; beneath this scene is another figure and the inscription: B'L KR. The last scene mentioned should then represent Melqart *redivivus* while the scenes 1-3 illustrate various episodes from the burning of Melqart, well known in the Classical litterature, e.g. Nonnos from Pannopolis who calls Heracles *anax pyros,* i.e. "Lord of fire",

---

25. DELCOR 1974, 68.
26. WELLHAUSEN 1897, 109-110; HÖLSCHER 1914, 132.
27. HEURGON 1966, 14, with reference to K. OLZSCHA, Interpretation der Agramer Mumienbinde, *Klio, Beih.* XL (1939), 55.
28. DELCOR 1974, 70.
29. HÖLSCHER 1914, 8-9; 132.
30. VERZÁR 1980, 37-54 and pl. I, 1-2.

which corresponds exactly to the Phoenician inscription B'L KR from Sidon.[31] Melqart-Heracles standing in flames may, according to Verzár, be depicted on another antefix from temple B;[32] this illustration however may – as demonstrated by R. Bloch – as well be a hint to the Etruscan sun-god Usil.[33] But whether KRR in the Pyrgi inscription means "the month of dance" or "the month of burning", it alludes to the cult of Melqart, to whom also the passage: "on the day of the burial of the deity" refers, as demonstrated by S. Ribichini.[34]

The name of the month KRR occurs in two Phoenician inscriptions, one from Idalion and another from Larnax tes Lapethou,[35] both places having a cult of Melqart.[36] KRR is furthermore attested at Altiburos (Tunisia) and at Constantine (Algeria).[37]

The ritus of *hieros gamos* has been adduced in favour of the presence of a Melqart cult in Pyrgi; this motif has been deduced from another rendering of line 6 in the Phoenician text: "because 'Ashtarte has been married by him", alluding to the *hieros gamos* of the goddess (*alias* Uni-Iuno Lucina) with the Etruscan Hercle (Melqart).[38] Be that as it may, the cultic and mythological elements in the Phoenician or Punic text from Pyrgi may point towards the Phoenician Cyprus and to Phoenicia proper, i.e. Tyre, the city of the Melqart cult *par exellence*. As for 'Ashtarte, her position is well proved in Tyre as well as in Cyprus where she is known at Kition already in the 9th cent. B.C.;[39] here we also find Melqart as early as in the 6th cent. B.C.[40]

As regards the Occident we find 'Ashtarte in Carthage, on the Douimēs pendant (probably of Cypriot provenance) from the 8th-7th

---

31. LIPINSKI 1969, 43-44, and DELCOR 1974, 68-74 and pl. XIX-XXI. Besides B'L KR alluding to the "Ba'al of the dance" we have B'L MRQD from Dēr el-Qal'a near Beirouth, cf. HÖLSCHER 1914, 132, note 4.
32. VERZÁR 1980, 65-70 and pl. I, 4.
33. BLOCH 1981, 126; *contra* this opinion: VERZÁR 1980, 62. The passage in the Pyrgi inscription: "in the month of the sacrifice to the Sun" may speak in favour of the opinion of BLOCH, unless Melqart is a deity of solar character which, however, is debated: *contra* DUSSAUD 1948, 207, while FERRON 1972, 202-204 argues in favour of Melqart as being a sun-deity.
34. RIBICHINI 1975, 45-46.
35. Idalion: *CIS* I, 92, 2; Larnax tes Lapetheu: HONEYMAN 1938, 285-298.
36. Melqart at Idalion: *CIS* I, 88; at Larnax tes Lapethou: HONEYMAN 1938, 290-297.
37. Altiburos: *KAI*, 159,5; Constantine: *EH*, 60, 4.
38. HOLLEMAN 1981, 42-47; cf. also FERRON 1972, 198-208.
39. DUPONT-SOMMER 1970, 15-25.
40. GUZZO AMADASI 1973, 93-94.

cent. B.C.;[41] and in Spain (Cerro del El Carambolo) we have the inscription dedicated to 'Ashtarte, the inscription probably being of Phoenician origin and dated to 8th-6th cent. B.C.:[42] So inscriptions from Phoenicia proper (or from Cyprus) are not unknown in the Occident.

As regards the type of characters and the language of the Pyrgi inscription, some elements point to the Phoenician inscriptions from Cyprus,[43], and it has been vigorously advocated that the Pyrgi inscription is of Cypro-Phoenician origin.[44] The rejoinder of G. Garbini: that the dedication formula "to the Great Lady" is unknown in Cyprus, is not quite correct; we know two or probably three similar formulae from Cyprus.[45]

What, then, are we to believe concerning the origin of the Pyrgi inscription – is it Phoenician (i.e. Cypro-Phoenician) or Punic?

If the inscription is Punic, it must be considered as a result of the relations between Carthage and the Etruscans reaching their climax about 535 (the naval action at Alalia) and thus in a period regulated by treaties between the Punic metropolis and Etruria.[46]

The inscription can not, of course, be separated from its archaeological context according to which it is dated to about 500 B.C., as already mentioned. Together with the political relations between Carthage and Etruria this may speak in favour of the inscription being Punic and so reflecting some Carthagenian elements of population in Pyrgi and Caere.[47] The affinity of the inscription to the Phoenician Cyprus may –

41. KRAHMALKOV 1981, 178-184.
42. RÖLLIG 1969, 141 sqq; GALLING 1972, 160; QUATTROCCHI PISANO 1974, 113-114 and LIPIŃSKI 1984, 116-117.
43. *KAI*, II, 330-332 PFIFFIG 1965, 8; FERRON 1965, 184-185; 195-196.
44. LEVI DELLA VIDA 1965, 37-38; 48-51.
45. GARBINI 1965, 36; the formula occurs *KAI*, 33 = *CIS* I, 10 (Kition); HONEYMAN 1938, 286 (Larnax tes Lapethou; the text is restored); HONEYMAN 1939, 104 (Idalion), all texts are from 4th cent. B.C.
46. GSELL 1913, 461, with reference to Aristotle, *Polit*. III, 5-10-11; cf. also COLOZIER 1953, 90-94; COLONNA 1965, 212; according to these authors the first treaty between Carthage and Rome in 509 was worked out having the treaties with the Etruscans as prototypes; for the date of the first treaty between Carthage and Rome, cf. CHARLES-PICARD/PICARD 1970, 72-79.
47. A female bronze figure of Etruscan origin (now in the Bardo-Museum) and – according to E. COLOZIER(-BOUCHER), *MEFR* 64 (1952), 59-65 – probably imported to Carthage from (or via Caere) has been taken as a testimony of the relations between Caere and the Punic metropolis, FERRON 1966, 700-701; the provenance of this bronze figure should, however, according to Professor P. J. Riis more likely be the region of Chiusi-Arezzo-Cortona-Perugia; I am very grateful to Professor Riis for his kind and very useful corrective (communicated in a letter to the present writer) to this special and difficult problem.

as maintained G. Charles-Picard/C. Picard – be accounted for by a Cypriotic element in Carthage.[48] But considered in relation to the inscriptions on the Praeneste and the Pontecagnano bowls from the 8th-7th cent., the Pyrgi inscription may as well be explained by the presence of Phoenician elements in Pyrgi – Phoenician *metoikoi* (as such elements are called by G. Buchner) established here a little before a Carthagenian influence began – just as is the case at Pithekoussai; here the Phoenician *metoikoi* are revealed by the above-mentioned graffiti as living in a Greek (Euboean) population.[49] This may also have been the case in Pyrgi-Caere where an Athenian colony had lived since the end of the 7th cent. B.C.[50]

The presence of Greeks in Pyrgi-Caere is reflected in Greek and Latin sources mentioning the goddesses Eileithyia and Leucothea.[51] These were goddesses of childbirth and daylight – so Dionysios from Halicarnassos calls Eileithyia *Heran phosphoran*, i.e. Iuno Lucina – and as for Leucothea, originally a maritime goddess, she is called Matuta by Ovid and Cicero,[52] and as Mater Matuta she is an Aurora, too.[53] The relations beetween Eileithyia (*alias* Iuno Lucina) – Leucothea (*alias* Matuta and Aurora) and Uni (*alias* 'Ashtarte) are rather complexed, and I shall confine myself to refer to the studies of R. Bloch, according to whom the identification of Uni with Eileithyia-Leucothea was preceded by an Etruscan identification of Uni with Iuno Lucina and Mater Matuta-Aurora (Theisan, the Etruscan Aurora is epigraphically attested in Pyrgi).[54]

The religious life of the community in Pyrgi has justly been characterized by K.-W. Weeber (cited above) as "a syncretistic jungle".[55] – Uni or Iuno is 'Ashtarte, as stated by St. Augustine: *Iuno sine dubitatione Astarte vocatur* (*Hept.* VII, 16) and now confirmed by the

---

48. CHARLES-PICARD/PICARD 1970, 70.
49. BUCHNER 1982, 295-296.
50. HEURGON 1966, 3 and GUARDUCCI 1952, 241-244.
51. The texts mentioning the Greek goddesses in Pyrgi are collected by BLOCH 1981, 129.
52. BLOCH 1976, 1-19; IDEM, 1981, 123-29; KRAUSKOPF 1981, 137-48.
53. BLOCH 1976, 6-8; IDEM, 1981, 125-26; COLONNA 1981, 34.
54. The name of Theisan is incised on a bronze lamina: BLOCH 1976, 7-8 and note 22; COLONNA 1981, 34 and pl. XXXI, c.
55. WEEBER 1985, 33.

Pyrgi inscriptions. But in addition to this we have got some new problems not yet sufficiently clarified.

University of Aarhus
Institute of Semitic Philology
DK-8000 Århus C

BIBLIOGRAPHY

Akten 1981	*Akten des Kolloquiums zum Thema Die Göttin von Pyrgi* (Tübingen 16-17 Januar 1979). Florence.
AVIGAD 1966	N. AVIGAD, Two Phoenician Votive Seals, *IsrExpl* 16, 242-51.
BARTON 1919	*apud* C. DENSMORE CURTIS, The Bernardini Tomb, *MAAR* 3, 44.
BLOCH 1976	R. BLOCH, *Recherches sur les religions de l'Italie antique*. Geneva.
BLOCH 1981	R. BLOCH, Le culte etrusco-punique de Pyrgi vers 500 J.C., *Akten* 1981, 123-29.
BUCHNER 1978	G. BUCHNER, Testimonianze epigrafiche semitiche dell'VII secolo A.C. a Pithekoussai, *PP* 33, 130-42.
BUCHNER 1982	G. BUCHNER, Die Beziehungen zwischen der euböischen Kolonie Pithekoussai auf der Insel Ischia u. dem nordwestsemitischen Mittelmeerraum in der zweiten Hälfte des 8. Jhs. v. Chr., *MBeiträge* 8, 277-306.
CHARLES-PICARD/ PICARD 1970	G. CHARLES-PICARD/C. PICARD, *Vie et mort de Carthage*. Paris.
CIS I	*Corpus Inscriptionum Semiticarum. Pars prima, Inscriptiones Phoenicias continens*. Paris.
COLONNA 1965	G. COLONNA, Il santuario de Pyrgi alla luce delle recenti scoperte, *StEtr* 33, 191-219.
COLONNA 1981	G. COLONNA, La dea di Pyrgi: bilancio aggiornato dei dati archeologici (1978), *Akten* 1981, 13-24.
COLOZIER 1953	E. COLOZIER, Les étrusques et Carthage, *MEFR(A)* 65, 63-98.
d'AGOSTINO 1977	B. d'ARGOSTINO, La patera orientalizzante da Pontecagnano riesaminata, *StEtr* 45, 51-58.
DELCOR 1974	M. DELCOR, Le hiéros gamos d'Astarté, *RStFen* 2, 63-76.
DUPONT-SOMMER 1970	A. DUPONT-SOMMER, Une inscription phénicienne archaïque récemment trouvée à Kition (Chypre), Extrait des *Mém. de l'Acad. des Inscriptions et Belles-Lettres*, t. 44. Paris.
EH	*Le Sanctuaire punique d'El-Hofra à Constantine*, par A. Berthier et R. Charlier. Paris 1955.
DUSSAUD 1948	R. DUSSAUD, Melqart, *Syria* 25, 205-30.
FERRON 1965	J. FERRON, Quelques remarques à propos de l'inscription phénicienne de Pyrgi, *OA*, 4, 181-98.
FERRON 1966	J. FERRON, Les relations de Carthage avec l'Etrurie, *Latomus* 25, 689-709.
FERRON 1972	J. FERRON, Un traité d'alliance entre Caere et Carthage, *ANWR* I, 1, 189-216.

GALLING 1972	K. GALLING, Der Weg der Phöniker nach Tarsis in literarischer u. archäologischer Sicht, *ZDPV* 88, 1-18 140-81.
GARBINI 1965	G. GARBINI, Considerazioni sull'iscrizione punica di Pyrgi, *OA* 4, 35-52.
GARBINI 1977	G. GARBINI, La patera orientalizzante de Pontecagnano riesaminata. L'iscrizione fenicia, *StEtr* 45, 58-62.
GARBINI 1978	G. GARBINI, Un' inscripzione aramaica a Ischia, *PP* 33, 143-50.
GARBINI 1980	G. GARBINI, *I Fenici. Storia e religione.* Naples.
GIBSON 1982	J. C. L. GIBSON, *Textbook of Syrian Semitic Inscriptions, 3.* Oxford.
GJERSTAD 1946	E. GJERSTAD, Decorated Metal Bowls from Cyprus, *SvInstSkrifter* XII, 1-18.
GRELOT 1972	P. GRELOT, *Documents araméens d'Egypte.* Paris.
GSELL 1913	S. GSELL, *Histoire ancienne de l'Afrique du Nord, t. I.* Paris.
GUARDUCCI 1952	M. GUARDUCCI, Iscrizioni greche su vasi locali di Caere, *ArchCl* 4, 241-44.
GUZZO AMADASI 1967	M. G. GUZZO AMADASI, *Le Iscrizioni fenicie e puniche delle colonie in Occidente.* Rome.
GUZZO AMADASI 1973	M. G. GUZZO AMADASI, Excavations at Kition (Cyprus), 1972, *RStFen* 1, 93-94.
HEURGON 1966	J. HEURGON, The Inscriptions of Pyrgi, *JRS* 56, 1-15.
HOLLEMAN 1981	A. W. J. Holleman, Lucretia u. die Inschriften von Pyrgi, *Latomus* 40, 37-47; Nachtrag, *ibid.* 830-31.
HONEYMAN 1938	A. M. HONEYMAN, Larnax tēs Lapēthou. A Third Phoenician Inscription, *Muséon* 51, 285-98.
HONEYMAN 1939	A. M. HONEYMAN, The Phoenician Inscriptions of the Cyprus Museum, *Iraq* 6, 104-08.
HÖLSCHER 1914	G. HÖLSCHER, *Die Propheten. Untersuchungen zur Religionsgeschichte Israels.* Leipzig.
KAI	H. Donner u. W. Röllig: *Kanaanäische u. Aramäische Inschriften,* I-III. Wiesbaden 1969.
KARAGEORGHIS 1976	V. KARAGEORGHIS, *Kition, Mycenaean and Phoenician Discoveries in Cyprus.* London.
KRAHMALKOV 1981	CH. R. KRAHMALKOV, The Foundation of Carthage, 814 B.C. The Douimës Pendant Inscription, *JSemSt* 26, 177-91.
KRAUSKOPF 1981	I. KRAUSKOPF, Leukothea nach den antiken Quellen, *Akten* 1981, 137-48.
LECLANT 1960	J. LECLANT, Astarté à cheval d'après les représentations égyptiennes, *Syria* 37, 1-67.
LEVI DELLA VIDA 1965	G. LEVI DELLA VIDA, apud GARBINI 1965.
LIPIŃSKI 1969	E. LIPIŃSKI, La fête de l'ensevelissement et de la résurrection de Melqart, ACTES DE LA XVIIᵉ RENCONTRE ASSYRIOLOGIQUE INTERNATIONALE (Bruxelles, 30-4 juillet 1969), 30-58 (ed. A. FINET). Ham-Sur-Heure.
LIPIŃSKI 1984	E. LIPIŃSKI, Vestiges phéniciens d'Andalousie, *OLP* 15, 81-132; pl. XI-XV.
MARKOE 1985	G. MARKOE, *Phoenician Bronze and Silver Bowls from Cyprus and the Mediterranean.* Berkeley-Los Angeles-London.
PALLOTTINO 1964	M. PALLOTTINO, Scavi nel santuario eetrusco di Pyrgi, *ArchCl* 16, 76-104.
PECKHAM 1968	J. B. PECKHAM, *The Development of the Late Phoenician Scripts.* Cambridge, Massachusetts.
PFIFFIG 1965	A. J. PFIFFIG, Uni-Hera-Astarte, *DenkschriftenWien* 88, 2, 1-55.
PUGLIESE	G. PUGLIESE CARRATELLI, Le stelle di Pyrgi, *PP* 20, 303-05.

CARRATELLI 1965 QUATTROCCHI PISANO	G. QUATTROCCHI PISANO, A proposito dell'Astarte di Siviglia, *RStFen* 2, 109-114.
RATHJE 1980	A. RATHJE, Silver Relief Bowls from Italy, *ARID* 9, 7-47.
RIBICHINI 1975	S. RIBICHINI, Melqart nell'iscrizione di Pyrgi? *Saggi Fenici – I* (ed. G. BENIGNI *et al.*), Centro di Studio per la Civiltà fenicia e punica. Rome.
RIX 1981	H. RIX, Pyrgi-Texte und etruskische Grammatik, *Akten* 1981, 83-98.
RÖLLIG 1969	W. RÖLLIG, Zur phönizischen Inschrift der Astarte-Statuette in Sevilla (Hispania 14), *MM* 10, 141-46.
TEIXIDOR 1979	J. TEIXIDOR, Bulletin d'épigraphie sémitique 1978-79, *Syria* 56, 353-405.
VACCARO 1963	A. VACCARO, La patera orientalizzante da Pontecagnano presso Salerno, *StEtr* 31, 241-47.
VERZÁR	M. VERZÁR, Pyrgi e l'Afrodite di Cipro, *MEFR(A)* 92, 35-84.
WEEBER 1985	K.-W. WEEBER, Die Inschriften von Pyrgi, *AW* 16, 29-37.
WEIPPERT 1975	M. WEIPPERT, Über den asiatischen Hintergrund der Göttin "Asiti", *OR* 44, 12-21.
WELLHAUSEN 1897	J. WELLHAUSEN, *Reste arabischen Heidentums*.² Berlin.

SOME OBSERVATIONS ON ETRUSCAN BOWLS WITH SUPPORTS IN THE SHAPE OF CARYATIDS OR ADORNED BY RELIEFS

by HELLE SALSKOV ROBERTS

The seminar held at the University of Copenhagen in April 1987 had as its theme "The Cultural Exchange between East and West in the Mediterranean Area in Antiquity".

The whole phenomenon of the Orientalizing period in Etruria is a striking example of such an exchange although in this instance we only have clear evidence of the East to West influence and largely have to guess what was exchanged in the other direction in those pre-monetary times.

We can discern a certain number of pieces of minor art of Oriental workmanship that found their way into Etruria in the 7th century B.C. and a much greater number of similar objects evidently inspired by, copied or derived from such imports. Examples are stands for cauldrons, cauldrons with animal protomes and bowls with ornamental supports, often in the shape of female figures.

It has, however, been called into queston whether in the first case the shape could rather be derived from the native Italic *calefattoio* (lately discussed by RATHJE 1986, SIEGFRIED 1986) and in the case of bowls no exact parallel in the Oriental world has so far been found. (Earlier discussions by *i.a.* BROWN 1960, 32-33, AUBET 1971, 200-201, RASMUSSEN 1979, 96).

Scholars dealing with the subject of cultural exchange may approach it from a variety of angles with a view to elucidating political, economic, aesthetic or sociological questions, and this has, indeed, been done.

In the case of Etruria the research was dominated for a long period by the desire to solve the question of ethnic origin against the background of the belief that, if the homeland of art, architecture and other manifestations of material culture could be determined the question of origin would also be answered. Later research has shown that the formation of Etruscan culture is far more complex and although political events in

Eastern empires may have influenced routes of trade and the movements of itinerant artisans, as we may be able to observe in certain fields of material culture, this is far from being equivalent to conquest, mass immigration or colonisation as we know it from other periods of ancient or more recent history.

Other scholars, fervent admirers of Oriental or Greek art, have only been able to evaluate the fidelity to the model and deplore the decline of artistic inspiration and workmanship (*e.g.* BROWN 1960, 21).

However, a certain transformation of a model and its fusion with elements supplied from native stock provide the best proof of the success of an imported type of object, *i.e.* its acculturisation.

An unpublished piece in the Danish National Museum may offer the opportunity of some comments on the bowl with four supports reaching from the bowl itself down to the standing surface.

Danish National Museum inv. no. 9182 is a fragmented bucchero bowl with four supports descending from the notched carination. *Plate* 2a-b. On the bowl, which is composed of several fragments, two horizontal wet-incised grooves and a notched band surrounded by two grooves. On the upper field two different designs of a bird are incised, one extremely simple and one somewhat more complex. The supports are broken at the top and partly missing. Fragments of two à-jour supports show these to have consisted of six panels arranged in two rows of three. *Plate* 3a-b. The decoration of one row is made up by a feline *passant* with raised paw walking upwards, a double palmette and a feline *regardant* with raised paw. The second row has one feline *passant* with raised paw, a winged goddess with raised arms and the hind quarters of a feline. The two other supports have been of a different kind, as appears from the rounded and much narrower preserved attachments.

The ware is rather thick with a good deal of mica. The inside has a central omphalos surrounded by a plain area and a concentric furrow from which rather broad furrows radiate.

H. of bowl: 9,5 cm. Diam.: 18,5-19 cm. Acquired in a sale in Paris, Collection de céramique antique; vente à Paris le 26 juin 1931, no. 13 (former no. 21).

A close parallel is the bowl Louvre C 665, which has one very similar bird design and two flat supports with six panels stamped with figures identical to those of Danish National Museum 9182. This piece has been clasified by Szilágyi as a work by "Il maestro dei calici pentapodi".[1]

H.: 18,5 cm. Diam.: 17,3 cm. CRISTOFANI & ZEVI 1965, type B 2 (not listed). BONAMICI 1974, no. 31, pl. XV, b. *Plate* 3c.

Louvre C 665 has, apart from the central conical support with cut-out triangles, two other supports in the shape of winged female caryatids having a polos with vertical striations and holding locks of hair over the breast.

The two missing supports af DNM 9182 are likely to have been similar female caryatids. The same bird design is found on the bucchero amphora Louvre C 565, CVA (20) IV Ba, pl. 20 and on the amphora S 4558 (*ibid.*, pl. 20) both the elaborate bird and the bird protome appear.

The two amphorae as well as the bowl 9182 should also be ascribed to the artisan named "Il maestro dei calici pentapodi". Two more examples in the reserves of the Villa Giulia are also likely to come from the same hand, and possibly also a bowl in Leningrad, inv. B 1335 (BONAMICI 1974, nos. 32, 33, 58).

The bowl Louvre C 664 has the same à-jour relief supports, but show some variations in the bird design. The central support does not reach the bottom of the bowl and has cut-out quadrangles instead of triangles. The caryatids are of a rather different kind, with large wings reaching to the ground and with different head-dress and hair style. The junction of torso and legs is marked by a sharply cut V-shaped line. This piece is classified by Szilágyi as "Near il Maestro dei calici pentapodi".

H.: 19 cm. Diam.: 17 cm. POTTIER 1897-1922, pl. 28. CRISTOFANI & ZEVI 1965, 24. CAPECCHI & GUNNELLA 1975, 74 no. 24. BONAMICI 1974, no. 30, type A, pl. III, 1, p. XV a.

A bowl in the Villa Giulia, Coll. Castellani 50365 has the same six stamps, but the supports are not à-jour. (Cf. RASMUSSEN 1979, 96). There are no bird incisions, but only three horizontal grooves on the bowl. There is no central support, but the four outer supports are joined by a ring-base. The caryatids are of the same type as those of Louvre C 665. *Plate* 4a.

---

[1]. Private communication during a visit to the Danish National Museum.

H.: 17,9 cm. Diam.: 17,5 cm. MINGAZZINI 1930, pl. I, 14 CRISTOFANI & ZEVI 1965 type B 2.

The affinity of the bucchero bowls with a central support and outer supports in the shape of female caryatids to the ivory bowls from the Praenestine Barberini Tomb has been evident to many scholars, although they do not agree as to which is copying which. (CURTIS 1925, nos. 31-38, pls. 12-14. HULS 1957, 157. CRISTOFANI 1969, 54. AUBET 1971, nos. 46-50, pls. 26-30, 200-201).

The ivory caryatids are wingless, but close to the bucchero examples in the gesture of the hands holding curved locks of hair and the manner of rendering the junction of torso and legs seen on *e.g.* Louvre C 664, which is indubitably influenced by carving, most likely in ivory. *Plate 4b.* (Cf. also the Dipylon ivories, RICHTER 1968, figs. 16-22).

There has also been a general agreement as to an Oriental inspiration, although it has not been possible to point to specific Oriental bowls supported by caryatids. (BROWN 1960, 33. RASMUSSEN 1979, 95-96).

There has, however, been less agreement as to the part played by Greece. RICHTER 1969, 27-31 lists a number of large stone perirrhanteria or basins supported by female figures found in Greek sanctuaries and presumably serving a ritual purpose, varying in size from 0,66 m to 1,26 m (Cf. also DUCAT 1964, 577).

There is no agreement as to the date of the Greek stone perirrhanteria with female caryatids, mainly ascribed by Richter to her Nikandre-Auxerre group and dated by her to the second half of the 7th century B.C. Brown, however, ascribes most of them to the 6th century B.C. (RICHTER 1968, 21-32, 52. BROWN 1960, 33).

Neither is the chronology of the Etruscan caryatid bowls firmly established although the evidence points to a period betweeen 620/10 B.C. and 570/60 B.C. (CRISTOFANI 1969, 70. RASMUSSEN 1979, 96). Accordingly, anteriority of appearance in Greece or Etruria does not help in solving the problem.

To the examples which have until now been discussed is this connection may now be added a polychrome terracotta bowl supported by female figures dressed in chitons and with their arms descending along the sides. This bowl, the height of which is 22,5 cm, was found during the excavations at Salamis, tomb 23, at the East coast of Cyprus, which is the easternmost provenance of caryatid bowls known so far. Tomb 23 is dated by Karageorghis to the 7th century B.C. (KARAGEORGHIS 1969, fig. 147; 1970, 51).

An example of two nude women forming the stem of a bowl also come from the excavations of Salamis, t. 47, likewise dated to the 7th century B.C. (KARAGEORGHIS 1967, pl. LXXIX).

The affinity of this last specimen to the ivory carytids found in the Burnt Palace af Nimrud seems undeniable, even if one has until now been a little reluctant to draw a parallel between the nude figures standing closely back to back and the usually dressed and often winged statuettes standing by themselves found in Etruria (BARNETT 1975, pl. LXXIV. MALLOWAN 1966, figs. 146-147).

Richter also lists two terracotta receptacles which are much closer in size to the Etruscan pieces varying in height from 17-19 cm and with a diameter of the rim of the bowl of also about 17-19 cm.

One receptacle (RICHTER no. 12) with four caryatids found in the Heraion alla Foce del Sele, is 17 cm high. The other (RICHTER no. 13) said to have been found in Rhodes, is 18 cm high.

The caryatids of these last two pieces differ from female figures considered so far in the position of arms and hands. Their arms are bent and they are holding their breasts with both hands.

In Etruria this gesture is found on the caryatids of the large vessel of hammered bronze known as the Vaso Castellani (COLONNA 1982, fig. 1).

It is understood as hieratic by Colonna, who accordingly explains the rather unique bronze specimen as having a ritual, more specifically a funeral character.

The receptacle from the Heraion alla Foce del Sele has also been interpreted as either a temple lamp or a bowl for holding holy water like the perirrhanteria from the sanctuariees in the Greek Motherland (ZANCANI MONTUORO 1960. RICHTER 1968, 30). Richter also puts forward the possibility of the female supports representing priestesses (*loc.cit.*, 28).

This leads to the question of the function of the bowls in Etruria. It seems to have been taken for granted that they were meant for drinking. The current terminology no doubt confirms that notion: cup, copa, chalice, calice con sostegni a cariatide, calice pentapodi or tetrapodi, and this has led to the conception of the vessel with supports as being just an ornate example of the chalice. Colonna, however, has convincingly shown that at least the bronze Vaso Castellani cannot have served as a drinking vessel, particularly in view of the flat horizontal rim with holes for attachments, which are now missing, but most likely have been rosettes (COLONNA 1982, 40).

The Barberini ivory specimens are not well-suited for drinking either. The rim may be less offensive to the lips of the drinker than the sharp horizontal rim of the Vaso Castellani would be, but the cable pattern carved just under the rim might create a problem for immediate comfort of the drinker as well as for eventual discolouring and wear of the bowl. To lift the vessel you would either have to insert a rather small hand between the stem and the caryatids or put both hands around the bowl with the carved frieze, that would soon show signs of wear. Finally, ivory being a porous substance, does not stand up too well to prolonged contact with liquids.

It can, of course, be argued that elaborate pieces like the Barberini ivories were not meant for much wear, but even ceremonial vessels would be expected to be suitable for their purpose and that must have included their ability to serve without too much lifting.

A bucchero or even an impasto chalice is indubitably – well suited for drinking, as testified by the frequent occurrence in *e.g.* the banquet service found at Ficana (RATHJE 1983). But it would be just as awkward to lift a bucchero chalice with five supports to ones lips for drinking as would be the case with ivory specimens.

Perhaps more than anything else the development in Etruria of the bowl with five supports to the one with four supports shows that the central support or stem did not serve any purpose, neither structurally for supporting the bowl nor for a person holding the vessel. Typologically, it appears at first as the central support not reaching the bowl and, finally, the central support disappears completely, leaving only the outer supports, *e.g.* Villa Giulia 50365, *plate* 4a. These, being often à-jour and rather frail, tend to break, as in the case of Danish National Museum 9182, *plate* 2a-b, 3a-b.

If these vessels were not used for drinking, what was their function? One would like to find representations in ancient art depicting such objects being used. To my knowledge this has not happened so far, but perhaps it is possible to draw a couple of relevant reliefs into the discussion.

From the Palace of Ashurbanipal at Niniveh comes a relief from about 645 B.C. showing the King and Queen celebrating a victory in the arbour. *Plate* 5a. The King reclines on a couch, while the queen is sitting on a throne with footstool. In the middle of a table in front of them stands a bowl (on a conical foot?) with flat supports reaching from the rim to the standing surface. On a tray carried by an attendant behind the Queen is a similar object. For drinking the Queen holds a flat phial with fluted bottom. The bowls with flat supports are most likely to hold things like nuts or dried fruit that you pick up from the bowl without lifting it. The Etruscan vessels with supports would be equally suited for such a purpose, although, of course, it is not the only one conceivable.

The vessels on the Assyrian relief do not seem to have caryatids. Whether the supports have any other decoration like reliefs it is impossible to tell.

Figures in the round or in relief are well represented in the Nimrud Ivories used as pure decoration of furniture, *e.g.* on the couch of Ashurbanipal, *Plate* 5b, or with a function as *e.g.* handles of household articles. MALLOWAN 1966, 480, pl. V, fig. 429. BARNETT 1975, pls. LXXIV-LXXVII, Cf. above p. 72.

The idea of using them as supports of bowls did, as we have just seen, occur to the potters of Cyprus.

There are also Oriental examples of using the actual figure as a receptacle, *e.g.* the ivory women-alabastra from the Burnt Palace of Nimrud, BARNETT 1975, pls. LVIII-LX.

Sometimes only part of a female figure is used, as in the terracotta cup from room S 32, Nimrud, in the shape of a woman's head (MALLOWAN 1966, fig. 313).

This idea caught on both in Greece, where especially head-shaped vases became very popular both in Protocorinthian as well as in East Greek Pottery, and on the Italian peninsula, where some interesting pieces, most likely Oriental imports, have been found. One example is an ivory mouth of an oinochoe from Pitino, San Severino Marche (RATHJE 1976, fig. 8), and another is a stone vase with the upper part in the form of a woman's head found in tomba degli Alari, Cerveteri (*ibid.* figs. 1-4).

Women-alabastra are also known both in Greece and in Etruria, but they did not become very popular. It may, however, be significant that the most obvious examples come from Populonia, a site particularly important for the overseas metal trade (MINTO 1943, pl. XXXI).

The Barberini caryatid bowls are considered to be actually produced in Etruria (AUBET 1971, 200-201), but the tongue-like fluting of the stem finds a close counterpart in the stands to either side of the central scene of the Ashurbanipal relief, *plate* 5a.

The fluting of the underside of the bowl possibly has its inspiration in metal bowls like the silver example, presumably from the booty captured by Sargon II in 714 B.C. from Urartu, and brought back by him to Nimrud. This booty comprised, according to the archives, of "hundreds of silver cups made in the lands of Assur, Urartu and Kilhu". (MALLOWAN 1966, fig. 357, 431). Mallowan also refers to the connection with finds in Italy and especially the Barberini tomb (*ibid.*, 431).

The ivory panels for couches and chairs found in room SW 7 at Nimrud are also likely to have been acquired by Sargon II as booty or tribute, in this case from North Syria, where they were presumably made and which is also a likely place of origin for many impulses of artistic style which reached Etruria (MALLOWAN 1966, 469. WINTER 1973).

Apart from the female caryatids of the Etruscan bucchero bowls the orientalizing character of the other supports with stamped or à-jour reliefs is evident, the main motifs being palmette-trees, winged goddesses and animals, often winged, *plate* 4a.

A less frequent, but no less orientalizing relief stamp is represented on a bucchero bowl with four supports in the Villa Giulia, no. 25105, *plate* 6a.

Villa Giulia 25105, CVA Villa Giulia fasc. 1, pls. 1, 3; 9; 2,4. CRISTOFANI & ZEVI 1965, 26, type E. CAPECCHI & GUNNELLA 1975, 63 no. 5. H.: 15 cm. Diam.: 15,5 cm.

The relief shows a woman (?) sitting on a throne with a footstool holding a staff finishing in a lily-like ornament. Her dress is patterned by cross-hatching. The legs of the throne are inverted cones and between them is a relief of a large bird. It looks as if there is a cushion provided.

There are several features in common with the enthroned Queen of the Ashurbanipal relief, *plate* 5b, although the woman is not holding a bowl for drinking and she is facing left.

Another Assyrian relief commenmorating the fall of Lachish in 701 B.C. shows King Sennacherib on a throne facing left, while the booty passes before him (BARNETT *APR*, figs. 69; 73).

Some ivory relief panels from Nimrud are in certain respects even closer to the bucchero stamp. MALLOWAN 1966, fig. 399 depicts an enthroned lady holding a lily in her left hand, not unlike the more staff-like shown on the Etruscan relief. The throne has a footstool and a sphinx in relief under the seat. *Ibid.* fig. 400 has a male counterpart facing left, with two birds adorning the throne. *Ibid.* 401-404 also have enthroned females, some with banquet-tables resting on the branches of trees or flowers. These panels were found in room SW 7 of the Palace at Nimrud, and the evidence suggests that they were executed a little before or a little after 730 B.C.

The identity of these ladies is enigmatic, suggestions ranging from queens to high priestesses, goddesses or protective spirits. Mallowan is inclined to interpret the females as supernatural because of the tables perched on what he understands as the tree of life (MALLOWAN 1966, 502). The Etruscan artisans and their patrons may not have had the same conception of the figure as the Oriental producers, but Mallowan's idea is certainly not incompatible with the hieratic character of the Etruscan pieces already suggested by the sometimes winged and sometimes breast-holding caryatids, which also frequently have a polos.

Stamps with a palmette-tree which were certainly regarded in the Orient as the tree of life are often used on the flat supports of bucchero bowls.

On the two bowls from Veio, Monte Michele tomb E (CRISTOFANI 1969, pl. 19, 1-4) there are palmette-tree stamps combined with caryatids holding locks of hair over the breast. The structure of the tree is basically the same as on the ivory bed-head from Nimrud SW 7 (MALLOWAN 1966, fig. 390) or the more elaborate plaque from SW 37 (*ibid.*, fig. 467). On the Veio bowl tomb E no. 3 the stamp is upside down.

Tomb E no. 2. H.: 17,7 cm. Diam.: 15,5 cm.

no. 3. H.: 17,8 cm. Diam.: 15,5 cm.

The main workshop which produced these bucchero bowls with elaborate supports, among the production of other shapes, is most likely to have been located at Cerveteri, as indicated by the find-spot of some of them: PARETI 317-20, tomba Regolini-Galassi, PARETI 528, tomba Calabresi, tomba IV del Colonnello (Villa Giulia 46779-46779 B; 46767 (RASMUSSEN 1979, 35-36. *Helbig, Führer* 1969, 550).

The other well-documented find-spot, Veio, which yielded the specimens from Monte Michele tomb E is not really contradicting the identification of Cerveteri as being the centre of production, as Veio seems to have been of minor autonomous importance from the last decades of the 7th century B.C. and under strong influence from Cerveteri (CRISTOFANI 1969, 70. Cf. however, BONAMICI 1975, 109).

The development of the bowls with ornamental supports represented by the examples from Veio tomb E is dated by Cristofani, *l.c.* to 610-590 B.C., and in the tomba del Colonnello from Cerveteri they were associated with late EC and MC material, also well into the 6th century B.C.

To settle the question of the function of these bowls it would be most desirable to find a scene showing them being used. Perhaps that wish is now partially fulfilled by the Murlo terracotta plaques showing banquet scenes and processions of women bringing objects for use during the banquet. *Plate* 6b. The mould-made relief plaques are not all equally clear, but on the better specimens one can observe women carrying deep bowls with a trumpet-shaped foot surrounded by flat supports reaching from the bottom of the bowl to the base. It is difficult not to see a certain parallel to the actual examples discussed here, although the bowl looks deeper and it is being carried by a handle. The proportions of the bowl are more reminiscent of the Chiusine buccheri pesanti, *e.g. CVA* Copenhagen, fasc. 5, pl. 215,9. Pottery bowls with a fixed handle are very rare in the Etruscan repertoire, and such vessels would only be suitable for very special purposes, but certainly not including drinking. As far as I know, no bowls with supports and with a handle reaching across the opening have ever been found in Etruria. One might suggest the possibility of removable handles being used for transport, as we know was the case of aryballoi and alabastra in Greece, and on the Balâwât Gates we see larger vessels like cauldrons and stands being carried by ropes (BARNETT *APR*, pl. 151).

The women on the Murlo plaques hold in their right hand a large fan, *plate* 6b, presumably to keep away insects from the contents of the vessel in the same way as one attendant on the Ashurbanipal relief, *plate* 5a holds a whisk or fan over the tray carried by the other.

The Murlo plaques, the final publication of which is still being prepared,[2] belong presumably to the second quarter of the 6th century

---

2. By Annette Rathje whom I thank for permission to publish the photograph as well as for many fruitful discussions. For previous publications see *Case e Palazzi* 1985.

B.C., a date not incompatible with the examples of bowls with four supports discussed here.

The Oriental ivories, which are likely to have played such a large part in the formation of Etruscan minor art, are a good deal older. The group of Nimrud ivories referred to here most frequently are dated to around 730 B.C.

Most of the material discussed in this paper point to North Syrian prototypes, the production of which is likely to have ceased by the end of the 8th century B.C. after the conquests by Sargon (WINTER 1973, 1), but the Phoenicians seem to have been engaged in sea trade in the 8th and 7th centuries B.C. (WINTER 1973, 510) and Phoenician inspiration is obvious in many other finds in Etruria in the 7th century B.C. (SALSKOV ROBERTS 1963, 178). Again, Cyprus has yielded important material for the development of *e.g.* the caryatid supports. During the vital period of the 7th century B.C. the Etruscan ivory carvers, bronze workers and potters transformed this and other Oriental motifs like the palmette-tree and the animal friezes to fit into a repertoire adapted to Etruscan needs and tastes.

BIBLIOGRAPHY

AUBET 1971	M. E. AUBET, *Los marfiles orientalizantes de Praeneste*. Barcelona.
BARNETT 1935	R. D. BARNETT, The Nimrud Ivories and the Art of the Phoenicians, *Iraq* II, 179-210.
BARNETT 1975	R. D. BARNETT, *Catalogue of the Nimrud Ivories.²* London.
BARNETT *APR*	R. D. BARNETT, *Assyrian Palace Reliefs*. London. Without year.
BONAMICI 1974	M. BONAMICI, *I buccheri con figurazioni graffite*. Firenze.
BROWN 1960	W. LLEWELLYN BROWN, *The Etruscan Lion*. Oxford.
Case e Palazzi 1985	*Case e Palazzi d'Etruria*, exhibition catalogue from Siena. Milano.
CAPECCHI & GUNNELLA 1975	G. CAPECCHI & A. GUNNELLA, *Calici di bucchero a sostegni figurati. Atti e Memorie dell'Accademia Toscana di Scienze e Lettere "La Colombaria"* XL, 35-105.
COLONNA 1982	G. COLONNA, Di Augusto Castellani e del cosidetto calice a cariatidi prenestino, *Studi in onore T. Dohrn*, 33-44, Rome.
CRISTOFANI & ZEVI 1965	M. Cristofani & F. Zevi, La tomba Campana di Veio. Il corredo, *ArchCl* 17, 1-35, 284-285.
CHRISTOFANI 1969	M. CRISTOFANI, *Le tombe da Monte Michele nel Museo Archeologico di Firenze*. Florence.
CURTIS 1925	C. D. CURTIS, The Barberini Tomb, *MAAR* V.
CVA	*Corpus Vasorum Antiquorum*
DUCAT 1964	J. DUCAT, Périrrhantèria, *BCH* 88, 577-606.

EC	Early Corinthian
Helbig, Führer 1969	W. HELBIG. *Führer durch die offentlichen Sammlungen klassischer Altertümer in Rom^2* III.
HULS 1957	Y. HULS, *Ivoires d'Étrurie*. Brussels.
IAArtifacts 1986	J. SWADDLING (ed.), *Italian Iron Age Artifacts in the British Museum. Papers of the Sixth British Museum Classical Colloquium.* London.
KARAGEORGHIS 1966	V. KARAGEORGHIS, Receent Discoveries at Salamis (Cyprus), *AA*, 210-255.
KARAGEORGHIS 1969	V. KARAGEORGHIS, *The Ancient Civilisation of Cyprus*. New York.
KARAGEORGHIS 1967	V. KARAGEORGHIS, *Excavations in the Necropolis of Salamis*, I, 3. London/Nicosia.
KARAGEORGHIS 1970	V. KARAGEORGHIS, *Excavations in the Necropolis of Salamis*, II, 4. Nicosia.
MAAR	*Memoirs of the American Academy in Rome.*
MC	Middle Corinthian
MALLOWAN 1966	M. E. L. MALLOWAN, *Nimrud and its Remains. I-II*. London.
MINGAZZINI 1930	P. MINGAZZINI, *Vasi della Collezione Castellani I-II*. Rome.
MINTO 1943	A. MINTO, *Populonia. La necropoli arcaica*. Firenze.
MONTELIUS 1895-1910	O. MONTELIUS, *La civilisation primitive en Italie depuis l'introduction des méteaux. I Italie Septentrionale*, Stockholm 1895. II *Italie Centrale*, Stockholm 1904, 1910.
Nuove scoperte 1975	*Nuove scoperte e acquisizioni nell'Etruria meridionale. Museo Nazionale di Villa Giulia*. Rome.
PARETI 1947	L. PARETI, *La tomba Regoloni-Galassi del Museo Gregoriano Etrusco*. Vatican City.
POTTIER 1897-1922	E. POTTIER, *Vases antiques du Louvre I-II*. Paris.
POULSEN 1912	F. POULSEN, *Der Orient und die frühgriechische Kunst*. Leipzig/Berlin.
RAMAGE 1970	N. HIRSCHLAND RAMAGE, Studies in Early Etruscan Bucchero, *BSR* 38, 1-61.
RASMUSSEN 1979	TOM B. RASMUSSEN, *Bucchero Pottery From Southern Etruria*. Cambridge.
RATHJE 1976	A. RATHJE, Some Unusual Vessels with Plastic Heads on their Necks, *Studia Romana in honorem Petri Krarup Sepetuagenarii*, Odense, 10-19.
RATHJE 1983	A. RATHJE, A Banquet Service from the Latin City of Ficana, *ARID* 12, 7-31.
RICHTER 1968	G. M. A. RICHTER, *Korai. Archaic Greek Maidens*. London.
SALSKOV ROBEERTS 1963	H. SALSKOV ROBERTS, Some Bronze Plaques With Repoussé Decoration in the Danish National Museum, *ActaArch* XXXIV, 1963, 135-184.
SIEGFRIED 1986	A. SIEGFRIED, Ein Holmos mit Greifenprotomenlebes: zur Frage des Verhältnisses zwischen Calefattoi und Holmoi, *IAArtifacts*, 249-255.
WINTER 1973	I. J. WINTER, *North Syria in the Early First Millennium B.C., with Special Reference to Ivory Carving*. Columbia University Ph.D. 1973, Fine Arts. Ann Arbor, Michigan.
WINTER 1976	I. J. WINTER, Phoenician and North Syrian Ivory Carving in Historical Context: Questions of Style and Distribution, *Iraq* 38, 1-22.
WOLDERING 1964	I. WOLDERING, *Festschrift Kestner-Museum*. Hannover.
ZANCANI MONTUORO 1960	P. ZANCANI MONTUORO, Lampada arcaica dello Heraion alla Foce del Sele, *AttiMGrecia*, N. S. III, 69-77.

Plate 1a. The Roundel **KH Wc 2104** from Khania. Along the edge is seen impressions from an amygdaloid seal with two lions and on one side of the roundel is incised the sign AB 61 (Godart-Olivier's nomenclature, cf. GORILA 5). The meaning of this isolated sign is unknown, but it is likely to have an ideographic value.

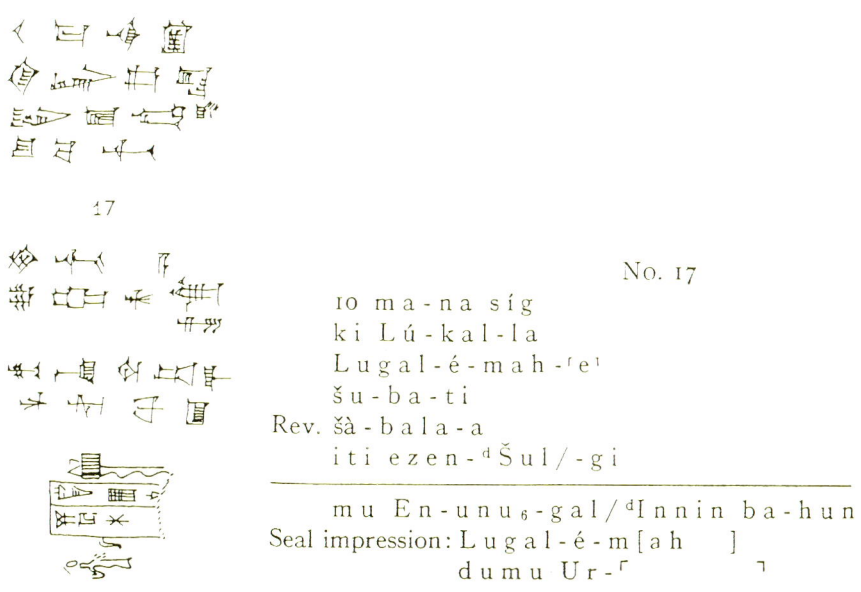

No. 17

10 ma-na síg
ki Lú-kal-la
Lugal-é-mah-ʼeʼ
šu-ba-ti
Rev. šà-bala-a
iti ezen-ᵈŠul/-gi

mu En-unu₆-gal/ᵈInnin ba-hun
Seal impression: Lugal-é-m[ah   ]
dumu Ur-ʼ   ʼ

Plate 1b. Simple sealed receipt from Umma during the Ur III Dynasty. The tablet reads: "Lugal-emahe received from Lukalla in the b a l a – (month) the tenth month of the fifth year of King AMAR-Sin: 10 pounds of wool. (Seal impression:) Lugal-emah, son of Ur ..." From HALLO 1958, document no. 17.

Plate 2a-b. Danish National Museum inv. no. 9182. Bucchero bowl. Photo HSR.

Plate 3a-b. Danish National Museum inv. no. 9182. Bucchero bowl. Photo HSR.

Plate 3c. Louvre C 665 (Coll. Campana 3052) Bucchero bowl. Museum Photo.

Plate 4a. Villa Giulia inv. no. 50365. Bucchero bowl. Photo HSR.

Plate 4b. Barberini ivory bowl, Curtis no. 37. Photo HSR.

Plate 5a. Relief from the Palace of Nineveh, showing King Ashurbanipal. British Museum no. 124920. Courtesy Trustees of the British Museum.

Plate 5b. Detail of plate 5a.

Plate 6a. Bucchero bowl Villa Giulia inv. no. 25105. Courtesy Soprintendenza alle Antichità dell'Etruria Meridionale.

Plate 6b. Terracotta plaque from Murlo. Courtesy Annette Rathje.

Plate 7. Ceramic banquet equipment from Ficana, Latium Vetus (RATHJE 1983).

Plate 8a. 'Phoenician' silver bowl from Cyprus, Cesnola 4555. The kings party (CULLICAN 1982).

Plate 8b. 'Phoenician' silver bowl from Cyprus, Cesnola 4555. The queens party (CULLICAN 1982).

Plate 9a. 'Phoenician' silver bowl from Tomba Bernardini, Palestrina. The kings meal/sacrifice (MARKOE 1985).

Plate 9b. 'Phoenician' silver mixing bowl and laddle from Tomba Bernardini, Palestrina (CANCIANI & v. HASE 1979).

Plate 10a. Banquet frieze from Poggio Civitate, Murlo. Detail-photo Chris Williams.

Plate 10b. Banquet Frieze from Poggio Civitate, Murlo; photo Chris Williams.

Plate 11a. Revetment plaque. W. 55,0 cm., H. 25,8 cm. Ny Carlsberg Glyptotek, HIN 709.

Plate 11b. Revement plaque. W. 54,9 cm., H. 26,0 cm. Ny Carlsberg Glyptotek, HIN 710.

Plate 12a. Revetment plaque. W. 55,3 cm., H. 25,4 cm. Ny Carlsberg Glyptotek, HIN 711.

Plate 12b. Fragment of processional frieze. Found in the Agora of Palmyra. H. 0.43 m. *Linzer-Forsch* 1987, 308.30.

Plate 13a. Beam relief: The Arabic procession. Bel temple of Palmyra. H. c. 2.00 m. WILL 1975, pl. 42.1.

Plate 13b. Merlon. Found in precinct of the Palmyrene Bel temple. *LinzerForsch* 1987, 85.55.

Plate 14a. From the tomb of Artaban. South-east necropolis of Palmyra. A.D. 125-150. *Linzer-Forsch* 1987, 279.3.

Plate 14b. The Konon frieze. Southern wall of naos in the Bel temple of Dura-Europos. Pr. h. 3.80 m. *LinzerForsch* 1987, 168.3.

Plate 15a. Head of stucco. Mekhasanda monastery, near Taxila. (After PUGACHENKOVA 1982, fig. 93).

Plate 15c. Seated Buddha. Gandhāra (exact provenance unknown). Oslo, Ethnographical Museum. (Museum Photo).

Plate 15b. Brahmā and Indra entreating the Buddha to preach. Butkara I. Museo Naz. d'Arte Orientale, Rome. (After LOUIZEN-de LEEUW 1981, fig. 12).

Plate 16.1. Bactria. Euthydemus II c. 200-170 B.C. Obv. Diademed bust of king r. Rev. Heracles standing facing, holding wreath, club and lion' skin; in field l., monogram. Greek legend (king's name and title). Tetradrachm, silver. *SNG* 264. Cop.

Plate 16.2. Bactria-India. Archebios. Obv. Bust of king r., wearing helmet. Greek legend (king's name and titles). Rev. Zeus standing facing, hurling thunderbolt and holding spear. Kharosti legend (king's name and titles). Tetradrachm, silver Cop. 9.92 g. Cf. MITCHINER 1975, type 359.

Plate 16.3. Bactria-India. Hermaeus and Kadphises. Obv. Diademed bust of Hermaeus r. Greek legend for Hermaeus. Rev. Heracles standing facing, holding club and lion's skin. Kharosti legend for Kujula Kadphises. Bronze. Cop. 17.49 g. Cf. BMC p. 120, 1.

Plate 16.4. Bactria-India. Kujula Kadphises. Obv. Diademed bust of king r. Greek legend (king's name and titles). Rev. Male figure seated on curule chair. Kharosti legend (king's name and titles). Bronze. Cop. 3.38 g. Cf. *BMC* p. 123.

Plate 16.5. Kushan kings. Vima Kadphises c. 166-230. Obv. King in biga r., holding club. Greek legend (kings name and titles). Rev. Siva standing facing holding trident and animal's skin; in field l. monogram or *tamga* (on the kings' personal tamgas, which appear on all the coins cf. Göbl 1984 pl. VIII), Kharosti legend (king's name and titles). Gold. GÖBL 1984 no. 5,1.

Plate 16.6. Kushan kings. Vima Kadphises c. 166-230. Obv. King seated crosslegged on cushion? holding club; flames on shoulders. Greek legend (king's name and titles). Rev. Siva standing as on no. 5 in front of humped bull. Kharosti legend (king's name and titles). Gold, double unit. GÖBL 1984 no. 10,1.

Plate 16.7. Kushan kings Vima Kadphises c. 166-230. Obv. King standing sacrificing over altar; in field l., trident; in field r., club. Greek legend (king's name and titles). Rev. Siva standing in front of humped bull. Kharosti legend (king's name and titles). Bronze. Cop. 16.47 g. Cf. GÖBL 1984 no. 762.

Plate 16.8. Kushan kings. Kanishka I 232-60. Obv. King emerging from wall of rocks, holding small club. Greek legend (king's name and titles). Rev. Siva standing as on no. 5. Kharoshti legend (king's name and titles). Gold. Cop. 6.95 g. GÖBL 1984, pl. 3, no. 15. ROSENFIELD 1967, 22.

Plate 16.9. Kushan kings. Kanishka I 232-260. Obv. Kings standing sacrificing over altar, holding elephant's goad and spear; flames on shoulders. Greek legend (king's name and titles). Rev. Nana, goddess of fertility, standing r., holding staff ending in horseprotome and bowl of box. Greek legend (name and title of goddess). Gold. Cop. 7.84 g. Cf. GÖBL 1984, no. 54. ROSENFIELD 1967, 90.

Plate 16.10. Kushan kings. Kanishka I 232-260. Obv. As preceding. Rev. Atsho god of fire standing l., holding diadem; flame on shoulder. Greek legend (name of god). Gold. Cop. 7.91 g. Cf. GÖBL 1984, no. 37. ROSENFIELD 1967, 76.

Plate 16.11. Kushan kings. Kanishka I 232-260. Obv. As preceding. Rev. Siva with four arms and halo standing l., holding vase, thunderbolt, trident and goat. Greek legend (name of god, Oesho). Gold. Cop. 7.90 g. Cf. GÖBL 1984, no. 62. ROSENFIELD 1967, 92.

Plate 17.12. Kushan kings. Kanishla I 232-260. Obv. As preceding. Rev. Pharro, god for "the kings' legitimacy and glory", standing r., holding flame and sceptre. Greek legend (name of god). Gold. Cop. 7.89 g. Cf. GÖBL 1984, no. 69. ROSENFIELD 1067, 96.

Plate 17.13. Kushan kings. Huvishka 260-92. Obv. King emerging from wall of rocks, holding small club. Greek legend (king's name and titles). Rev. Ardoxsho, goddess of fortune, standing r. with halo, holding cornucopiae. Greek legend (name of goddess). Gold. Cop. 7.84 g. Cf. GÖBL 1984, no. 154. ROSENFIELD 1967, 74.

Plate 17.14. Kushan kings. Huvishka 260-92. Obv. As preceding with different headgear; king wears halo and holds small club and sceptre Ardoxsho standing l., holding cornucopiae. Greek legend (name of goddess). Gold. Cop. 7.92 g. Cf. GÖBL 1984, no. 157. ROSENFIELD 1967, 74.

Plate 17.15. Kushan kings. Huvishka 260-92. Obv. As no. 13. Rev. The gods Skando-Komaro, Massena and Bizago (three aspects of Kartikkeya, god of wars) standing on dais in aedicule. Greek legend (names of gods). Gold. Cop. 7.90 g. Cf. GÖBL 1984, no. 157. ROSENFIELD 1967, 99.

Plate 17.16. Kushan kings. Kanishka II 332-350. Obv. King with halo standing l., sacrificing over altar and holding staff with ribbon in field l., trident with ribbon. Greek legend (king's name and titles. Rev. Ardoxsho, goddess of fortune, seated on throne holding wreath and cornucopiae. Greek legend (name of Goddess). Gold. Cop. 7.94 g. Cf. GÖBL 1984, no. 541.

Plate 17.17. Kushan kings after Vasudeva III 4. cent. A.D. Obv. As preceding but no legend. Rev. As preceding but no legend. Gold. Cop. 7.87 g. GÖBL 1984, no. 589, 3.

Plate 17.18. Rome. Augustus 27 B.C.-14 A.D. Obv. Victory standing r. on prow. Rev. Emperor r. in triumphal quadriga, holding branch. Aureus, gold. Cop. 3.75 g. Cf. *RIC* 7.

Plate 17.19. Rome. Caracalla in the reign of Septimius Severus 193-211. Obv. Bust of Emperor r. Rev. Emperor in triumphal quadriga r., holding eagle-tipped sceptre. Aureus, gold. BM. Cf. *RIC* 87.

Plate 17.20. Rome. Julia Domna in the reign of Septimius Severus 193-211. Obv. Bust of empress r. Rev. Diana Lucifera holding torch. Aureus, gold. Cop. 7.28 g. Cf. *RIC* 548.

Plate 17.21. Rome. Septimius Severus 193-211. Obv. Head of emperor r. Rev. Emperor standing l. sacrificing over altar and holding spear. Aureus, gold. Cop. 7.50 g. Cf. *RIC* 167.

Plate 17.22. Rome. Vitellius 68 A.D. Obv. Head of emperor r. Rev. Libertas standing r. holding pileur and spear. Aureus, gold. Cop. 7.46 g. Cf. *RIC* 17.

Plate 17.23. Rome. Elagabal 218-222. Obv. Bust of emperor r. Rev. Salus standing r., feeding snake. Aureus, gold. Cop. 6.22 g. Cf. *RIC* 136.

Plate 17.24. Rome. Numerian 282-83. Obv. Bust of emperor r. Rev. Abundantia standing l. pouring fruits from cornucipiae. Aureus, gold. Cop. 4.03 g. Cf. *RIC* 451.

Plate 17.25. Rome. Hadrian 117-138. Obv. Head of emperor r. Rev. Hercules and two nymphs standing in distyle temple; beneath them, rivergod. Aureus, gold. BM. Cf. *RIC* 59.

Plate 18. South-wall of the fortified camp. The wall is preserved up to a height of 4 metres. In the foreground the rubbish-dump that is now being excavated. (Photo: AB-J, 1983).

MANNERS AND CUSTOMS IN CENTRAL ITALY IN THE ORIENTALIZING PERIOD: INFLUENCE FROM THE NEAR EAST

by ANNETTE RATHJE

The impact of the change in the material culture of Central Italy in the 8th-7th century B.C. can be studied by close analyses of the imports from the Near East and their imitations. As we are dealing with the 1st millenium B.C. this phenomenon, and the long-distance trade and its conditions, has attracted very little attention from the orientalists, but this is changing in accord with the increasing interest in the Phoenician expansion in the Mediterranean.

In Central Italy the orientalizing period covers the end of the 8th century and the whole of the 7th century B.C. and it represents the genesis of the Etruscan culture as a process of amalgamation of a local Iron Age culture and oriental influence on one hand and Greek culture on the other. We must bear in mind that the Greek culture of this time is orientalizing, too. In other words we are dealing with an orientalizing process which is both direct and indirect.

This orientalizing period has mostly been the subject of studies of a more stylistic kind, including the study of the forms and shapes adopted from the new repertoire that flooded the market. Typological detail-studies enable us to trace a regular import of goods and techniques from the Near East but it enables us to place these objects in a social context too, so that we can ask the question: how were these objects acquired? (CRISTOFANI 1975, *Formazione* 1980, 138-145). Some objects passed through several hands, as can be seen from the oriental inscriptions on the Phoenician silver bowls found in Italy(HVIDBERG-HANSEN this journal 58-60).

I have concentrated here on a different approach by studying the consequences of the contacts with the outer world which reflect an interior transformation of society. This transformation has been identified by analysing the archaeological material of the finds from tombs as well as dwellings. In other words, I think that the oriental influence on Central Italy is demonstrated by the incorporation of eastern customs in society. This contribution is a further development of my discussion in the seminar held in Rome 1984 entitled "Aspetti delle aristocrazie fra VIII e VII secolo a. C." and of the questions asked in the "premesse" (*Aspetti* 1984, 231-33, RATHJE 1984).

We are witnessing the introduction of luxury (*tryphe*), represented by objects of bronze, precious metals, ivories and exotica such as glass and shells etc. (RATHJE 1979, 1980, 1986). To this group belong objects which increased in value because they were given as gifts (1984, 915-916). To this discussion of value and quality that of luxury involving quantity must be added, for instance the Castel di Decima tomb 153 (*CLP* 1976, 91) contained about 100 objects, although 10 might have been sufficient.

This is just the phenomenon described by Braudel "Luxury then can take on many guises, depending on the period, the country or the civilisation. What does not change by contrast is the unending social drama of which luxury is both the prize and the theme, a choise spectacle for sociologists, psychologist, economist and historian" (BRAUDEL 1979, 184).

The person who demonstrates luxury shows where he or she belongs in the social hierarchy. This demonstration takes place in the lifetime of the person involved as well as after death in the tomb! What is meant as luxury in this context includes precious garments (RATHJE 1984, 346-347), and objects that belong to the ruler or to court-culture: sceptres (BOITANI 1985, 545) thrones (STRØM 1988), carts and horses (BARTOLINI & GROTTANELLI 1984), precious furniture (MACINTOSH 1981, RATHJE 1984, 346) and vessels with a considerable ideological value as metal bowls (ZACCAGNINI 1984). These luxury items separated the persons of status, the *"aristoi"* from the rest of society (AMPOLO 1984, 469-476).

I am not going to discuss all these categories here, nor the oriental influence on warfare, arms and armour (STARY 1979, 1980, 1981) but will concentrate on a specific aspect: the banquet, the feast as a token of an ideology of representation; dialectically speaking the banquet gives status to the host and to the participants.

It has been noted that the change in the material culture reflects a change in the eating and drinking habits (*Formazione* 1980, GRAS 1983, 1074).[1] The repertoire of shapes of the Iron Age were quite abruptly

---

1. This is a well known social-anthropological fact cf. GOODY 1982, passim.

replaced by quite different types, the origin of which is either Greece or the Near East. In this connection it is worth noticing how many of the imported objects are ones used for banqueting purposes (RATHJE 1984, 344-346) and that it has been stated that parts of drinking sets are the favorite items in East-West trade (MOOREY 1980, 181).

Another very important class of imports is wine, well known from the Old Testament e.g. Ezekiel 27, 18 (ZACCAGNINI 1984, 238). Imported wine was a status symbol equal to many of the imports with which the elite surrounded itself, as can be learned from the description of the treasury of Odysseus, his *thalamos:*

> "A wide room where gold and bronze lay piled and rainment in chests and stores of fragrant oil. There, too, stood great jars of wine, old and sweet, holding within them an unmixed divine drink, and ranged in order along the wall" (Od. II, 337-347).

It is significant that quite a few of the so called phoenician wine amphorae have been found in the recent excavations of *Latium Vetus*, the oldest being the ones found in Castel di Decima (Tomb 15, and 101, GRAS 1986, 293). We are, however, allowed to assume that these amphorae and their contents were exported to Etruria, too. It is the extremely low interest taken in the undecorated ceramics the so-called domestic ware in Etruria that has caused the negative evidence from there, but it is significant that the Etruscan wine amphorae are imitations of the Phoenician types (GRAS 1986, 319).

But even if we are dealing mostly with drinking vessels and vessels for mixing and serving of the wine which may indicate complicated drinking rituals, it is of uttermost importance to stress that we are dealing with *syndeipnon* not the *symposion,* well known from Greece (SCHMITT RANTEL 1985, 145, 148, MURRAY **). Other objects point to the actual eating: vessels for cooking, fire-dogs, spits and plates and dishes.

Banquet equipment has been well-known from the tombs of Central Italy, but are now recently appearing in the settlement-excavations of our time. We may mention the equipment found at ancient *Ficana* Latium Vetus (RATHJE 1983) *(plate 7)*. It has been found in connection with the foundations of a building which most resonably can be ascribed as a dwelling of the local elite. It is interesting to note a close analogy. A study of the very fragmentary finds from the old excavations near the Faustina and Antoninus' temple at Forum Romanum, made by Giacomo Boni in the beginning of this century, show the presence of a similar banquet-equipment connected with the Archaic house found there.[2] Both the house from Forum and the one from *Ficana* must be dated to the last half of the 7th century B.C.

The banquet equipment from *Ficana* (*plate* 7) was meant for more than 30 persons, 4 big *holmoi* or stands for mixing-bowls were found, a type well-known from the famous imported items found in the princely tombs of Palestrina. The main part of vessels that make up the set are of red impasto, a well-polished ware that enters the scene as a complete novelty in the 7th century B.C.

Of special interest in this connection are chalices and plates. The stemmed chalice with its characteristic carinated body has long been connected with the Orient, especially with Assyrian forms (HIRSCHLAND RAMAGE 1970, 25-26). The plate on ringfoot or high-stemmed foot with a sharply carinated shoulder is very similar to the characteristic Phoenician plates of the so-called red-slip ware, which have been found in great quantity in the Western Phoenician colonies and on the isle of Ischia, where a local production has been claimed (BUCHNER 1982). It is not inconceivable that Pithekoussai, the international Greek emporion, has played a part in the distribution of this form, but it is not the occasion to discuss the key-position of Pithekoussai in the East-West connection.[3]

The banquets, as we know them from the written sources, indicate clearly an internal hierarchy. One must ask the question: can we ever realize this in the archeological material? It is worth keeping an eye on this problem when involved in comparative analyses of banquet equipments. Different mixing bowls in the same set for instance, could be the token of hierarchic differences, i.e. some got the best wine and some, of course, got the best pieces of meat. Other differences may be due to the division of drinking habits of the sexes, as it is known that in some cases women were not allowed to drink wine unless it was imported (GRAS 1986, 1070-72).

---

2. I have been able to study the finds in the Forum Antiquarium.
3. I refer to the brilliant synthesis made by D. Ridgway in 1984 especially 121-134.

This elite-culture under discussion here has been compared to the description of the *"aristoi"* in the Homeric epic and we may talk about an Homeric "style of life" as discussed by Finley in his brilliant study "The World of Odysseus", in which he focuses on the guest-friendships and the gift-exchange and the exhibition of status (FINLEY 1977).

The orientals we meet in the Homeric world are Phoenicians and the image we have of them is that they are hospitable and givers of gifts. They produce the highly valued objects of precious metals as for instance the royal krater which Menelaos gives to Telemachos in Od IV (613-19). Furthermore the Phoenicians in the epos are interested in wine and slaves, just as the Greeks are.

It is well known that the Phoenicians did not have a Dark Age, as was the case with the Greeks after the fall of the Mycenean Empire. Therefore, it is not difficult to assign them a primary role in the circulation of goods and ideas from East to West as Coldstream has argued, comparing the Euboians and the Phoenicians "As traders both people were energetic middlemen, frequently meeting one another in most parts of the Mediterranean, except perhaps in the extreme West. Thus the record of Tyre, Kition and Motya is complementary to that of Eretria, Lefkandi, Pithekoussai and Eastern Sicily" (COLDSTREAM 1982, 263).

It is relevant to ask if it is possible to trace an oriental influence on the Homeric epic. It is striking that there are parallels between the innumerable Homeric banquets and the feasts described in the Mesopotamic, Ugaritic and Hebrew texts (LICHTENSTEIN 1968, 24 note 24). The feast is everywhere based on meat and wine, as for instance in the more detailed description in the old Testament:

> those who lie upon beds
>   of ivory
> and stretch themselves
>   upon thir couches
> and eat lambs from the
>   flock
> and calves from the midst
>   of the stall;
> who sing idle songs to the
>   sound of the harp.

> ...
> Who drink wine in
>   bowls
> and annoint themselves with
>   the finest oils ...

This passage (Amos 6:4-6) gives a vivid description of the banquet in a very luxurious setting accompanied by music. It has to be compared with the banquet of the suitors (*Od.* I 150-54) and the banquet of the court of the Phaeacians (*Od.* VIII 61-70; IX, 1-11).

We are now led to the question as to how the banquets were actually held. The solitary oriental banquet as seen on the famous garden party of Assurbanipal and his Queen (SALSKOV ROBERTS this journal *plate* 5) has been contrasted to the collective banquet of the Greeks (STOPPONI 1983, 58). However, an elaborate and detailed representation of a collective feast is seen on the charming narrative friezes on the newly-cleaned silver-bowl from Cyprus (CULICAN 1982, 13-32).

On this bowl (*plate* 8a-b) a party is seen leaving town in a cart and a chariot for a picnic in the open in the first frieze. In the second frieze the "King" is seen reclining under the vine accompanied by musicians. He is served with a cup and a jug by a servant who serves from a table of jars. Behind this table is seen the outline of a mixing bowl on a stand, comparable to the bronze stands found in the princely tombs of Palestrina in *Latium Vetus* (RATHJE 1979, 160). In the approximately opposite position of the frieze the "Queen" is seen sitting in a throne at a loaded table in the shadow of a parasol. In the frieze below various people (the "courtiers") are reclining, accompanied by music.

The reclining banquet has been known from the Orient from the 8th century B.C. but this habit does not seem to affect the meal and its significance, as has been clearly shown (DENTZER 1982, 52). In the Phoenician sphere both sitting and reclining banquets are practised, as can be seen from the ivories (BARNETT 1975, 118, DENTZER 1982, 54 especially note 21).

This silver bowl belongs to the Cypro-phoenician group, of which several have been found in Italy. The extraordinary figured scenes can best be compared to the bowl with the narration of the : "Kings Hunting-day" (RATHJE 1980, 9 B 4, MARKOE 1985, 191 E 2) from Palestrina,

Tomba Bernardini). The king is sitting at his meal/sacrifice.[4] Before him is a stand with a deep mixing-bowl and ladle (*plate* 9a), comparable to the set actually found in the same tomb (*plate* 9b) (CANCIANI and v. HASE 1979, 41 no. 27). On the Cyprus bowl with the picnic party the participants are seen drinking from hemishperical bowls. This is a very well-known type of drinking vessel in the Near East. An actual imported one made of blue glass was found in the Tomba Bernardini (CANCIANI and v. HASE 1979, 77 no. 148). This cup was imitated in silver somewhere in Etruria (RATHJE 1984, 345)[5] and the same type is seen on the banquet of the architectural terracotta frieze that belonged to the upper building complex at Poggio Civitate Murlo (*plate* 10a).

This figurative scene (*plate* 10b) is the oldest representation of a reclining banquet in Central Italy. The terracotta friezes from Murlo are generally dated to the beginning of the 6th century B.C. In the 7th century, however, sitting banquets are represented (RATHJE **), a fact that accords well with the Homeric banquets and the Latin descriptions of the habits of "old days" cfr. Ovid, *Fasti* VI 301 ff. "It used to be the habit to sit on long benches in front of the hearth".

As an iconografic motif, however, the reclining banquet seems to be very popular in the Archaic period of Etruria (STOPPONI 1983, 58-65), and it must be allowed to assume that the popularity of this motif reflects the real importance of this habit in life and the afterlife.

It is important to stress that the banquet service represented on the tables in front of the reclining participants in the Murlo frieze has actually been found at the excavation (*Case e Palazzi* 1985, 138-146). The terracotta frieze adorned the "upper building" (second building-phase at the site), a complex which belongs to the 'bīt hīlanī' type of palace-architecture. The "lower building", from the first building phase (ca. 640-600 B.C.) also represents a big complex of rooms around an open courtyard, although we are not able to distinguish its plan in any detail. The extraordinary finds, including various items of banquet equipment, vessels for cooking and for storing (*Case e Palazzi* 1985, 65, 80-88) leave, however, the idea of a very "orientalized" elitist society.[6] So the complex of Murlo must be viewed in the light of continuity

---

4. The distinction between meal and sacrifice being of a very subtle nature, it is not considered in this study.

5. We must add the newly-found item found in the aristocratic female tomb of Roca di Papa, which also contained imports from the Near East, several bronze cauldrons and parts of a richly-decorated garment (GHINI 1987, fig. 8).

6. Cf. also RYSTEDT 1984.

as stressed by the excavators (*Case e Palazzi* 1985, 64). There is good reason to hope that further studies will enable us to understand the finds from Murlo and similar large buildings, whether they are private or public, and consequently to settle if the banquets held in these surroundings belonged to the private or the public sphere. It is, however, not always easy to make a separation: the private and the public sphere being very much entangled.

I do agree with Torelli that the architectural model of Murlo does not represent an isolated phenomenon, and we cannot but regret the paucity of evidence from the orientalizing period in the Etruscan *poleis* in Southern Etruria (TORELLI 1983, 482). I do think, however, that the evidence from Murlo supports the point of view that the banquet represents an oriental style of life as adopted by the elites of Central Italy in the 7th century B.C.

University of Copenhagen
Institute of Classical Archaeology
Vandkunsten 5
DK-1467 Copenhagen K

BIBLIOGRAPHY

AMPOLO 1984	C. AMPOLO, Il lusso nelle società antiche, *Aspetti*, 469-76.
Aspetti 1984	Aspetti delle aristocrazie fra VIII e VII secolo a.C., *OPUS* III, 231-476.
Aufnahme 1981	*Die Aufnahme fremder Kultureinflüsse in Etrurien und das Problem des Retardierens in der etruskischen Kunst*, Mannheim.
BARNETT 1975	R. D. BARNETT, *A Cataloque of the Nimrud Ivories*, London.
BARTOLONI & GROTTANELLI 1984	G. BARTOLONI & C. GROTTANELLI, I carri a due ruote nelle tombe femminili del Lazio e dell' Etruria, *Aspetti*, 383-410.
BOITANI 1985	F. BOITANI, Veio: La Tomba "Principesca" della Necropoli di Monte Michele, *StEtr*. LI.
BRAUDEL 1985	F. BRAUDEL, *The Structures of Everyday Life*, London, Fontana ed.
BUCHNER 1982	G. BUCHNER, Die Beziehungen zwischen der euböichen Kolonie Pithekoussai auf der Insel Ischia und dem norwestsemitischen Mittelmeerraum in der zweiten Hälfte des 8. Jhrs. v. Crh., *MBeiträge* 8, 277-298.
CANCIANI & VON HASE 1979	F. CANCIANI and F. W. VON HASE, *La Tomba Bernardini*, Rome.

Case e Palazzi 1985	Case e Palazzi d'Etruria, exhibition cataloque from Siena, Milan.
CLP 1976	Civiltà del Lazio Primitivo, exhibition cataloque, Rome.
COLDSTREAM 1982	J. N. COLDSTREAM, Greeks and Phoenicians in the Aegean, MBeiträge 8, 261-275.
CRISTOFANI 1975	M. CRISTOFANI, Il "dono" nell'Etruria arcaica, PP 30, 132-152.
CULICAN 1982	W. CULICAN, Cesnola Bowl 4555 and other Phoenician Bowls, RStFen X, 13-32.
DENTZER 1982	J. M. DENTZER, Le motif du banquet couché dans le proche-orient et le monde grec du VIIe au IVe siecle avant J. C., Rome.
FINLEY 1977	M. I. FINLEY, The World of Odysseus, New York.
Formazione 1980	La formazione delle città nel Lazio, DdA 1-2.
GHINI 1987	G. Ghini, Recupero di una tomba orientalizzante presso Rocca di Papa; il corredo, QuadAEI 14, 213-217.
GOODY 1982	J. GOODY, Cooking, Cuisine and Class. A Study in Comparative Sociology, London.
GRAS 1983	M. GRAS, Vin et société à Rome et dans le Latium à l'époque archaïque, Modes de contacts et processus de transformation dans les sociétés anciennes – Actes du colloque de Cortone 1981, Pisa-Rome, 1067-1075.
GRAS 1986	M. GRAS, Trafics tyrrhéniens archaïques, Rome.
HIRSCHLAND RAMAGE 1970	N. HIRSCHLAND RAMAGE, Studies in Early Etruscan Bucchero, BRS 38, 1-61.
IAArtifacts 1986	Iron Age Artifacts in the British Museum. J. SWADDLING ed., London.
IbR 1979	D. RIDGWAY-F. R. RIDGWAY (eds.), Italy before the Romans. The Iron Age, Orientalizing and Etruscan Periods, London.
LICHTENSTEIN 1968	M. LICHTENSTEIN, The Banquet Motif in Keret and Proverbs 9, JANES 1, 19-31.
MACINTOSH 1981	J. MACINTOSH, Review of STEINGRÄBER 1979, Gnomon, 717-719.
MARKOE 1985	G. MARKOE, Phoenician Bronze and Silver Bowls from Cyprus and the Mediterranean, University of California Publications: Classical Studies vol. 26.
MOOREY 1980	P. R. S. MOOREY, Metal Wine sets in the Ancient Near East, IrAnt 15, 181-197.
MURRAY**	O. MURRAY, The Deipnosophistae: a Symposium on the Greek Symposium. (Forthcomming) Oxford.
PARISE 1984	N. PARISE, Sacrificio e misura del valore nella Grecia antica, Quaderni storici 57, 913-923.
RATHJE 1979	A. RATHJE, Oriental Imports in Etruria in the Eight and Seventh Centuries B.C.: their Origins and Implications, IbR, 145-183.
RATHJE 1980	A. RATHJE, Silver Relief Bowls from Italy, ARID, IX, 7-47.
RATHJE 1983	A. RATHJE, A Banquet Service from the Latin City of Ficana, ARID XII, 7-31.
RATHJE 1984	A. RATHJE, I Keimelia orientali, Aspetti 341-354.
RATHJE 1986	A. RATHJE, Five Ostrich Eggs from Vulci, A Tridacna Squamosa Shell, IAArtifacts, 393-404.
RATHJE**	A. RATHJE, The Adoption of the Homeric Banquet in Central Italy in the Orientalizing Period, in MURRAY**
RIDGWAY 1984	D. RIDGWAY, L'Alba della Magna Grecia, Milan.
RYSTEDT 1984	E. RYSTEDT, Architectural Terracotta as aristocratic Display: the case of seventh Century Poggio Civitate (Murlo), Aspetti, 367-376.

SCHMITT PANTEL 1985	P. SCHMITT PANTEL, Banquet et citè greque, quelques questions suscitées par les recherches récents, *MEFRA* 97, 135-158.
STARY 1979	P. STARY, Foreign Elements in Etruscan Arms and Armour 8.-3. Centuries B.C., *ProcPrHist Soc* 45, 179-206.
STARY 1980	P. STARY, Orientalische Einflüsse in der Früh-etruskischen Bewaffnung, *HamBeitrA* 7, 23-27.
STARY 1981	P. STARY, Orientalische und Griechische Einflüsse in der Etruskischen Bewaffnung und Kampfesweise, *Aufnahme*, 25-40.
STEINGRÄBER 1979	S. STEINGRÄBER, *Etruskische Möbel*, Rome.
STOPPONI 1983	S. STOPPONI, *La Tomba della Scrofa Nera*, Rome.
STRØM 1971	I. STRØM, *Problems concerning the Origin and Early Development of the Etruscan Orientalizing Style*, Odense.
STRØM 1988	I. STRØM, Orientalizing Bronze Reliefs from Chiusi, *ARID* 17.
TORELLI 1983	M. TORELLI, Polis e "Palazzo". Architettura, ideologia e artigianato greco tra VII e VI secolo a.C. *Architecture e société de l'archaïsme grec à la fin de la République romaine*, Paris-Rome, 471-499.
ZACCAGNINI 1984	C. ZACCAGNINI, La Circolazione dei beni di lusso nelle fonti neo-assire (IX-VII sec. A.C.), *Aspetti*, 235-252.

SOME EARLY ETRUSCAN REVETMENT PLAQUES IN THE NY CARLSBERG GLYPTOTEK*

by JETTE CHRISTIANSEN

Among the Etruscan architectural terracottas in the Ny Carlsberg Glyptotek in Copenhagen are four revetment plaques, two by two with the same motif: a pair of walking bulls and a procession of warriors, two driving a biga, one mounted on horseback. Of the latter type, one is in a very fragmentary state. All four plaques are moulded and have a forward curving sima with 18 convex strigils, a slightly raised groundline and decoration in very low, in places almost indiscernible relief, emphasized with added black and cream paint on a red-to-orange-red background. Accordance in technique and measurements makes it probable that the plaques belonged to the same building (*plates* 11a-b, 12a).

Of the two friezes represented, processions with bulls are rarely seen on Etruscan revetment plaques. Warrior friezes, however, occur in several variations. Among those which iconographically are closest to the plaques in the Glyptotek are the friezes from the so-called *oikos* at Piazza d'Armi in Veji. Two different series are distinguishable, but they have essentially the same motif. The earlier is dated around 600 B.C., while the later probably belongs to the second quarter of the 6th cent. Stylistically the warrior plaques in the Glyptotek should be placed somewhere between the two Veji types. This implies a date about 575 B.C. for the plaques here considered, the bull friezes included.

Southern Etruria is assumed to be the most probable place of origin for the plaques in the Glyptotek. By technique and material they are related to the 7th cent. B.C. white-on-red ware from Caere. The plaques might represent a 6th cent. survival of that technique, in this case applied to architectural revetment plaques.

It is suggested that both the warrior- and the bull-motifs owe their iconography to orientalizing models of the 7th cent. B.C., in spite of apparent Greek elements in the equipment of the warriors.

With reference to the relief-decorated plaques from Murlo where the scenes have been interpreted as depicting important events in the life of the rulers, it is considered whether other early Etruscan revetment plaques might derive from buildings which, as is probably the case at Murlo, served both a sacred and a secular (residential?) purpose for the ruling aristocracy.

Until recently the Near Eastern impact on the Etruscan aristocratic environment in the Orientalizing period has mostly been attested by the abundant grave gifts in the tombs of local chieftains. The Murlo site gives a hint of what kind of residence these sovereigns might have had. The interpretation of the Murlo plaques means that not only the iconography, but also the ideology behind the narrative friezes and the various symbols of power and prestige reflect Near Eastern practice which has been adapted to Etruscan society.

Ny Carlsberg Glyptotek
Dantes Plads 7
DK-1556 Copenhagen V.

*These lines are a summary of an article which will be published in *ARID* 17, 1988.

THE WISDOM OF THE CHALDAEANS. MESOPOTAMIAN MAGIC AS CONCEIVED BY CLASSICAL AUTHORS

by MARIE-LOUISE THOMSEN

ABSTRACT
The people of ancient Mesopotamia are connected with magic, astrology and divination by several classical authors. However, their descriptions of Chaldaean astrologers or Assyrians and Babylonians performing love magic and necromancy have little in common with the information in cuneiform texts from Mesopotamia. These texts contain incantations and ritual instructions to avert illness and all sort of misfortune by reconciling the gods with offerings and prayers and purificating the afflicted person. It must therefore be concluded that the content of the old Mesopotamian literary tradition concerning these matters was not known to the classical world and probably did not survive beyond the end of cuneiform writing.

It is noteworthy that in our modern highly technological time the fascination of magic and occult phenomenons is as widespread as ever, although – or just because – science can explain things which were earlier considered supernatural or inexplicable. A whole literary genre is devoted to such themes using magic and sorcerers as elements in order to produce excitement. In films, nowadays also in computer games, exotic and ancient cultures are often preferred as a background to occult rites and fantastic events: there are films about American Indian medicine men, voodoo and zombies, Egyptian mummies, the curse of Pharaoh and so on. Ancient Mesopotamia also belongs to this modern occult universe of the entertainment business, but the connection between the ancient cultures of Mesopotamia and magic, demonology, divination and astrology is of course not new. In the Old Testament there are many allusions to fortune-tellers, soothsayers and dream-readers at the court of the Babylonian king (e.g. the books of Daniel and Isaiah) and Greek and Latin authors mention the knowledge of Assyrians, Babylonians and Chaldaeans about astrology and magic. It is therefore worth while to investigate the oldest stages of this long tradition in order to prove what the scholars and authors in Antiquity really knew about the ancient Mesopotamian teachings in these fields, especially concerning magic, and whether parts of these sciences in some way or other continued after the end of the cuneiform tradition.[1]

---

1. A thorough study of this subject is in preparation.

Concerning the character of magic in antiquity I quote Kleine Pauly under the catchword *Zauberei:* "Die hauptsächl. Anwendungsgebiete sind: Liebeszauber, Wetterzauber, Geisterbeschwörung (Goetie) und philos. angehauchte Theurgie" (vol. 5, 1460), and I would add necromancy. These magic methods are often connected with the *Magi,* originally an Iranian tribe or class of priests already mentioned by Herodotus as diviners and conjurers (VII 113; 191). The *Magi* were confused with the Chaldaeans and the terms "Assyrians" and "Babylonians" are moreover used in almost the same meaning, namely about Orientals or persons who were occupied with Oriental (Babylonian or Persian) magic practices and astrology. To illustrate this I shall give an account of some references in classical authors to Mesopotamians and *Magi* in connection with magic and divination:

Theocritus gives a rather detailed description of love magic. At the end of this the woman who performs the ritual tells that she got some "evil drugs" (κακὰ φάρμακα) from an Assyrian (Idyll 2: Φαρμακεύτρια, 161-162).

In his description of Babylon Strabo tells that in this city there was a special residential quarter for the Chaldaeans who were occupied with observations of the stars, and that some of them claimed to foretell the future on the basis of these observations. Strabo also informs that the Chaldaeans were a Mesopotamian tribe and, moreover, that there were different schools of astrologers distinguished according to their home cities: Borsippa, Uruk and some others (XVI 1, 6).

In *De divinatione* Cicero mentions several times the astronomical observations of the Assyrians and Babylonians saying that they were the first to make such observations and that they had put them down during several thousands of years. The *Magi* he calls dream-readers and augurs.[2]

In the work of Diodorus of Sicily there is a remarkable passage about the Chaldaeans:

"Now the Chaldaeans, belonging as they do to the most ancient inhabitants of Babylonia, have about the same position among the divisions of the state as that occupied by the priests of Egypt; for being assigned to the service of the gods they spend their entire life in study, their greatest renown being in the field of astrology. But they occupy

---

2. *De divinatione* I 2; 90-91; 93; II 97.

themselves largely with soothsaying as well, making predictions about future events, and in some cases by purifications, in others by sacrifices, and in others by some other charms they attempt to effect the averting of evil things and the fulfilment of the good. They are also skilled in soothsaying by the flight of birds, and they give out interpretations of both dreams and portents. They also show marked ability in making divinations from the observation of entrails of animals, deeming that in this branch they are eminently successful" (II 29, 2-3).[3]

In another context Diodorus tells that the Chaldaeans originally were colonists from Egypt; they were led to Babylon by Belus, where they pursued the study of astrology which they had learned from the Egyptian priests (I 28, 1; 81, 6).

In the 30th book of his Natural History Pliny the Elder gives an account of the origins and development of magic. According to him it was founded by Zoroaster in Persia and later introduced to the Greeks by Ostanes who attended the campaign of Xerxes. Pythagoras, Empedocles, Democritus and Plato also went to the Orient in order to study magic. Pliny renders many methods and remedies presumably deriving from the *Magi,* not only in this book, although he does not believe in them.

The Roman historian Quintus Curtius Rufus describes the entry of Alexander the Great in Babylon and tells that he was met by singing *Magi,* by Chaldaeans and by Babylonian diviners. Further he states that the Chaldaeans made observations of the stars (V 3).

Another historian, Arrian, tells that the Chaldaeans once dissuaded Alexander from proceeding Babylon from a certain direction, since they have been warned by Belus that this would be unfavourable at that moment. Alexander nevertheless entered the city where he died soon afterwards (*Anabasis* VII 16, 5-8).

Iamblichus the Syrian (2nd Century A.D.), the author of a romantic novel with the title *Babyloniaka*, was born in Syria but brought up by a slave who came from Babylonia. Iamblichus pretends to have learned the language and customs of Babylonia from this slave. However, the novel, as it has survived until today, contains no piece of original

---

3. The translation is by C. H. Oldfather in the *Loeb Classical Library, Diodorus Siculus*, Books I-II, 34. Cambridge, Mass. and London 1968, 445-447.

Mesopotamian literary or historical subject matter. Moreover, it mentions various *Magi* acting against locusts, lions, mice, hailstorms and snakes and performing necromancy. Iamblichus, calling himself a Babylonian, claims to have got instructions in these fields.[4]

At last I shall mention Lucian's satire *Necyomantia*.[5] Menippos visits in Babylon Mithrobarzanes (an Iranian name), being a Chaldaean and disciple of Zoroaster; he agrees to lead Menippos to the netherworld. Lucian now describes the preparations for this venture rather circumstantially. Menippos bathes daily at sunrise in the Euphrates twenty-nine days from the day of the new moon on; during the bath Mithrobarzanes murmurs incantations and at last he spits in Menippos' face three times. In this period they must both observe a diet and sleep outdoors. After all these preparations the journey itself begins with lustrations: a bath and a cleansing with incense, also accompanied by incantations. At dawn they go by boat to a solitary place in the marsh where they dig a hole, slaughter an animal and let its blood flow into the hole. Then the earth quakes and opens and the descent to the netherworld can begin.

Now, for these aspects of ancient Mesopotamian life we are not obliged to rely on classical authors only. On the contrary there is a large amount of authentic cuneiform texts from Assyria and Babylonia dealing with magic and divination. It is thus natural to compare these texts with the information from other ancient sources.

The cuneiform texts contain incantations and instructions for the performance of rituals to heal or to avert sickness, demons, witchcraft, misfortune and accidents, shortly, everything negative or dangerous which could harm a human being. In connection with this a large literature of manuals has developed: diagnostic texts, hemerologies, collections of medical recipes, catalogues of plants and stones used as remedies, etc. The methods described in these texts reflect the cosmological system of the Mesopotamians and their understanding of causality between man's behavior and sickness, misfortune etc. and of the relation between man and god.[6] Normally, it was thought, man was

---

4. HABRICH 1960, 32. For Iamblichus' work in general see SCHNEIDER-MENZEL 1948, 48-92.
5. HARMON 1925, 72-109.
6. See THOMSEN 1987a, 11-13; THOMSEN 1987b.

protected by the gods, first of all by his personal god, but if he committed a sin, for instance by breaking a taboo, the gods would draw back and now being without protection the man could be afflicted by demons, witches and so on. The disharmony in the relation between man and the gods might be expressed in an omen like the birth of a malformed animal or the occurrence of a wailing cat in the man's house. A serious and persistent illness was also the sign that the relations were disturbed. In these cases a ritual should be performed in order to purify the man, to reconcile the gods and to re-establish the good connections. This was obtained by offerings and by bathing or cleansing with incense followed by some rather symbolic acts like destroying figurines of the supposed witches or throwing a clay figure of the above-mentioned cat into the river. These actions are not really magic since it was not thought that they alone could affect the witches or other evil-doers, rather their purpose was to demonstrate to the gods the wanted result of the ritual.[7]

Both the background and aims of the Mesopotamian rituals are thus fairly different from the magic of classical antiquity. The Mesopotamian texts give no directions for the performance of witchcraft, for the control of gods and demons or for necromancy, only love magic is rather sparsely represented. But there are some at least seeming resemblances. The purifications described by Lucian, but not Menippos' purpose, are thus similar to Mesopotamian practices. The methods and remedies in Pliny claimed to derive from the *Magi* are in principle very like the medical recipes in cuneiform texts, but I have not been able to find a single case of identity. Burning of wax figures or binding of knots on a cord spun of more than one colour mentioned by Vergil in connection with love magic[8] is also known in Mesopotamian literature, but here these actions are performed in a totally different context. And conversely, Mesopotamian directions for love magic are quite different.[9] In Greek magical papyri the name of the Mesopotamian goddess Ereškigal occurs sometimes;[10] she is the queen of the netherworld and is identified with Hecate. In Mesopotamian rituals and incantations,

---

7. For the use of figurines see DAXELMÜLLER and THOMSEN 1982; THOMSEN 1987b.
8. Vergil, *eclogue* 8, see LUCK 1962, 6-15, espec. p. 9.
9. For Mesopotamian examples of love magic see BIGGS 1967, 70-78.
10. For instance PREISENDANZ 1973, 83; 121; 151; 197.

however, Ereškigal is seldom mentioned. In defiance of the numerous references to Babylonians, Assyrians and Chaldaeans, these descrepancies suggest that the connection between the classical authors and the old Mesopotamian tradition is rather thin.

The Mesopotamian incantations and ritual instructions were already early written down; parts of the literary tradition go back as far as the third millennium B.C. Most of these texts, however, date to the first millennium B.C. when Sumerian, one of the languages connected with this tradition, was already long a dead language, and the other, Babylonian gradually ceased to be spoken, displaced by Aramaic. In spite of this the ancient literary tradition is continued as long as the cuneiform writing is still used, i.e. until approximately 100 B.C., perhaps a little longer. This tradition certainly does not represent popular belief, folk medicine, still less superstition as it is sometimes asserted; on the contrary, it was the tradition of the intellectual elite of the Mesopotamian society. The texts were copied and studied and sometimes commented on by the learned experts at the royal court or in the service at one of the big temples. We know for certain that the rituals were performed under the Assyrian kings Esarhaddon (680-669 B.C.) and Assurbanipal (668-627 B.C.), but we cannot decide whether it also was the case in later periods. Possibly, in the Seleucid period, at the end of cuneiform tradition, the texts had no practical use any more.

Dating to the second and early first centuries B.C., at the same time as the latest cuneiform documents were written, there is a small number of clay tablets with Sumerian and Babylonian texts written with Greek letters, among them two or three incantations.[11] Transliterations with both Greek and Aramaic characters written on perishable materials like leather and papyrus have probably existed in a greater number, but are not preserved due to climatic conditions. In any case they were not written by or for Greeks who wanted to learn the Sumerian and Babylonian texts. On the contrary, they were made by Babylonians mainly for practical purposes at a time when cuneiform writing was about to be given up and when the old writing and languages were no longer under-

---

11. For these "Graeco-Babyloniaca" see SOLLBERGER 1962; GELLER 1983; BLACK and SHERWIN-WHITE 1984. The tablet published by Geller, a Babylonian incantation with Greek transliteration, is according to the Greek script not older than the first century A.D., a surprisingly late date for these documents; see GELLER 1983, 114.

stood very well.[12] On this basis we cannot conclude that there was an interest among the Greeks for the old Mesopotamian texts.

The fact that the Mesopotamian literary tradition concerning incantations and rituals apparently ceases at the same time as the cuneiform writing is given up, depends probably on the special religious background of the rituals. Since an important theme was the re-establishing of the good relations between human beings and the gods, the ritual practices could not immediately be transformed to groups or societies not familiar with the Mesopotamian culture. Moreover, the texts were written in two dead languages, and it is not surprising that no translations are known, not only because of understanding difficulties, but also because just the original wording of the incantation is important, not the content. Thus the old Sumerian incantations were also retained in their original form and the Babylonian interlinear translations were not recited during the ritual, but added as an aid for the understanding only. But even if incantations were not translated for these reasons, it might be expected that some narrative elements at least were transformed and used in the classical tradition, for instance the dialogue between the god Enki and his son Asalluhi, the divine exorcist, a motif very common in Sumerian incantations.[13] However, neither this typical theme nor other literary motifs seem to be known in ancient magical texts outside Mesopotamia.

It can therefore be concluded that if magic of classical antiquity contained elements from the Mesopotamian tradition, as it is sometimes postulated by classical authors, these are either changed in such a way that it is impossible to identify them, or they stem from a tradition other than the literary which is the only one known to us. What survives from the Mesopotamian tradition concerning magic is apparently not the methods or the literary tradition which the ancient Assyrians and Babylonians themselves studied and tried to keep for posterity but a quite different literary topic: the image of the conjuring Chaldaean, observing the stars and commanding demons and ghosts. This image was also in the minds of the early Assyriologists first studying the religious cuneiform texts found in Ninive in the last century. Compare

---

12. See OELSNER 1971.
13. This literary motif is described in FALKENSTEIN 1931, 53-58.

for instance the title of François Lenormant's study *La magie chez les chaldéens et les origines accadiennes*, published as early as 1874. Finally we can state that this image still lives today when the discovering of a figurine representing an ancient Mesopotamian demon is used as prelude to the film "The Exorcist" (W. Friedkin, 1974), or when the heroine in the comedy "Ghostbusters" is obsessed by a demon with a name which the film claims to be Sumerian.

The Carsten Niebuhr Institute
of Ancient Near Eastern Studies
University of Copenhagen
Njalsgade 78
DK-2300 Copenhagen S

BIBLIOGRAPHY

BIGGS 1967	Robert D. BIGGS, *ŠÀ.ZI.GA. Ancient Mesopotamian Potency Incantations*. (Texts from Cuneiform Sources, 2) New York.
BLACK and SHERWIN-WHITE 1984	J. A. BLACK and S. M. SHERWIN-WHITE, A Clay Tablet with Greek Letters in the Ashmolean Museum and the "Graeco-Babyloniaca" Texts. *Iraq* 46, 131-140.
DAXELMÜLLER & THOMSEN 1982	Christoph DAXELMÜLLER & Marie-Louise THOMSEN, Bildzauber im alten Mesopotamien. *Anthropos* (Fribourg) 77, 27-64.
FALKENSTEIN 1931	Adam FALKENSTEIN, *Die Haupttypen der sumerischen Beschwörung literarisch untersucht*. (Leipziger semitistische Studien, neue Folge 1) Leipzig.
GELLER 1983	Markham J. GELLER, More Graeco-Babyloniaca, *ZA* 73, 114-120.
HABRICH 1960	Elmar HABRICH, *Iamblichi Babyloniacorum Reliquiae*. Leipzig.
HARMON 1925	A. M. HARMON, *Lucian*. (Loeb Classical Library). London, New York.
Kleine Pauly	*Der kleine Pauly. Lexikon der Antike in fünf Bänden*. Munich 1975.
LENORMANT 1874	François LENORMANT, *La magie chez les chaldéens et les origines accadiennes*. Paris.
LUCK 1962	Georg LUCK, *Hexen und Zauberei in der römischen Dichtung*. Zürich.
OELSNER 1971	Joachim OELSNER, Zur Bedeutung der Graeco-Babyloniaca für die Überlieferung des Sumerischen und Akkadischen. *MIO* 17, 356-364.
PREISENDANZ 1973	Karl PREISENDANZ, *Papyri Graecae Magicae. Die griechische Zauberpapyri*. I. (2. verbesserte Auflage). Stuttgart.
SCHNEIDER-MENZEL 1948	Ursula SCHNEIDER-MENZEL, Jamblichos' Babylonische Geschichten. In: Franz ALTHEIM, *Literatur und Gesellschaft im ausgehenden Altertum*. Halle/Saale, 48-92.

SOLLBERGER 1962	Edmond SOLLBERGER, Graeco-Babyloniaca. *Iraq* 24, 63-72.
THOMSEN 1982	See DAXELMÜLLER and THOMSEN 1982.
THOMSEN 1987a	Marie-Louise THOMSEN, *Zauberdiagnose und Schwarze Magie in Mesopotamien.* (*Carsten Niebuhr Institute Publications,* 2), Copenhagen.
THOMSEN 1987b	Marie-Louise THOMSEN, Magi og Videnskab. En analyse af de mesopotamiske besværgelsesritualer. *Chaos. Dansk-norsk tidsskrift for religionshistoriske studier* 7, 69-81.

THE FOUR SONS OF PHRAATES IV IN ROME
by ELISABETH NEDERGAARD

1. Introduction
Phraates IV was king of Parthia from 37 to 2 B.C. In Roman terms the period of his reign coincided with the last six years of the civil wars which followed the death of Caesar in 44 B.C. and with the first 29 years of the long reign of Augustus (31 B.C.-A.C. 14). Some time during his reign (see below), Phraates IV sent his four sons, Seraspadanes, Rhodaspes, Phraates and Vonones, together with two daughters-in-law and four grandsons to Augustus in Rome (*Aug. Res Gest.* 32,2; *Eutr.* VII,9; *Joseph. Ant.* XVIII, 42; *Justinus* XLII, 5, 12; *Oros.* VI, 21, 29; *Strabo* VI, 4, 2; XVI, 1, 28; *Suet. Aug.* XXI, 3; XLIII, 4; *Tac. Ann.* II, I; *Vell. Pat.* II, CXIV, 4; *Victor Ep.* I, 8). The purpose of this article is to examine the circumstances of this event closer: In the first part of the article the gesture will be considered in context of the development of political relations between Rome and Parthia in the first century B.C. Secondly the status of the four sons and their families during the period spent in Rome will be examined. Thirdly and finally it will be considered, how the stay in Rome influenced the lives of the four princes.

II. The four princes in Rome and the political relations between Rome and Parthia[1]
In the second century B.C. Rome had greatly extended its territory towards the East, thus coming into the sphere of interest of the Parthian Empire. Parthia was at that time a powerful nation with diplomatic relations reaching as distant a country as China (DEBEVOISE 1938, 43). The first contact was established in the mid-nineties B.C. and was of purely diplomatic character (*Ampel.* 31, 2; *Liv. Per.* LXX; *Plut. Sulla* V, 3-6; *Ruf. Fest.* XV; *Vell. Pat.* II, XXIV, 3). After that about 40 years passed with only minor disturbances that were all settled through di-

---

1. ANDERSON 1934, 254-265; COLLEDGE 1967, 34-48; DEBEVOISE 1938, 46-53, 70-155; SCULLARD 1959, *passim*; TARN 1932, 603-612; TIMPE 1962; TIMPE 1975; WISSEMANN 1982, 3-13; WOLSKI 1976.

plomacy. From 69 B.C. the river Euphrates was officially recognized as the border between the territories of Rome and Parthia (ZIEGLER 1964, 27; cf. also *Cass. Dio* XXXVII, 5, 2-6, 3; *Plut. Pomp.* XXXIII, 6).

This treaty was violated in 54 B.C., when the *triumvir* M. Crassus invaded Parthia with an army of 40,000 men (main sources: *Cass. Dio* XL, 12-27; *Plut. Crass.* XVI-XXXIII; other sources: *Ampel.* 31,3; *App. B.C.* II, 18; *Caes. B.C.* III, 31; *Cic. Div.* II, 22; *Cic. Fin.* III, XXII; *Eutr.* VI, 18; *Flor.* I, 46 (= III, 11); *Joseph. Ant.* XIV, 105-109; XIV, 119; *Joseph. Bell.* I, 179-180; *Justinus* XLII, 4, 4-5; *Liv. Per.* CV; CVI; *Nic. Dam. F GR HIST* II A, 378 fr. 79; *Obseq.* CXXIV (63); *Oros.* VI, 13; *Petr. Sat.* CXX; *Plut. Caes.* XXVIII; *Plut. Cic.* XXXVI; *Polyaen. Strat.* VII, 41; *Ruf. Fest.* XVII; *Sen. Ep.* IV, 7; *Serv. Comm. in Verg. Aen.* VII, 606; *Strabo* XVI, 1, 23; *Vell. Pat.* II, XLVI, 2-4; *Zonar.* V, VII). The decisive battle took place in 53 B.C. near Carrhae in Mesopotamia and was a catastrophe for the Romans: Of the 40,000 men that Crassus had brought over the Euphrates, only about 10,000 returned to Rome, 20,000 died on the battlefield and 10,000 were taken prisoner by the Parthians. Furthermore, the Parthians had captured the standards of the Roman army (the *aquilae* and the *signa cohortium*), creating for the Romans a 'Parthian problem' that was to remain unsolved for a long time.

Caesar was preparing a large scale invasion in Parthia when his death in 44 B.C. put a definite end to these plans (*App. B.C.* II, 110; III, 24; IV, 58; *Cass. Dio* XLIII, 51; XLIV, 15; XLV, 3, 1; *Cic. Att.* XIII, XXVII; XIII, XXXI; *Flor.* II, 13 (= IV, 2); *Nic. Dam. F GR HIST* II A, 398, 401, F 130 (XVI; XVIII), *Plut. Brut.* XXII, 2; XXV, 2; *Plut. Caes.* LVIII; LX, 1-2; *Suet. Aug.* VIII, 2; *Suet. Caes.* XLIV; LXXIX, 3; *Vell. Pat.* II, LIX, 4). In the civil wars that followed, the Parthians first lent their support to the murderers of Caesar (*App. B.C.* IV, 63; IV, 88; IV, 99; *Cass. Dio* XLVIII, 24, 4-5; *Justinus* XLII, 4, 7). After the defeat of Brutus and Cassius, however, they invated Syria and Asia Minor in joint command with Q. Labienus, an officer from the army of Cassius, who had fled to Parthia. The invasion took place in 40 B.C. (*App. B.C.* V, 10; *Cass. Dio* XLVIII, 24, 3-27; *Flor.* II, 19 (= IV, 9); *Joseph. Ant.* XIV, 330-364; XX, 245; *Joseph. Bell.* I, 248-270; *Justinus* XLII, 4, 7; *Liv. Per.* CXXVII; *Plut. Ant.* XXVIII, 1; XXX; *Ruf. Fest.* XVIII; *Strabo* XII, 8, 9; XIV, 2, 24; *Tac. Ann.* II, 62; *Vell. Pat.* II, LXXVIII, 1; *Zonar.* X, XXII). The eastern Roman legions were not able to withstand the attacks of the invading army; the general in charge, L. Decidius Saxa, was captured and killed, and all of Rome's eastern provinces were conquered by the Parthians. More standards had been lost. The Romans then sent P. Ventidius Bassus with reinforcements to the East, and under his command the Parthians were expelled from the newly conquered territories (*Ampel.* 31,4; *App. B.C.* V, 65; *Cass. Dio* XLVIII, 39-41; XLIX, 19-22; *Eutr.* VII, 5; *Flor.* II, 19 (= IV, 9); II, 20 (= IV, 10); *Frontin. Strat.* I, I, 6; II, V, 36-37; *Fronto ad Ver.* II, 1(ed. C. R. HAINES (Loeb) vol. II, 137); *Gell.* XV, IV; *Joseph. Ant.* XIV, 392-395; XIV, 420; XIV, 434; *Joseph. Bell.* I, 284-292; I, 317; *Justinus* XLII, 4, 7-11; *Liv. Per.* CXXVII; CXXVIII; *Oros.* VI, 18, 23; *Plin. Nat. Hist.* VII, 135; *Plut. Ant.* XXXIII-XXXIV; *Ruf. Fest.* XVIII; *Strabo* XVI, 2, 8; *Tac. Germ.* 37; *Tac. Hist.* V,9; *Val. Max.* VI, 9, 9; *Vell. Pat.* II, LXV, 3; II, LXXVIII, 1; *Zonar.* X, XVI; X, XXIII). In 38 B.C. Ventidius could return to Rome to celebrate a triumph (cf. also *Fasti Triumphales Capitolini*, fr. XL (DEGRASSI 1947, 86-87); *Fasti Triumphales Barberiniani* (DEGRASSI 1947, 342-343)).

Ever since Octavian and Antonius had divided the responsability for Roman state affairs between them, Antonius had been in charge of all eastern questions. Thus, the 'Parthian problem' was in reality his to solve. Having relieved Ventidius in 38 B.C., he offered the Parthians peace on condition that they gave back the standards and the Roman prisoners of war (*Cass. Dio* XLIX, 23, 5-24; *Plut. Ant.* XXXVII). When this failed, he invaded Parthia. The invasion took place in 36 B.C. and did not prove successful (main sources: *Cass. Dio* XLIX, 25-31; *Plut. Ant.* XXXVII, 2-LI; other sources: *App. B.C.* V, 132-133; *Eutr.* VII, 6; *Flor.* II, 20 (= IV, 10); *Frontin. Strat.* II, III, 15; II, XIII, 7; IV, I, 37; *Justinus* XLII, 5, 3; *Liv. Per.* CXXX; *Oros.* VI, 19, 1; *Ruf. Fest.* XVIII; *Strabo* XI, 13, 3-4; XI, 14,9; XVI, 1, 28; *Tac. Hist.* III, 24; *Vell. Pat.* II, LXXXII, 1-3; *Victor Vir. Ill.* 85, 4; *Zonar.* X, XXVI; *Zos. Hist.* III, XXXII, 3). On the march Antonius split up the army, making the main part of the forces march quickly towards the provincial capital Praaspa. The heavier train of military equipment and supplies followed more slowly, escorted by two legions. The Parthians made their attack on the latter part of the Roman army, the two legions were completely annihilated, and the military machines and the supplies never reached the soldiers waiting outside besieged Praaspa. As winter drew nearer the siege had to be raised and the Romans withdrew through the mountains of Armenia with heavy losses. More standards had fallen into the hands of the Parthians.

Rome was now facing the final encounter between Octavian and Antonius. With the battle of Actium in 31 B.C. and the subsequent conquest of Egypt in 30 B.C., the whole Roman world was now in Octavian's power and the 'Partian problem' his. Unexpectedly, fortune lent him a helping hand: In Parthia Phraates IV, who had reigned since 37 B.C. was having trouble with a rival for the throne, Tiridates (*Cass. Dio* LI, 18, 2; *Justinus* XLII, 5, 4-6; *Plut. Ant.* LIII, 6). Already before the battle of Actium, both parties had asked Octavian for military support. He, however, did not take sides in the conflict. In 31 B.C. Tiridates dethroned Phraates IV. The latter took refuge with the Scythians, but as early as 30 B.C. was able to reconquer the throne. At that time Octavian was passing through the eastern Roman provinces on his way from Egypt, and he was again contacted by both Tiridates and Phraates (*Aug. Res Gest.* 32, 1; *Cass. Dio* LI, 18, 3). Tiridates came in person as a refugee to Syria, where he was granted asylum, while Phraates sent delegates to Octavian to enter into negotiations. In 29 B.C. the gates of the temple of Janus in Rome were closed: Peace had been established in the whole Roman world – and also with the Parthians (*Aug. Res Gest.* 13 (cf. also 10); *Cass. Dio* LI, 20, 1-4; *Liv. A.U.C.* I, 19, 3; *Oros.* VI, 20, 8; *Suet. Aug.* XXII).

In 27 B.C. Tiridates returned from his exile in Syria (*Isid. Char.* I) and again succeeded in driving Phraates IV from the throne of Parthia. Coins were struck commemorating this event (SCHOFF 1914, 25; SELLWOOD 1971, 166-167; TIMPE 1975, 155-158). On these Tiridates appears not only as ΒΑΣΙΛΕΥΣ ΒΑΣΙΛΕΩΝ, the traditional title for the Parthian king, but also as ΦΙΛΟΡΩΜΑΙΟΣ, friend of the Romans, a highly unusual epithet for a Parthian ruler. The period of his reign this time too was only short. In 26 B.C. Phraates was back in power, and Tiridates again sought refuge with Augustus. He brought with him the youngest son of Phraates IV, whom he had kidnapped (*Justinus* XLII, 5, 6).

In Rome the Parthian civil war was discussed at a meeting of the Senate in 23 B.C. (*Cass. Dio* LIII, 33, 1-2; *Justinus* XLII, 5, 7-9; cf. also *Aug. Res Gest.* 32, 1). Tiridates was present and asked the Romans for help in his efforts to gain power in Parthia. Phraates had sent delegates, who demanded that Tiridates as well as the kidnapped son should be surrendered. The Senate let Augustus decide the matter, and he on the one hand declined Tiridates' wish for military support, but on the other hand he let him stay within Rome's frontiers for as long as he wanted with all expenses paid by the Roman state. Thus Augustus did not comply with Phraates' request, that Tiridates should be sent back to Parthia. The son however, was returned, but only on condition that Phraates IV gave back the Roman standards and prisoners of war.

Phraates did eventually fulfill this condition, but not until 20 B.C. and only when the Romans made a grand show of force near the Parthian border (*Aug. Res Gest.* 29, 2; *Cass. Dio* LIV, 8, 1-2; *Cassiodorus Chron.* 385E; *Eutr.* VII, 9; *Flor.* II, XXXIX, 65; *Justinus* XLII, 5, 10-11; *Liv. Per.* CXLI; *Oros.* VI, 21, 29; *Strabo* VI, 4, 2; XVI, I, 28; *Suet. Aug.* XXI, 3; *Suet. Tib.* IX, 1; *Vell. Pat.* II, XCI, 1). Both Augustus and the young Tiberius participated in the eastern expedition of 20 B.C., and in Rome the return of the standards and the prisoners of war treated as if it had been the long expected final military victory over Parthia (*Hor. carm.* IV, 5, 25; IV, 14, 42 & 46; IV, 15, 6-8 & 22-23; *Hor. carm. saec.* 54; *Hor. ep.* I, 12, 25-29; I, 18, 56-57; *Ovid Fasti* V, 545-498; *Ovid Tristia* II, 227-228; cf. also *Prop.* III, 4; IV, 6, 79-84. The standards were placed in the Temple of Mars Ultor (the Avenger) in the Forum of Augustus (*Aug. Res Gest.* 29, 3; ZANKER 1970), a triumphal arch was built in the Roman Forum (*Cass. Dio* LIV, 8, 3; *Schol. Ver. ad Verg. Aen.* VII, 606), the return of the standards was depicted on the cuirass of the statue of Augustus from Prima Porta (KÄHLER 1959) and coins were struck in all parts of the Roman world commemorating the event (*BMCRE* I, *passim*)). In the *Res Gestae* (29, 2) Augustus proudly states that he forced the Parthians to give back the booty and the standards they had taken from three Roman armies and to beg for the '*amicitia*' of the Roman people.

Most of the sources refer to the surrender of the four princes and their families in the same breath as the restitution of the standards and the prisoners of war in 20 B.C. (*Eutr.* VII, 9; *Justinus* XLII, 5, 12; *Oros.* VI, 21, 29; *Strabo* VI, 4, 2; *Suet. Aug.* XXI, 3). These two events, however, do not necessarily coincide chronologically. The fact that they are mentioned together may merely mean that they were seen in the same political context. Only Strabo gives more precise chronological indications (XVI, 1, 28): He writes that Phraates IV summoned the legate of Syria, M. Titius, to a conference and gave the four sons and their families into his charge. The problem with this is, that there is no secure date for the Syrian command of M. Titius (CORBISHLEY 1934; HANSLIK 1937, 1562; TAYLOR 1936). Generally it is placed around 13-10 B.C., but it has been suggested that he was also in command in Syria in 20 B.C. (TAYLOR 1936).

However this may be, it seems clear that Phraates IV must have had a reason, a serious reason, for sending his four sons off to Rome, just as Augustus on his side must have had a specific motive for welcoming them there.

As to Phraates' motives, the sources offer several different explanations. Augustus (*Res Gest.* 32,2) writes that Phraates wanted the friendship of the Roman people, here again using the expression '*amicitia*', and he states that the sons were to be considered as tokens – '*pignora*' – of this '*amicitia*'. This interpretation is repeated by Strabo (VI, 4, 2; XVI, 1, 28) and Tacitus (*Ann.* II, I), but both of these authors also suggest a totally different explanation: Phraates' fear of internal revolts in Parthia and of the eventual rôle of his sons in such revolts. Strabo stresses the importance of the *arsacides* for the kingdom of Parthia (XVI, 1, 28; cf. also *Joseph. Ant.* XVIII, 44): Only members of this family could hold the kingdom, and only a revolt supporting such a member could ever succeed. According to Tacitus (*Ann.* II, I) Phraates' fear of an internal revolt was a more important reason for sending his sons to Rome than his fear of a Roman invasion in Parthia. This latter motive is, however, mentioned by other sources as the most important (*Justinus* XLII, 5, 10-12; *Vell. Pat.* II, XCIV, 4). Finally, Josephus (*Ant* XVIII, 42) tells yet another story: The four Parthian princes had a half-brother, Phraataces, whose mother, Thesmusa, was a slave girl that Augustus had sent to Phraates IV as a gift. After the birth of Phraataces, Thesmusa was given status as queen and, according to Josephus, it was she, who persuaded Phraates to send the four legitimate princes away, thus securing the throne for her own son, Phraataces.

Of Augustus' reasons for welcoming the sons in Rome, the sources make no mention, at least not explicitly. Nevertheless, much can be deduced from the way the four sons were treated in Rome and from their fate.

III. The status of the princes in Rome

As we have seen, Augustus speaks of the four princes as *'pignora'* – 'tokens' – of the *'amicitia'* between Rome and Parthia (*Res Gest.* 32, 2), He has chosen his words with care to create a positive atmosphere around the event. The rest of the Roman sources, however, most often call the princes *'obsides'*, that is to say 'hostages' (*Eutr.* VII, 9; *Justinus* XLII, 5, 12; *Oros.* VI, 21, 29; *Suet. Aug.* XXI, 3; LIII, 4; *Tac. Ann.* II, I; *Vell. Pat.* II, XCIV, 4; *Victor Ep.* I, 8). Similar expressions are to be found in the Greek sources (*Joseph. Ant.* XVIII, 42; XVIII, 46; *Strabo* VI, 4, 2; XVI, 1, 28). In a very interesting passage, Tacitus lets the Parthians express their view of the event: They speak about *'servitus'* – 'slavery' – and refer to one of the princes as Augustus' *'mancipium'*, which means 'private property', i.e. 'slave' (*Tac. Ann.* II, II; cf. also *Joseph. Ant.* XVIII, 47).

Strabo (XVI, 1, 28) states, that the Parthian princes were treated according to their rank at the expense of the Roman state (he uses the word 'βασιλεκῶς' – 'in a royal manner'). Furthermore, one of the sons must have had enough funds to finance the construction of a temple – perhaps dedicated to the goddess Isis – in the sanctuary of Diana at Nemi, as can be deduced from an inscription found there, commemorating Hadrianic restoration of the building (CIL XIV, 2216; ILS 843).

Modern discussions of the subject tend to emphasize that Phraates IV was acting of his own free will, when he sent his sons away (TAYLOR 1936, 162), that they on their side were content to go to Rome (ANDERSON 1934, 265; ZIEGLER 1964, 52), and that the princes in Rome were treated in a manner befitting their rank (DEBEVOISE 1938, 144; ZIEGLER 1964, 52). It is thus proposed that the princes were not hostages in the full sense of the word (DEBEVOISE 1938, 144 n. 5; ZIEGLER 1964, 52). One scholar has come to the conclusion that Phraates sent his sons to Rome to study (MELLA 1979, 319). A closer examination of the sources shows, however, that even though the Parthian princes could maintain a royal standard of living in Rome, there still were justifications for the use of the term 'hostages'.

In the first place, it is clear that the Parthians could not return to their native country without Augustus' assent (*Aug. Res Gest.* 33; *Cass. Dio* LV, 10, 20; *Joseph. Ant.* XVIII, 46; *Strabo* VI, 4, 2; *Tac. Ann.* II, I-II). Secondly, Suetonius describes how Augustus presented the Parthian '*obsides*' to the Romans at a public display (*Suet. Aug.* XLIII, 4). They were led through the middle of the arena for everyone to see and thereafter placed in the second row of seats right behind Augustus himself. This little story forms part of a larger description, which shows Augustus as always eager to present new phaenomena to the Romans, things that were of interest because they had never before been seen in Rome. Immediately before the reference to the Parthian '*obsides*' Suetonius has mentioned the presentation of a two-foot tall dwarf, who weighed only 17 pounds, but had an astonishingly powerful voice (*Suet. Aug.* XLIII, 3), and immediately after he refers to a rhinoceros, a tiger and a snake 50 cubits long (*Suet. Aug.* XLIII, 4). With regard to the Parthians it is stressed that they were the first Parthian '*obsides*' that had ever come to Rome (*Suet. Aug.* XLIII, 4; cf. also *Eutr.* VII, 9). Their novelty value may also have consisted in their appearance in native dress.

To get a clear picture of the situation and status of the four Parthian princes in Rome, all the evidence must be taken into account. Despite the fact that they were supplied with ample funds, the public presentation and the restrictions on their freedom of movement lead to the conclusion that they were in fact hostages – in the full sense of the word.

IV. *The fate of the princes*

The Parthian princes in all probability came to Italy somewhere between 20 and 10 B.C. (see above). It is known that two of them remained there until they died. The inscription from their grave has been found (CIL VI, 1799; ILS 842). The two princes in question are Seraspadanes and Rhodaspes. Each is mentioned in the inscription as '*Phraatis/Arsacis regum regis f(ilius)/Parthus*', the Latin translation of their official Parthian title. Their death is not mentioned in the literary sources.

Vonones, the eldest of Phraates' sons, returned to Parthia as king about A.D. 7 (*Aug. Res Gest.* 33; *Joseph. Ant.* XVIII, 46; *Tac. Ann.* II, I-II; COLLEDGE 1967, 48; DEBEVOISE 1938, 151; WISSEMANN 1982, 13; ZIEGLER 1964, 56). In 2 B.C. Phraataces had murdered Phraates IV and married his own mother, after which he reigned as Phraates V for about four years (*Joseph. Ant.* XVIII, 39-43; COLLEDGE 1967, 47; DEBEVOISE 1938, 147-151; WISSEMANN 1982, 12-13; ZIEGLER 1964, 53-56). With his assumption of power, relations between Rome and Parthia again became strained (*Cass. Dio* LV, 10, 18-21; LV, 10a, 3-4; *Ovid A.A.* I, 117-228; *Ovid Rem.* 155-158; *Vell. Pat.* C, 1; CI). After the fall of Phraataces a certain Orodes III reigned until he too was murdered in A.D. 6 (*Joseph Ant.* XVIII, 44-45; COLLEDGE 1967, 47-48; DEBEVOISE 1938, 151; WISSEMANN 1982, 13; ZIEGLER 1964, 56). The Parthians now sent for Vonones, who returned home after at least 15 years in the Roman capital. It soon turned out that life in Rome had left its mark on him. Tacitus (*Ann.* II, II) writes, that the Parthians found his foreign manners very strange. He did not show interest in horses, he did not like hunting, he disliked the food and he was carried around in a litter. Soon dissatisfaction was rife, and Parthia had to face new dynastic trouble (*Joseph. Ant.* XVIII, 48-50; *Suet. Tib.* XLIX; *Tac. Ann.* II, III-IV; COLLEDGE 1967, 48; DEBEVOISE 1938, 151-153; WISSEMANN 1982, 13; ZIEGLER 1964, 56-57). About A.D. 12 a rival to the throne, Artabanus III, came into power, and Vonones fled to Armenia, where he became king. He was, however, forced to abdicate in A.D. 15-16 under pressure from Artabanus III, who had great influence in Armenia (*Joseph. Ant.* XVIII, 50-52; Tac. Ann. II, IV; II, LVI). Vonones now fled to Syria, where he was given permission to stay retaining his riches as well as his title of king (*Tac. Ann.* II, IV; cf. VI, XXXI). At the request of Artabanus (Tac. Ann. II, LVIII) Vonones was later moved further away from Parthia to Cilicia, where he was actually held prisoner. In one last attempt to regain position and power Vonones in A.D. 19 bribed his guards and fled. When he reached the river Pyramus, he was, however, already expected. All bridges had been cut by the Romans, and Vonones was surrounded and killed (*Suet. Tib.* XLIX; *Tac. Ann.* II, LXVIII; DEBEVOISE 1938, 155; ZIEGLER 1964, 58-59).

The last of the Parthian princes, Phraates, was, like Vonones, called back to Parthia to become king (*Cass. Dio* LVIII, 26, 2; Tac. Ann. VI, XXXI-XXXII; COLLEDGE 1967, 48; DEBEVOISE 1938, 157-158; ZIEGLER 1964, 60). This happened in A.D. 35, when he had been in Rome for at least 45 years. He died suddenly in Syria, and like Seraspadanes and Rhodaspes never saw his native land again.

V. *Conclusion*
The four sons of Phraates IV had the status of privileged hostages in Rome. Privileged they were, because they kept their titles and rank and

lived royally at the expense of the Roman state. Hostages they were because of the restrictions on their freedom: They could not return to Parthia without Augustus' consent (and three of them in fact never did), and it was within Augustus' power to make a public display of them.

Augustus presented the princes as proof of what he called a relation of *'amicitia'* between Rome and Parthia. It is evident from his words that this relation was not an equal one. Rome was clearly to be considered the strongest partner and could force the second party into the relation of *'amicitia'*, as was the case in 20 B.C., when Parthia gave back the captured standards and prisoners of war to the Romans. It is hardly a coincidence that Augustus uses the word *'amicitia'* in connection both with the restitution of the standards and with the surrender of the four princes, and the fact that most of the sources mention the two events nearly as one should not be underestimated. There must be a clear connection between them. The background for both of them must, I think, be sought in the internal dynastic conflicts in Parthia. The key to the whole question may be Tiridates, the king living in exile within the Roman Empire, the ΦΙΛΟΡΩΜΑΙΟΣ: He had already twice proved that his support among the Parthian nobility was strong enough to enable him to dethrone Phraates IV. Rome knew from bitter experience that invasions in Parthia were likely not to succeed, but with Tiridates as ally the situation could be quite different (for this, see also DĄBROWA 1983, 41, 62-63 n. 191). Phraates IV must have been aware of this, and, as far as I can see, a threat from Augustus of the Romans lending their support to Tiridates must have been the reason why Phraates finally gave back the standards and the prisoners of war and sent his sons to Rome as hostages. It is difficult to believe that he would have wanted to hand over the legitimate heirs to the Parthian throne to Augustus of his own free will, and it is just the fact that they were the legitimate heirs to the throne that explains why Augustus was so eager to receive them, and why they were treated so well. Through these princes Rome could hope to be able to influence Parthian affairs also in the future (cf. also ANDERSON 1934, 265; WISSEMANN 1982, 11; ZIEGLER 1964, 52). Vonones is the clear example that things did not quite turn out as planned.

The four Parthian princes and their families with their unfamiliar looks and ways added a touch of an unknown oriental world to Augustan Rome, and Vonones, the only of the four sons that ever returned to

Parthia, had by then been so influenced by Roman habits that he seemed a stranger in his own country. Life and values of Augustan Rome were clearly much different from those of the Parthia of Phraates IV.

Odense Universitet
Department of Classical Studies
Campusvej 55
DK-5230 Odense M

BIBLIOGRAPHY

Ampel	L. Ampelius: Liber memorialis. (Lucii Ampelii Liber Memorialis, ed. E. ASSMANN, (Teubner) Stuttgart 1976 (1935)).
ANDERSSON 1934	ANDERSSON, J. G. C.: CAH X, 239-283, Cambridge (1966).
App. B.C.	Appianus: Bella Civilia. (Appian's Roman History, Vol. III-IV, ed. H. WHITE, (Loeb) London/Cambridge Mass. 1961-64 (1913)).
Aug. Res Gest.	Augustus: Res Gestae. (Velleius Paterculus, Compendium of Roman History; Res Gestae Divi Augusti, ed. F. W. SHIPLEY, (Loeb) London/Cambridge Mass. 1961 (1924)).
BMCRE I	Coins of the Roman Empire in the British Museum I, Augustus to Vitellius, ed. H. MATTINGLY, London 1976 (1923).
Caes. B.C.	Caesar: Commentarii de Bello Civili. (C. Iulii Caesaris Commentarii de Bello Civili, ed. F. KRANER, F. HOFFMANN, H. MENSEL, Berlin 1963 (1890)).
CAH	Cambridge Ancient History.
Cass. Dio	Cassius Dio: Ῥωμαϊκά. (Dio's Roman History, ed. E. CARY, (Loeb), London/Cambridge Mass. 1961 (1914-27)).
Cassiodorus Chron.	M. Aurelius Cassiodorus: Chronikon. (J. P. MIGNE: Patrologia, series latina, 69, 1213-1248, Paris 1865).
Cic. Att.	Cicero: Epistulae ad Atticum. (Cicero: Letters to Atticus, ed. E. O. WINSTEDT, (Loeb) London/Cambridge Mass. 1960-62 (1913-18)).
Cic. Div.	Cicero: De divinatione. (Cicero: De senectute, de amicitia, de divinatione, ed. W. A. FALCONER, (Loeb) London/Cambridge Mass. 1964 (1923)).
Cic. Fin.	Cicero: De finibus bonorum et malorum. (Cicero: De finibus bonorum et malorum, Ed. H. RACKHAM, (Loeb) London/Cambridge Mass. 1961 (1914)).
CIL	Corpus Inscriptionum Latinarum.
COLLEDGE 1967	COLLEDGE, M.A.R.: The Parthians, London.
CORBISHLEY 1934	CORBISHLEY, T.: A Note on the Date of the Syrian Govenorship of M. Titius, JRS XXIV, 43-49.
DĄBROWA 1983	DĄBROWA, E.: La politique de l'État Parthe à l'égard de Rome – d'Artaban II à Vologèse I (ca. 11-ca. 79 de n.e.) et les facteurs qui la conditionnaient, Krakow.

DEBEVOISE 1938	DEBEVOISE, N. C. : *A Political History of Parthia,* Chicago.
DEGRASSI 1947	DEGRASSI, A.: *Inscriptiones Italiae* XIII, I: Fasti Consulares et Triumphales. Rome.
Eutr.	*Eutropius: Breviarium ab urbe condita.* (*Eutropi breviarium ab urbe condita,* ed. F. RUEHL, Darmstadt 1975 (Leipzig 1887)).
F GR HIST II A	*Die Fragmente der Griechischen Historiker,* II A, ed. F. JACOBY, Leiden 1961 (1925)).
Flor.	*Florus: Epitome de Tito Livio.* (*Florus: Oevres,* vol. I-II, ed. P. JAL, (Budé) Paris 1967).
Frontin. Strat.	*Frontinus: Strategematon.* (*Frontinus: The Strategems and the Aqueducts of Rome,* ed. C. E. BENNETT, (Loeb) London/Cambridge Mass. 1961 (1925)).
Fronto ad Ver.	*M. Cornelius Fronto: Epistulae ad imp. Verum.* (*The Corrispondence of Marcus Cornelius Fronto,* ed. C. R. HAINES, (Loeb) London/Cambridge Mass. 1962-63 (1919-20)).
Gell.	*Aulus Gellius: Noctes Atticae.* (*The Attic nights of Aulus Gellius,* ed. J. C. ROLFE, (Loeb) London/Cambridge Mass. 1960-61 (1926-27)).
HANSLIK 1937	HANSLIK, R.: Titius 18), *RE* VI, A.2, 1559-1562.
Hor. carm.	*Horatius: Carmina.* (Q. Horatii Flacci opera, ed. C. WICKHAM, Oxford 1947 (1901)).
Hor. carm. saec.	*Horatius: Carmen saeculare.* (*O. Horatii Flacci opera,* ed. C. WICKHAM, Oxford 1947 (1901)).
Hor. ep.	*Horatius: Epistulae.* (*Q. Horatii Flacci opera,* ed. C. WICKHAM, Oxford 1947 (1901)).
ILS	*Inscriptiones Latinae Selectae,* ed. H. DESSAU.
Isid. Char.	*Isidorus Characenus:* Σταθμοί Παρθικοί. (SCHOFF 1914).
Joseph. Ant.	*Josephus: Antiquitates Iudaicae.* (*Josephus,* ed. H. ST. J. THACKERAY, R. MARCUS, A. WIKGREN, L. H. FELDMANN, vol. IV-IX, (Loeb) London/Cambridge Mass. 1930-65).
Joseph. Bell.	*Josephus: Bellum Judaicum.* (*Josephus,* ed. H. ST. J. THACKERAY, vol. II-III, (Loeb), London/Cambridge Mass. 1927-28).
Justinus	*Justinus: Epitoma historiarum philippicarum Pompei Trogi.* (*M. Iuniani Iustini epitoma historiarum philippicarum Pompei Trogi accedunt prologi in Pompeium Trogum,* ed. F. RUEHL, O. SEEL, (Teubner) Stuttgart 1972).
KÄHLER 1959	KÄHLER, H.: *Die Augustusstatue von Prima Porta,* Cologne.
Liv. A.U.C.	*Livius: Ab urbe condita.* (*Livy,* vol. I-XIII, ed. B. O. FOSTER, F. G. MOORE, E. T. SAGE, A. C. SCHLESINGER, (Loeb) London/Cambridge Mass. 1919-1951).
Liv. Per.	*Livius: Periochae librorum XLVI-CXLII.* (*Livy,* vol. XIV (Summaries, Fragments and Obsequens), ed. A. C. SCHLESINGER, (Loeb) London/Cambridge Mass. 1959).
MELLA 1979	MELLA, F. A. A.: *L'Impero Persiano,* Milano.
Nic. Dam.	*Nicolaus Damascenus.* (*F GR HIST* II A, 324-430).
Obseq.	*Iulius Obsequens: Ab anno urbis conditae DV prodigorum liber.* (*Livy,* vol. XIV (Summaries, Fragments and Obsequens), ed. A. C. SCHLESINGER, (Loeb) London/Cambridge Mass. 1959).
Oros.	*Orosius: Historiarum adversum paganos libri VII.* (*Paulus Orosius: Historiarum adversum paganos libri VII accedit eiusdem liber apologeticus,* ed. C. ZANGEMEISTER, Hildesheim 1967 (Wien 1882)).
Ovid A.A.	*Ovidius: Ars Amatoria.* (*P. Ovidi Nasonis amores, medicamina faciei femineae, ars amatoria, remedia amoris,* ed. E. J. KENNEY, Oxford 1965 (1961)).

Ovid Fasti	Ovidius: Fasti. (*Ovid's Fasti*, ed. J. G. FRAZER, (Loeb) London/Cambridge Mass. 1959 (1931)).
Ovid Rem.	Ovidius: Remedia Amoris. (*P. Ovidi Nasonis amores, medicamina faciei femineae, ars amatoria, remedia amoris*, ed. E. J. KENNEY, Oxford 1965 (1961)).
Ovid Tristia	Ovidius: Tristia. (*Ovid: Tristia, ex Ponto*, ed. A. L. WHEELER, (Loeb) London/Cambridge Mass. 1965 (1924)).
Petr. Sat.	Petronius: Satyricon. (*Pétrone: Le Satiricon*, ed. A. ERNOUT, (Budé) Paris 1962 (1923)).
Plin. Nat. Hist.	Plinius: Naturalis Historia. (*Pliny: Natural History*, ed. H. RACKHAM, W. H. S. JONES, D. E. EICHHOLZ, (Loeb), London/Cambridge Mass. 1938-1963).
Plut. Brut.	Plutarchus: Brutus. (*Plutarch's Lives*, vol. VI, ed. B. PERRIN, (Loeb) London/Cambridge Mass. 1961 (1918)).
Plut. Caes.	Plutarchus: Caesar. (*Plutarch's Lives*, vol. VII, ed. B. PERRIN, (Loeb) London/Cambridge Mass. 1971 (1919)).
Plut. Cic.	Plutarchus: Cicero. (*Plutarch's Lives*, vol. VII, ed. B. PERRIN, (Loeb) London/Cambridge Mass. 1971 (1919)).
Plut. Crass.	Plutarchus: Crassus. (*Plutarch's Lives*, vol. III, ed. B. PERRIN, (Loeb) London/Cambridge Mass. 1958 (1916)).
Plut. Pomp.	Plutarchus: Pompeius. (*Plutarch's Lives*, vol. V, ed. B. PERRIN, (Loeb) London/Cambridge Mass. 1968 (1917)).
Plut. Sulla	Plutarchus: Sulla. (*Plutarch's Lives*, vol. IV, ed. B. PERRIN, (Loeb) London/Cambridge Mass. 1959 (1916)).
Polyaen. Strat.	Polyaenus: Στρατηγήτα. (*Polyaeni strategematon libri octo*, ed. E. WOELFFLIN, J. MELBER, (Teubner) Stuttgart 1970 (1887/1901).
Prop.	Sextus Propertius. (*Propertius*, ed. H. E. Butler, (Loeb) London/Cambridge Mass. 1962 (1912)).
RE	Paulys Realencyclopädie der classischen Altertumswissenschaft.
Ruf. Fest.	Rufius Festus: Breviarium. (*The Breviarium of Festus*, ed. J. W. EADIE, London 1967).
SCHOFF 1914	SCHOFF, W. H.: *Parthian Stations by Isidore of Charax*, London (Chicago 1974).
Schol. Ver. ad Verg. Aen.	Scholia Veronensia ad Vergilii Aineida. (*Servii Grammatici qui feruntur in Vergilii carmina commentarii*, vol. III, fasc. II: Appendix Serviana – ceteros praeter Servium et Scholia Bernensia Vergilii commentatores continens, ed. H. Hagen, Leipzig 1902.
SCULLARD 1959	SCULLARD, H. H.: *From the Gracchi to Nero – A History of Rome from 133 B.C. to A.D. 68*, London (1976).
SELLWOOD 1971	SELLWOOD, D.: *An Introduction to the Coinage of Parthia*, London.
Sen. Ep.	Seneca: Epistulae morales. (*Sénèque: Lettres à Lucilius*, vol. I, ed. F. PRÉCHAC, H. NOBLOT, (Budé) Paris 1964 (1945)).
Serv. Comm. in Verg. Aen.	Servius: Commentarii in Vergilii Aeneida. (*Servii Grammatici qui feruntur in Vergilii carmina commentarii*, vol. II (Aeneidos librorum VI-XII commentarii), ed. G. THILO, Hildesheim 1961 (Leipzig 1883-84)).
Strabo	Strabo: Γεωγραφικά. (*The Geography of Strabo*, ed. H. L. JONES, (Loeb) London/Cambridge Mass. 1954-61 (1917-32)).
Suet. Aug.	Suetonius: Divus Augustus. (*Suetonius*, ed. J. C. ROLFE, vol. I, (Loeb) London/Cambridge Mass. 1964 (1913)).

Suet. Caes.	Suetonius: Divus Iulius. (Suetonius, ed. J. C. ROLFE, vol. I (Loeb) London/Cambridge Mass. 1964 (1913)).
Suet. Tib.	Suetonius: Tiberius. (Suetonius, ed. J. C. ROLFE, vol. I, (Loeb) London/Cambridge Mass. 1964 (1913)).
Tac. Ann.	Tacitus: Annales. (Tacitus, vol. II (The Histories IV-V, ed. C. H. MOORE; the Annals I-III, ed. J. JACKSON), vol. III (The Annals IV-VI; XI-XII, ed. J. JACKSON), (Loeb) London/Cambridge Mass. 1962-63 (1931-37)).
Tac. Germ.	Tacitus: Germania. (Publius Cornelius Tacitus: Germaniens historie, geografi og befolkning, ed. N. W. BRUUN, A. A. LUND, Aarhus 1974.
Tac. Hist.	Tacitus: Historiae. (Tacitus, vol. I (The Histories I-III, ed. C. H. MOORE), vol. II (The Histories IV-V, ed. C. H. MOORE; the Annals I-III, ed. J. JACKSON), (Loeb) London/Cambridge Mass. 1962 (1925-31)).
TARN 1932	TARN, W. W.: *CAH* IX, 574-613, Cambridge (1966).
TAYLOR 1936	TAYLOR, L. R.: M. Titius and the Syrian Command, *JRS* XXVI, 161-173.
TIMPE 1962	TIMPE, D.: Die Bedeutung der Schlacht von Carrhae, *MusHelv* XIX, 104-129.
TIMPE 1975	Zur augusteischen Partherpolitik zwischen 30 und 20 v.Chr., *WürzJbAltWiss*, N.F. I, 155-169.
Val. Max.	Valerius Maximus: Facta et dicta memorabilia. (Valerii Maximi factorum et dictorum memorablium libri novem, ed. C. KEMPF, (Teubner) Stuttgart 1966 (1888)).
Vell. Pat.	Velleius Paterculus: Historia romana. (Velleius Paterculus, Compendium of Roman History; Res Gestae Divi Augusti, ed. F. W. SHIPLEY, (Loeb) London/Cambridge Mass. 1961 (1924)).
Victor Vir. Ill.	Victor: De viris illustribus urbis Romae. (Sexti Aurelii Victoris liber de Caesaribus, ed. F. PICHLMAYR, R. GRUENDEL, (Teubner) Leipzig 1966 (1911)).
Victor Ep.	Epitome de Caesaribus (libellus de vita et moribus imperatorum breviatus ex libris Sexti Aurelii Victoris). (Sexti Aurelii Victoris liber de Caesaribus, ed. F. PICHLMAYR, R. GRUENDEL, (Teubner) Leipzig 1966 (1911)).
WISSEMANN 1982	WISSEMANN, M.: *Die Parther in der augusteischen Dichtung*, (Europäische Hochschulschriften XV, 24), Frankfurt am Main/ Bern.
WOLSKI 1976	WOLSKI, J.: Iran und Rom, Versuch einer historischen Wertung der gegenseitigen Beziehungen, *ANRW* II, 9, 1, 195-214, Berlin/ New York.
ZANKER 1970	ZANKER, P.: *Forum Augustum – Das Bildprogram*, Tübingen.
ZIEGLER 1964	ZIEGLER, K.-H.: *Die Beziehungen zwischen Rom und dem Partherreich*, Wiesbaden.
Zonar.	Zonaras: Χρονικόν. (J. P. MIGNE: *Patrologia*, series graeca, vol. 134, Turnout 1966).
Zos.	Zosimus: Ἱστορία νέα. (Zosime: Histoire nouvelle, ed. F. PASCHOUD, (Budé) Paris 1971-86).

AUGUSTUS AND THE HELLENISTIC KINGS
A NOTE ON AUGUSTAN PROPAGANDA
by SANNE HOUBY-NIELSEN

This paper will attempt a definition of the levels on which the propaganda of the Hellenistic kings may have influenced Augustan propaganda.

The concluding argument of the paper will be: I) that Augustan propaganda was influenced by the politics of the Hellenistic rulers in the East to such a degree that even when Augustus acted most convincingly like a Roman emperor, this was rooted in his knowledge of Hellenistic ruler politics II) that Augustan propaganda in the West was different from Augustan propaganda in the East.

Below follows a survey of the spheres of propaganda alike in the Hellenistic kingdoms and Augustan Rome, which seemed to me the most important for the present study.

Images of the king/emperor
As is well-known Roman commanders adopted the characteristics from the Greek idealistic portrait. Famous examples are the image of Titus Quinctius Flaminius, Sulla, Marius, Pompeius Magnus, Caesar, Marcus Antonius and Augustus. In this connection it is of special interest that the Hellenistic ruler as well as Augustus (especially the Actium-type) used allusions to Alexander the Great in their portraits (MICHEL 1967, ZANKER 1973 p. 34, SMITH 1983, MEGOW 1985 p. 480-1, HANNESTAD 1986 p. 48). Other formal[1] similarities are the material and the size of the images. Literary and archaeological sources attest images of the Hellenistic king and the Roman emperor in all kinds of materials and in all possible sizes. Plinius (NH 7.125) tells us, that only Lysippos was allowed to make images of Alexander in the round, only Apelles from Cos to paint portraits and only Pyrgoteles to carve his image, in this way giving us the impression of a very systematic and well-considered

---

1. I use the word "formal" in the same sense as PANOFSKY 1962 p. 3.

image-distribution and -production. Likewise in Ptolemaic Egypt the image of the ruler was presented in all sizes ranging from the colossal to miniature and in all kinds of material (KYRIELEIS 1975 p. 27), as was the image of Augustus and his family (ZANKER 1979a).

Also, when regarding the context of the images we can observe certain similarities. During the Hellenistic period, starting with Alexander, people in the East had been acquainted with the image of the ruler in sanctuaries, in public areas of profane character, in private houses, within the army and, of course, within the court. This image-distribution was imitated by Augustus. A very striking example of contextual similarity is the "Philippeion" in Olympia, the "Ptolemaion" in Alexandria, the "Heroon" in Pergamon, the later "Caesareion" in Alexandria and the exedrae in the Forum of Augustus (HÖLSCHER 1971 p. 29, KYRIELEIS 1975 p. 139), in which not only images of the king/emperor were exhibited, but also images of his family.

Axiality between commemorative monuments and buildings in marketplaces/fora:
Axiality between monuments in order to express a political message is probably known since the 5. cent. B.C. in Greece (SCHALLES 1986 p. 53 note 337 for further literature), and it was used already in the 3. cent. B.C. on the Forum Boarium in Rome (HÖLSCHER 1978 p. 320-22).

According to P. Zanker the images of Augustus' ancestors, placed in the exedrae of the portici on the Forum of Augustus, stood in an axial connection with the gods in the pediment of the Mars Ultor temple, the cult statues and the quadriga in the middle of the Forum. This axiality turned the whole Forum into a propaganda programme, which legitimated the power of Augustus through his halfdivine ancestry, great achievements and victories and celebrated him as Pater Patriae (ZANKER 1968, HANNESTAD 1986 p. 83-90).

In Hellenistic Athens a similar use of axiality within an architectural setting has recently been argued for by H.-J. Schalles, who interpreted the Attalid alterations on the Athenaion Agora as propaganda for a mythological genealogy of the Attalids (SCHALLES 1982 p. 97-116).

Architectural layout of the house of the king/emperor:
Another very important similarity between Pergamenian and Augustan propaganda has recently been pointed out by Zanker (ZANKER 1983 p.

21-40). Zanker argues very convincingly that the house of Augustus was not deliberately built near the legendary hut of Romulus – as mentioned by Dio Cass. 53, 16,5 – but also that its architectural connection with the temple of Apollo is directly relatable to the Attalid royal palace in Pergamon situated on the same terrace as the sanctuary of Athena and with a direct access from the palace to the sanctuary through a propylon. The justification of this comparison was further strengthened by the argument that both in Pergamon as well as on the Palatine, libraries were installed in the portici surrounding the temenos.

Equestrian statues:
From the end of the 4th cent. it was customary for a city in Greece to honour a person of high rank with an equestrian statue for his benefits towards the city.[2] This type of monument remained the normal way for the Greeks to honour their foreign rulers, the Hellenistic kings, until the 2. cent. B.C., when the foreign control of Greece changed hands from the East to the West. Thus Roman Republican commanders of the 2. cent. B.C. set up equestrian statues of themselves as victory monuments in all the main sanctuaries of Greece. This practise was continued by the Roman emperors such as Augustus and Tiberius, the last mentioned was even given the Hellenistic honourary titles of "Soter" and "Euergetes", as was before him Sulla and Agrippa (SIEDENTOPF 1968).

Gates/triumphal arches carrying images of the king/emperor:
In 300 B.C. the Athenians erected an equestrian bronzestatue for Demetrios Poliorcetes and placed it on a gate instead of on a high plinth as was the usual practise. Foundation-remains of this gate built immediately to the west of the Stoa Poikilé on the Agora of Athens and fragments of the bronzestatue have recently been excavated (CAMP 1986 p. 162-5).

The earliest known monuments in Rome of a similar kind is the arch erected by L. Sternius in 190 B.C. and Fornix Fabianus erected by Q. Fabius Maximus in 121 B.C. (COARELLI 1985 P. 347). Hereafter a regular series of triumphal arches began starting with the Arch of Actium built by Augustus in 29 B.C. (HANNESTAD 1986 p. 58).

---

2. For archaic equestrian statues on the Acropolis of Athens, see PAYNE 1936 pl. 133, 3-4, -140, SCHRADER 1939 p. 273-6.

Shields placed on public buildings:

An important victory could also be commemorated by placing the shields taken from the enemy on a temple or a public building, a practise known to the Greeks since the 5. cent. B.C.[3]

Alexander the Great had shields placed on the Parthenon after his victory at Granikos in 334 B.C. (ZANKER 1968 p. 13); the Roman commander L. Mummius imitated this Greek practise by placing shields on the temple of Zeus in Olympia after he had slain the Achaeans in 146 B.C. (HERRMANN 1972 p. 182). In Rome a similar way of commemorating a victory is first heard of in 310 B.C., when golden shields were placed on the "Tabernae" (Livius does not tell us which) after L. Papirius Cursor's victory over the Samnites (HÖLSCHER 1978 p. 320 n. 19); later, in 78 B.C., Aemilius placed shields on the Basilica Aemilia (ZANKER 1968 p. 13, COARELLI 1985 p. 203), and on the attica of the portici on the Forum of Augustus decorative shields in the Pergamenian Baroque style depicting Zeus Ammon alluded to Augustus' many victories (ZANKER 1968 p. 13).

Public exhibition of beaks from ships:

In Greece as well as in Rome a naval victory was commemorated by exhibiting the beaks of the conquered ships in public places. The common symbol of a naval victory was the protective city god/goddess or Nike holding a beak in his/her hand or standing upon a prow. On some early Classical vases Athena is shown holding an aphlaston in her outstretched hand symbolizing the victory at Salamis in 480 B.C. (HAUSMANN 1957), and in Delphi Herodotus saw a 5,35 m. high statue of Apollon likewise holding an aphlaston (Hdt. VIII 121, GAUER 1968 p. 71). On coins struck in Macedonia between 306-283 B.C. Nike is shown standing on the prow of a ship (FRANKE/HIRMER 1964 fig. 174), as was Demetrios Poliorcetes' huge Nike-monument off Cyprus from 306 B.C. (POLLITT 1986 p. 113-4).

In the 3. cent. B.C. Roman coins depicting a prow became widely distributed (HANNESTAD 1986 p. 20), probably symbolizing Rome as a seapower. Around two centuries later Augustus issued a denar with Nike standing on a ship's prow, and he placed the beaks won at Actium

---

3. For further literature, see HÖLSCHER 1978 p. 350 n. 171.

on the Rostra of the temple of Divus Iulius on Forum Romanum (ZANKER 1972 p. 13, HANNESTAD 1986 p. 57 fig. 36).

Allusion to a mythological-genealogical ancestry:
As is well-known Alexander traced his family back to Heracles; he was worshipped as Dionysos and often depicted with the attributes of Zeus (HÖLSCHER 1971, POLLITT 1986 p. 25). This way of legitimating the power of the ruler was imitated by the Hellenistic Kings. Thus the Seleucids traced their dynasty back to Apollo, the Attalids and Ptolemies to Dionysos (MICHEL 1967 p. 126, POLLITT 1986 p. 271). In Rome during the 4. and 3. cent. B.C. the fight for the most important and prestigous "gens" often resulted in the maintenance of a divine ancestry (LAHUSEN 1985). In the late Republican period C. Caesar was accepted as descending from Venus, and in Ephesos he was greated as the son of Aphrodite and Ares (MICHEL 1967 p. 67). Augustus, divi Iuli filius, not only traced his family back to Aeneas and Romulus, but also associated himself with Apollo (SIMON 1957 p. 30-44, ZANKER 1983a), while Marcus Antonius was celebrated as Neos Dionysos in the East (MICHEL 1967 p. 126). This divine genealogy was propagated in much the same way in the East and in the West: One way was to liken the portrait of the king/emperor to the portrait of a desired god or hero – but also vice versa. This was the case in the relation between the portrait of Alexander – Heracles and Augustus – Apollo (HÖLSCHER 1971 p. 43-44). Other means were:

The use of divine attributes:
Within iconography we often see divine attributes either carried by the king/emperor or in association with him. (Alexander depicted with the horns of Zeus Ammon or as Keranophoros with a thunderbolt; Augustus shown next to a thunderbolt, ect.). Another more subtle way of achieving the same effect – namely the transference of the achievements and strength of the god to oneself – was to place one's image beside the image of the god, one wished to be assimilated to. Thus Attalos I erected a colossal statue representing himself beside a statue of Apollo in Sikyon (ALLEN 1983 p. 147).

Official myths:
Official myths stating the divine origin of the king/emperor have also

come down to us. The one concerning Alexanders semidivine birth was closely imitated by the later Hellenistic kings, which inspired Augustus to do the same thing (SIMON 1957 p. 15-29).

Rulercult:
The Hellenistic kings as well as Augustus were worshipped as gods, the main difference being that Augustus was deified after his death in Rome (but worshipped in the East during his lifetime, always together with Dea Roma however) while the Hellenistic kings could be worshipped in life.

The king's/emperor's use of theatrical effects:
One very important similarity between the Eastern kings and the Romans emperors is their use of theatrical effects when appearing in public.

A thorough analysis of the portrait of Alexander, as done by B. Fehr (FEHR 1979 p. 69-84) with reference to the literary sources concerning Alexander's behaviour, shows us an actor rather than a true person. This is not surprising as Alexander was a devoted admirerer of the theatre. He arranged huge theatre festivals, and at banquets he would dress up as Heracles, Hermes, Zeus Ammon or even Artemis (HÖLSCHER 1971 p. 39). Furthermore literary sources tell us that Demetrios Poliorcetes had his hair coloured, used make-up and star embroidered garments when he appeared in public (HÖLSCHER 1971, WALLACE-HADRILL 1982 p. 33-34). Such theatrical behaviour designed to attract as much attention as possible fits very well into the picture of the late Classical and early Hellenistic Greece, where the self-advertisement of artists, politicians etc. in their struggle to win public favour is a well-known phenomenon. (HÖLSCHER 1974 p. 97-8, HARWARD 1982 p. 7-50).

The Roman commanders and emperors acted in very much the same way. Marcus Antonius rode through Alexandria dressed up as Dionysos, Pompeius Magnus drove in an elephant-drawn quadriga thus reminding the audience of Alexander and Dionysos (MICHEL 1967 p. 37, 129); Augustus is known to have used high heels – as had already Persian kings in the 5. cent. B.C. (ALFÖLDI 1970 p. 16, WALLACE-HADRILL 1982 p. 33, 40) – and Caligula, Nero and Commodus entered the amphitheatre disguised as Heracles (PALAGIA 1986).

The use of specific artistic styles to express political messages:
Archaism and classicism was known from the 5. cent B.C. and was much used in the Hellenistic period (WEBSTER 1966 p. 175-79, POLLITT 1986 p. 175-185), but evidence of a political use of old fashioned artistic styles is scant. One case worthy of mention, however, is the archaistic cult statue in the temple of Athena in Pergamon, the style of which has long been interpreted as politically motivated (SCHALLES 1985 p. 13 n. 69). Furthermore, the colossal statue of Athena on the terrace of her temple in Pergamon – if she ever existed – most likely imitated the high Classical style of Athena Promarchos in Athens (SCHALLES 1985 p. 53-6).

The choice for the oldfashioned doric order instead of a ionic for the temple of Athena in Pergamon was probably meant to give the impression of a long history of the cult thereby hightening its prestige (SCHALLES 1985 p. 21).

No doubt Attalos I chose the archaizing (or classicizing) letters for the votive inscription on his stoa in Delphi out of political reasons (SCHALLES 1985 p. 109).

Ever since the expansion of the Roman empire began in the 3. cent. B.C., Greek art objects of all periods had been collected intensively. Nevertheless, as P. Zanker has shown, it was Augustus, who initiated a systematic use of Greek art in his political propaganda for the Principate. Not only did Augustus mainly select pieces of art from the Archaic or Classical period, but he also created an Augustan classicizing style, a true "empire art" (ZANKER 1979b, HANNESTAD 1986 p. 89 for the term "empire art").

In all of these cases summarized above we meet similar means of propaganda in Rome and in the Hellenistic East – when speaking on a formal or primary level.[4] On which socio-cultural levels are these similarities to be understood?

In my opinion we should not attempt to explain the means of Roman propaganda by seeking its roots, but rather analyse its contemporary context and function and thus determine, how it was perceived by the public. To do such an analysis we need to study thoroughly the iconography of the monuments in question in order to define their messages.

---

4. For this term, see note 1.

One and the same monument need not, or rather will never be perceived in the same way by peoples living in separate countries with an independent historical and cultural background, even though they have many characteristics in common.

The late Republican period and the age of Augustus in so many ways constitutes a total break with the early and middle Republic that we cannot possibly equate the intellectual milieu in Rome in these two periods no less than we can equate our modern way of thinking with e.g. the 19. cent.

As mentioned above the Roman nobility had collected Greek art intensively since the 3. cent. B.C. Instruction in Greek art, philosophy and literature belonged to the education of every Roman nobleman, a situation which must have changed people's way of thinking. Nevertheless, it was precisely in the way in which Greek art was received and used, that the "Roman mind" showed its face (ZANKER 1979b). It was this fascination with and snobbishness for the Greek world in the late Republic, which enabled Augustus to create his classicistic "empire" art. All of a sudden classicizing images of the imperial family were distributed en masse: in miniature on coins, on glasspasta vases, cameos – this being a totally new medium probably introduced from the newly conquered Egypt – in colossal sizes in marble, precious metals, on paintings, etc. (ZANKER 1979a). As pointed out earlier in this paper a similar distribution of the Hellenistic ruler-portrait had a long tradition in the East, but certainly not in the West, where C. Caesar was the first person to be allowed to have his image struck on coins (HANNESTAD 1986 p. 27).

Therefore we have to ask ourselves, how a Roman citizen perceived e.g. colossal statues of Augustus or equestrian statues? How would an Eastern Greek citizen perceive them? Since early times in the Eastern Greek world the colossal scale had allusions to the divine sphere, as had e.g. the use of precious metals and the chryselephantine technique. These connotations were very well-known to Alexander and his followers, when they had their images carried out in such sizes and materials. The equestrian statue, originally a religious monument, later became a special monument erected only for men of high rank, who had benefitted a city in one way or another, often as a "soter"/liberator from an enemy, disease or hunger, while in Rome it was used primarily as a victory monument (SIEDENTOPF 1968 p. 20-3). Likewise, when

Sp. Carvilius Maximus placed his image beside the colossal statue of Juppiter on the Capitol made out of the booty taken from the Samnites in 293 or 272 B.C., or when Fabius Maximus placed his equestrian statue beside Lysippos' colossal statue of Heracles brought as booty to Rome from Tarent in 209 B.C., these two Roman commanders did this in order to present themselves as victors rather than to propagate a heroical ancestry, which was the case of Attalos I (see above) (HÖLSCHER 1978 p. 323-4).

Turning to the portrait of Augustus we will meet a similar problem. Augustus and several Hellenistic kings employed elements from the image of Alexander in their portraits. In the Greek world the characteristics of Alexander's portrait alluded to heros and gods, especially Heracles, Helios and Dionysos (HÖLSCHER 1971, FEHR 1979). But in describing Augustus' look Sueton emphasized Augustus' expression of "serenity" (Suet. Aug. 79). Certainly this is a Roman intellectual characterizing Augustus, while a Greek would have noted Augustus' divine looks.

This ambiguity in the message of Augustus seems to me a basic feature of Augustan propaganda. Manifestations of propaganda could be understood in one way in the East, in another in the West, as they appealed to local emotive values. This ambiguity even went so far that different means of propaganda were used in the East and in the West. It is this appeal to local emotive values which in my opinion constitutes the basis in Roman propaganda, and the Romans learned it in the East.

Thus the Ptolemies made use of two strictly different portrait-styles namely the Hellenistic and the Pharaonic, in order to reach both the local Greek and Macedonian elite as well as the native Egyptian population. This "stylistic duality" – as Pollitt calls it – is well documented by portraits of Arsinoe II and Ptolemaius II – Ptolemaius III. The Ptolemies also exhibited family-portraits in order to emphasize that the kingship did not depend on individuals, but on inherited legitimacy appealing to the strong feeling for inherited rulership in the Egyptian people. (KYRIELEIS 1975 p. 146, POLLITT 1986 p. 250-64).

As a ruler cult never gained as strong a foothold in Macedonia as in Egypt, the Macedonian rulers preferred an image, which alluded to the Greek ideal of a strong, heroic man. Demetrios, Philip V and Perseus therefore appear as commanders not as gods. The Seleucids stuck to the single-portrait leaving out the queen in contrast to the Ptolemaic family-representations; their appearance resembles that of the Macedonian kings (KYRIELEIS 1975 p. 146-49, p. 160-4).

In the same way as the image of the Hellenistic kings embodies the spirit of their time, the image of Augustus exemplifies/is the Augustan spirit (HÖLSCHER 1971 p. 39).

Another example of true Hellenistic capability to appeal to local emotive values is the foreign policy of the Attalid king Philetairos. In the hard competition for prestige and acceptance going on among the Hellenistic kings in Greek sanctuaries, Philetairos is noted for his modest behaviour, which was no doubt deliberate (SCHALLES 1985 p. 38-41). Philetairos also had the dedicatory inscription on his monument written in the local dialect thereby addressing himself directly to the local population. Furthermore he equated his victories over the Galatians with the Greek victory over the Persians thereby appealing to the strong national sentiment of the Greeks (SCHALLES 1985 p. 38-42, 53).

Examples which clearly proove that the Romans fully understood the "deeper meaning" of the Hellenistic propaganda, are the many cases of direct Roman reuse of Hellenistic monuments in the late Republic and early Empire. In Athens statues of Attalos and Eumenes had been transscribed into statues of Marcus Antonius; in Milet the consul Ahenobarbus not only reused a plinth for his statue, which originally belonged to a very famous general, Lichas, he even reused the votive-inscription of Lichas. In Athens this same Ahenobarbus had a statue transscribed into a statue representing himself (FELTEN 1985 p. 133). A colossal statue of Augustus was erected on the circular base, which most likely once supported a colossal statue of Athena set up by the Attalids in Pergamon after they had defeated the Galatians (see above). The portrait of Augustus from Sakka, now in Stuttgart, with a diadem has been shown to be a reworked portrait of a Ptolemaic king, and the "head of Attalos I" in Berlin has been reworked into a portrait of Marcus Antonius (FELTEN 1985 p. 135). In the Amphiareion near Oropos a whole series of equestrian statues, originally meant to honour Hellenistic kings, were transcribed to honour Roman commanders (SEIDENTOPF 1968 p. 15), and in Rome C. Caesar placed his own portrait on an equestrian statue of Alexander erected on the Forum Iulium (FELTEN 1987 p. 114).

I think, we should interpret these cases of transcription as a Roman wish to transfer to themselves not only the prestige, fame and achievements connected with the original owners of the monuments, but also to convey their previous emotive values to the public.

In the light of these cases of transcription I consider the equestrian statue in Delphi erected by L. Aemilius Paullus on a high plinth, which was originally meant to carry an equestrian statue of his besieged enemy Perseus a true Roman monument.[5] The definite Greek workmanship of the frieze contrasts with its definite Roman subject (POLLITT 1986 p. 157). I interpret this as a deliberate use of a local art tradition in much the same way as Philetairos had his dedicatory inscription written in a local Greek dialect (see above).

It is within the frame of a deliberate East-West policy that Augustan propaganda should be interpreted. Such a policy is reflected in the portrait-production and -distribution of the later emperors. Thus Hadrian, Antonius Pius and Septimius Severus presented themselves as princepes inter pares in Rome and in the East as Hellenistic kings by adding divine characteristics to their portraits (ZANKER 1983b).

In Rome Augustus is princeps inter pares: he cultivates the virtue "recusatio" by rejecting more honorary titles than he receives (WALLACE-HADRILL 1982 p. 36); he acts according to the much praised ideal "civilis" (WALLACE-HADRILL 1982 p. 43) – to be on equal footing with the citizens – by showing great respect towards the senate and the Roman people; when he comes into power, he – very wisely indeed – is very attentive towards the old traditions thus giving the impression that the Republic continues; he lives on the Palatine as did Romulus and connects his house with the sanctuary of Apollo, but at the same time he is famous for his modest way of living (HANNESTAD 1986 p. 40); he rejects a personal cult; he is careless about his looks (Suet. Aug. 79, HÖLSCHER 1971 p. 39 n. 134).

Turning to the East we meet a different Augustus, an Augustus who would appear as "basileus" in Asia Minor (e.g. the portrait of Augustus from Samos with pronounced Alexander-features (ZANKER 1983b, pl. 29.I)) or as a pharaoh in Egypt (in Egypt Augustus was called "Lord of the Diadems" (ALFÖLDI 1970 p. 265) and he reused a Ptolemaic portrait of a king with a diadem – the Sakka-head (see above); a basalt-statue from Karnak no doubt represents Augustus (STROCKA 1980. For this

---

5. For a different opinion, see HANNESTAD 1986 p. 38.

identification see also MEGOW 1985 p. 480)), an Augustus, who was worsipped as a god (although always together with Dea Roma), who paid exaggerated attention to the most devotedly worshipped king of all kings in the East, the fabled Alexander the Great.

Sanne Houby-Nielsen
Institute of Classical Archaeology
Vandkunsten 5
DK-1467 Copenhagen K

BIBLIOGRAPHY

ALFÖLDI 1970	A. ALFÖLDI, *Die monarchische Repräsentation im römischen Kaiserreiche*, Darmstadt.
ALLEN 1983	R. E. ALLEN, *The Attalid Kingdom. A Constitutional History*, Oxford
CAMP 1986	J. M. CAMP, *The Athenaion Agora. Excavations in the Heart of Classical Athens*, London.
COARELLI 1985	F. COARELLI, *Il Foro Romano. Periodo Republicano e Augusteo*, Rome.
FEHR 1979	B. FEHR, *Bewegungsweisen und Verhaltensideale. Physiognomische Deutungsmöglichkeiten der Bewegungsdarstellungen an griechischen Statuen des 5. und 4. Jhr.. Chr.*, Bad Bramstedt, Germany
FELTEN 1985	F. FELTEN, *Römische Machthaber und hellenistische Herrscher. Berührungen und Umdeutungen*, Öjh 56, Beiblatt, p. 109-154
FRANKE/HIRMER 1964	P. R. FRANKE, M. HIRMER, *Die Griechische Münze*, Munich
GAUER 1968	W. GAUER, *Weihgeschenke aus den Perserkriegen*. IstMitt Beih. 2.
HANNESTAD 1986	N. HANNESTAD, *Roman Art and Imperial Policy*, Aarhus.
HARWARD 1982	V. J. HARWARD, *Greek Domestic Sculpture and the Origins of Private Art Patronage*, Harvard Diss.
HAUSMANN 1957	U. HAUSMANN, *Akropolisscherben und Eurymedonkämpfe*, Charites. Studien zur Altertumswissenschaft. Festschrift für E. Langlotz. Ed.: K. Schauenburg, Bonn.
HERRMANN 1972	H.-V. HERMANN, *Olympia. Heiligtum und Wettkampfstätte*, Munich.
HÖLSCHER 1971	T. HÖLSCHER, *Ideal und Wirklichkeit in den Bildnissen Alexanders des Grossen*, Heidelberg.
HÖLSCHER 1973	T. HÖLSCHER, *Griechische Historienbilder des 5. und 4. Jhs. v. Chr.*, Würzburg.
HÖLSCHER 1974	T. HÖLSCHER, *Die Nike der Messenier und Naupaktier in Olympia. Kunst und Geschichte im späten 5. Jahrhundert v. Chr. JdI* 89, 70-111.
HÖLSCHER 1978	T. HÖLSCHER, *Die Anfänge römischer Repräsentationskunst*, RM 85, 315-357

KYRIELEIS 1975	H. KYRIELEIS, *Bildnisse der Ptolemäer*, Berlin
LAHUSEN 1985	G. LAHUSEN, Zur Funktion und Rezeption des römischen Ahnenbildes, *RM* 92, 261-289.
MEGOW 1985	W. MEGOW, Zu einigen Kameen späthellenistischer und frühaugustäischer Zeit, *JdI* 100, 445-496.
MICHEL 1967	D. MICHEL, *Alexander als Vorbild für Pompeius, Caesar und Marcus Antonius, Collection Latomus*, XCIV, Brussel.
PALAGIA 1986	O. PALAGIA, Imitation of Heracles in Ruler Portraiture. A Survey from Alexander to Maximus Daza, *Boreas* 9, 137-51.
PANOFSKY 1962	E. PANOFSKY, *Studies in Iconology. Humanistic Themes in the Art of the Renaissance*, New York
PAYNE/YOUNG 1936	H. PAYNE, G. M. YOUNG, *Archaic Marble Sculpture from the Acropolis*, London.
POLLITT 1986	J. J. POLLITT, *Art in the Hellenistic Age*, Cambridge.
SCHALLES 1982	H.-J. SCHALLES, Die Hellenistische Umgestaltung der Athener Agora im 2. Jhr. v. Chr. – Ausdruck von Rationalität oder Entpolitisierung? *Hephaistos* 4, 97-117.
SCHALLES 1985	H.-J. SCHALLES, Untersuchungen zur Kulturpolitik der Pergamenischen Herrscher im dritten Jahrhundert vor Christus, *IstForsch* 36.
SCHRADER 1939	H. SCHRADER et al., *Die archaischen Marmorbildwerke der Akropolis*, Mainz.
SIEDENTOPF 1968	B. SIEDENTOPF, *Das hellenistische Reiterdenkmal*, Waldsassen.
SIMON 1957	E. SIMON, *Die Portlandvase*, Mainz.
SMITH 1983	R. R. R. SMITH, *Sculptural Portraits of the Hellenistic Kings ca. 330-30 B.C.*, Oxford.
STROCKA 1980	V. M. STROCKA, Augustus als Pharao, in *Eikones. Festschrift Hans Jucker, AntK* 12. Beiheft.
VERSNEL 1970	H. S. VERSNEL, *Triumphus. An Inquiry into the Origin, Development and Meaning of the Roman Triumph*, Leiden.
WALLACE-HADRILL 1982	A. WALLACE-HADRILL, Civilis Princeps: Between Citizen and King, *JRS* LXXII, 32-49.
WEBSTER 1966	T. B L. WEBSTER *Hellenimus*, Baden-Baden.
ZANKER 1968	P. ZANKER, *Forum Augustum. Das Bildprogram*, Tübingen.
ZANKER 1972	P. ZANKER, *Forum Romanum. Die Neugestaltung durch Augustus*, Tübingen.
ZANKER 1973	P. ZANKER, *Studien zu den Augustus-Porträts I. Der Actium-Typhus*, Göttingen.
ZANKER 1979a	P. ZANKER, *Die Bildnisse des Augustus. Herrscherbild und Politik im kaiserlichen Rom. Sonderausstellung der Glyptothek München Dezember 1978 bis März 1979*, Munich.
ZANKER 1979b	P. ZANKER, Zur Funktion und Bedeutung griechischer Skulptur in der Römerzeit, *Fondation Hardt. Entretiens sur l'antiquité classique* XXV
ZANKER 1983a	P. ZANKER, Der Apollotempel auf dem Palatin. Ausstattung und politische Sinnbezüge nach der Schlacht von Actium, in *Città e Architectura nella Roma Imperiale, ARID Suppl.* X, 21-40.
ZANKER 1983b	P. ZANKER, *Provinzielle Kaiserprotraits. Zur Rezeption der Selbstdarstellung des Princips*, Munich.

EAST SYRIAN ART OF 1ST CENT. B.C.-2ND CENT. A.D.
by GUNHILD PLOUG

ABSTRACT
In this study it is asserted that the early Palmyrene art (late 1st cent. B.C. – late 1st cent. A.D.) amalgates Greek, Achaemenian and western Semitic traits, thus not reflecting contemporary Mesopotamian art, which, according to archaeological evidence, is in Hellenistic tradition. It is also pointed out, that none of the Mesopotamian, i.e. Parthian, sculptures, appearing in a linear style reminding of Palmyrene art, can be dated earlier than 2nd cent. A.D., likewise that true Parthian traits do not show in Palmyrene art before the 2nd cent. A.D.

The aim of this article is to suggest a possible revision of some of the prevailing views on the relationship between the art of eastern Syria and that of Upper- and Lower Mesopotamia in the period 1st cent. B.C.-2nd cent. A.D.

An assessment of a such relationship is somewhat hampered by a lack of contemporaneous remains from the said regions. From two localities in the Syrian desert, Palmyra and Dura Europos, has come down to us an abundance of monuments comprising architecture, sculpture and frescoes, dating 1st cent. B.C.-3rd cent. A.D. In Parthian Hatra in northern Mesopotamia was excavated a number of statues and reliefs dating 2nd-3rd cent. A.D., from nearby Parthian Assur three sculptures: two of 1st cent. B.C., one of 2nd cent. A.D. From the Parthian winter capital Ctesiphon in Lower Mesopotamia no finds are recorded, from Seleucia-on-the-Tigris and from Babylonia only examples of minor arts. Despite the scant material evidence it is generally accepted, that the art of Palmyra and Dura is reflecting the art of Mesopotamian metropoles.

According to I. M. Rostovzeff (1935) the finds from Dura were largely in accord with those from Palmyra, the major arts from the two appeared to him to possess a mutual style. The style he termed Parthian, and he held the finds from Palmyra and Dura to be representative of the extinct art of Mesopotamian Ctesiphon and Seleucia, in his views the originators of the style. In Rostovtzeff's assertion this Parthian style was uniform throughout Mesopotamia and Iran. Its governing principle he considered to be frontality and frontality he finds evident in the Syrian representations from early 1st cent. A.D.

In publishing the finds from Foundation T, a depot from the precinct of the Bel temple in Palmyra, H. Seyrig (1941) supplied fresh material for the discussion on the origin of Palmyrene art. Seyrig's interpretation of the finds supports the views held by Rostovtzeff. The finds derive from a structure, that was demolished owing to rearrangement of the precinct in Flavian times; they comprise fragments of mouldings with various decorative patterns, fragments of friezes with human figures, some of which are depicted en face and also an inscription datable to 44 B.C. Seyrig sums up its evidence thus:

"At the time it became a city, Palmyra was entirely under the ascendance of Lower Mesopotamia. Its policy looked towards Ctesiphon. Its religion was strongly influenced by Babylonian religion. The costume of its wealthier classes copied that of Parthian noblemen or Greek merchants who were to be met with in the Hellenistic colonies on the Tigris. Its artists learned sculpture and architecture from the Graeco-Iranian workshops which developed that peculiar art which we begin to know as having been that of the Parthian empire. Of western influence we perceive nothing: even the Hellenism of Palmyra came from the East" (SEYRIG 1950, 6).

Seyrig is unable to refer the Foundation T finds to Mesopotamian parallels; in Gandharan architecture, however, he observes mouldings that remind him of the above late 1st cent. B.C. fragments:

"... a likely explanation would be that Palmyra and North-west India in those days belonged to a single cultural circle or sphere of influence, the centre of which most probably was in the Graeco-Parthian towns of Lower Mesopotamia" (loc.cit.). The Gandharan material of the comparison according to Seyrig is datable to 2nd cent. A.D.

Seyrig's opinion on the subject met with general accept (INGHOLT 1954, 4) also from D. Schlumberger and according to his works on the Hellenized civilizations of the East (SCHLUMBERGER 1960, 1970). He, and others with him, however fail to agree with Rostovtzeff's , by Seyrig supported, claim to a Parthian origin of the art of Palmyra and Dura. Though they retain the term, "Parthian" is modified by being put in inverted commas; Schlumberger comments:

"... cette appellation ... je la crois bonne, pour peu qu'il soit entendu qu'il ne s'agit point la d'un art dont les Parthes seraient les auteurs, mais seulement de l'art des pays qu'ils sont dominés ou qui ont été soumis à leur influence" (SCHLUMBERGER 1960, 134). In Schlumberger's view "Parthian" does not comprise a uniform style, it was open to influence from local trends. As the place of origin for this "Parthian" art Schlumberger (1970, 151-152) too points to Lower Mesopotamia, presumably with Ctesiphon playing a leading part. Unlike Rostovtzeff, Schlumberger (1970, 196-201) does not regard the introduction of frontality into eastern art as an eastern achievement, but rather as a result of Greek influence on the art of Lower Mesopotamia. This point of view has recently been refuted by M. A. R. Colledge (1976, 126-127), in whose opinion frontality has merged into Mesopotamia and Iran from Semitic Syria.

It should be apparent from the above summary, that to the present writer chronology is of primary importance. For want of contemporaneous comparative material as basis for their theories, the cited authors have made comparisons between monuments in some cases centuries apart, and on such premises professed cultural intercourse between their places of origin. The following is a brief account on such aspects that in my opinion have not enjoyed due consideration in the studies of style (iconographic and artistic) of the art of eastern Syria.

The earliest examples of sculpture pertinent to our views are the Foundation T and associated fragments from Palmyra. An inscription of 44 B.C. indicates a date of mid 1st cent. B.C. for the finds, but only some finds can be that early (SEYRIG 1941, 31-33, SABEH 1953, 17-18 pl. 1.1): the fragments of friezes with worshippers casting incense, *plate 12b*. Seyrig has already pointed to the similarity between the positioning of the worshippers on these early fragments to that of the figures depicted on cylinder seals (SEYRIG 1941, 32-33, figs. 1-2, pl. 1.1). The drapery style of the worshippers likewise depend on ancient Near Eastern traditions: the rendering of the unbroken folds, especially on the himation of the men and on the veils of the women from waist down, is very like that appearing on Achaemenian seals (WISEMAN 1958, Nos. 101, 103, 104). Like all Achaemenian figures some of the Palmyrene worshippers are depicted in profile, others, however, en face. These Palmyrene sculptures and the South Arabian votive steles with frontal busts, the earliest of which date from 1st cent. B.C. (PIRENNE 1960, 329-330, pls. 14.3, 15.4), constitute the first examples of frontality we know of in eastern art. The remaining sculptures (SEYRIG 1941, 33-44, figs. 3-6, 10-11, pls. 1.2-3, 2-3), most of them from Fondation T, are all younger than the earliest fragments. Although not all of the younger fragments are contemporary, they will be referred to as the younger group. In contrast to the older fragments the younger group comprises only frontal figures, the spacing of which is wider than that of the figures on the older fragments. The drapery style displayed by the younger group is similar to that of the older, although less rigid. The narrow, unbroken pleats depicting the tunics of the older fragments likewise characterize the tunics of the younger reliefs, those of the horseriders in particular. Such pleats are also present on South Arabian sculptures: one of late 1st cent. B.C./early 1st cent. A.D. (PIRENNE 1962, 259, pl. 15.11), another dated 5-4th cent. B.C. (CONTENSON 1962, 84 pl. 5). In addition to the Greek dresses the younger fragments include oriental dresses worn by camel- and horseriders: trousers concealed beneath leggings, the latter of Achaemenian origin, and the short Arabic skirt. Further details on the younger fragments – the halo hair style, the large rosettes and the animals – also derive from Achaemenian models, others, however, correspond to the decorative patterns of mouldings framing wall niches, likewise from Foundation T (SEYRIG 1940, 282-297, figs. 3-7, pls. 29-30). Seyrig, saw these mouldings and certain Gandharan mouldings of 2nd cent. A.D. as influenced by the architecture of Lower Mesopotia. E. Will (1975, 177-184), who has recently examined the niches of the Bel temple in Palmyra, does not actually oppose Seyrig's views, but concludes:

"... l'on est ainsi amené à penser que, s'il existait un modèle hellenistique mésopotamien de genre de cadres décorés, il en existait un autre dans la Syrie occidentale dont on placera l'origine à Antioch même" (op.cit. 181) and finally:

"L'origine de ses cadres de niche très décorés reste encore obscure" (op.cit. 182). Thus the subject, which is of such importance to Seyrig's theory, is still open to discussion.

The overwhelming influence Achaemenian art has had on Palmyrene and other Near Eastern art, is due to the fact that the conquering Seleucids and their successors, the Parthians, were recreating the ruined monuments in their original style (WILL 1975, 163 note 6). As late as 1st cent. B.C. therefore art and architecture in Achaemenian style was still in existence. In Palmyra, once part of the Achaemenian empire, a monumental tomb of ancient Mesopotamian style (FELLMANN 1970, 111, 118, 129) demonstrates connections still in the 2nd cent. B.C. with the ancient culture of Mesopotamia, so it is not unnatural that the earliest examples of 1st cent. B.C. Palmyrene sculpture closely reflect

Achaemenian art, *plate* 12b. In fact, as the Palmyrene community seems to have possessed no previous tradition of stone-carving (COLLEDGE 1976, 235), the artists carving the early friezes, copying Achaemenian models, very likely learned the art from Mesopotamian artists. However, the younger group of fragments does not appear as copies of Achaemenian art; in spite of several Achaemenian signs being present in the friezes, the younger fragments have but a distant likeness to Achaemenian art. Generally, importance has not been attached to this difference between the fragments, on the contrary they are usually being looked upon as one entirety: due to the obvious Mesopotamian influence on the older friezes all the fragments are held to mirror "Parthian" art, the assumed origin of which is said to be in Ctesiphon in Lower Mesopotamia (COLLEDGE 1976, 236).

As mentioned earlier, no sculptural remains have come down to us from Ctesiphon. The two Parthian steles from Assur (ANDRAE 1938, 175, pl. 80.b-c), dated 89/88 B.C., are in Hellenistic tradition, as also most of the statuettes from Lower Mesopotamia, excepting some depicted in Late Parthian style, 2-3rd cent. A.D. (e.g. COLLEDGE 1967, pls. 19, 20.b-c). The Mesopotamian material is indeed scant, but if "Parthian" art existed in Lower Mesopotamia already in 1st cent. B.C. and subsequently became the prevailing tradition of the region, we should expect the minor arts to reflect a such tradition. However, a linear character, apparent already in the Palmyrene style of 1st cent. B.C., does not appear in the Mesopotamian material until 2nd quarter of 2nd cent. A.D. and then, as instanced by the third Assur stele (ANDRAE 1938, 175, pl. 8.a) and a Hatra statuette dated A.D. 137, *infra* 136, in the material from Upper Mesopotamia, *infra* 138. More likely, having learned the technique of the craft from Mesopotamian artists, it was the Palmyrene sculptors of late 1st cent. B.C., who combined Greek and Mesopotamian motifs, adding, moreover, elements conditioned by western Semitic tasts, frontality, *infra*, and the prevalence of pleats.

From 1st cent. A.D. Syrian finds have come down to us from Palmyra and Dura. In Palmyra the most significant sculptural remains are the friezes with human figures from the Bel temple, dedicated in A.D. 32 (WILL 1975). Although it is adjusted to Oriental needs the temple design is largely Greek, likewise the decorative patterns. The temple friezes, however, mix western and oriental motifs, just as the friezes of 1st cent.

B.C. The most conspicuous feature in the majority of the figures is the frontality. In many of the figures one foot points more or less forwards, the other turns slightly or strongly sidewards, a few figures, however, have both feet pointing forwards (WILL 1975, pl. 15.l). Colledge (1976, 126-128) emphasizes that the former pose is Greek, the latter Semitic. In his opinion the principle of frontality seems to have arisen due to Semitic needs, the foot pose, however, being Hellenized after the arrival of the principle. The Semitic pose is depicted on certain 1st century reliefs of Palmyra (COLLEDGE 1976, 45-46, pl. 36) and Hauran (*Nabatäer* 1981, pl. 68), but seems to disappear during 1st cent. A.D. As to the frontal figures of the Palmyrene sculptures of 1st cent. B.C., none of their feet remain.

In the friezes of the Bel temple western influence is visible in types of dress and drapery style. The Bel priests (WILL 1975, pl. 42.2) like those on the fragments of 1st cent. B.C., *plate* 12b, are wearing the himation, the Bel priests, however, in a distinct Greek manner: the right arm rests in the sling of the himation and the bunch of folds falling from the left wrist has moved from the centre of the figure to his left side. The western stamp on the drapery style is noticeable in the broken folds of different sizes, imparting irregularity to the drapery. A ceiling relief revealing this stamp is stylistically related to that of a contemporary sculpture from Heliopolis in Northern Syria (SEYRIG 1939; ceiling relief: WILL 1975, pl. 39). The fall of unbroken folds appearing extensively in the temple reliefs indicates, however, that western influence was not prevailing. In the frieze with the Arabic procession, *plate* 13a, the fall of unbroken folds in a skirt-like garment is related to that of the drapery on the fragments of 1st cent. B.C. In fact the stylistics are so closely related, that the drapery style of the younger relief must have developed from that of the older. Likewise the fall of the unbroken, slightly curved folds in the veil covering the upper half of the women on the early fragment must be considered a predecessor of that of the veiled women in the Arabic procession. On the other hand the spectacular fall of folds concealing the heads of the latter women may have had a contemporary model, perhaps the spiral ornaments of the temple merlons, *plate* 13b, in marked contrast to the more natural rendering of the headveil on a fragment of a somewhat later frieze from the Allat temple (*LinzerForsch* 1987 314.37).

Fairly contemporary with the reliefs on the Bel temple are two reliefs found in Dura (PERKINS 1973, 76-79 pls. 30-31). The sculptural evidence from Dura is otherwise scant; the poor quality of the local stone has not encouraged extensive sculptural activities. The two reliefs are fine works, they are not, however, made of local stone, but of a stone supposed to come "from somewhere in the neighbourhood" (PERKINS 1973, 70-71). Judging by the style they were probably carved by Palmyrene sculptors. In fact the true fame of the finds from Dura is solely based on the fresco paintings. The remains of the earliest depict one foot of the colossal, frontal figure of a god, flanked by the preserved lower half of two small worshippers, portrayed in profile and clad in the characteristic Parthian tunics with ornamental borders (CUMONT 1926, 74-76, 140-142, 296-298, pl. 43). Based on epigraphic and genealogical evidence this painting from the Durene Bel temple is dated A.D. 80. In Parthian rock reliefs, Hellenistic and of 1st cent. A.D., profile view dominates, so including the above frontal figure with Greek foot pose in a late 1st century painting, the artist in Dura, which until A.D. 164 was under Parthian rule, must have been inspired by Palmyrene tradition.

The purpose of my comments on the friezes of the Bel temple in Palmyra is to show the continuity of the style of the sculptures from 1st cent. B.C. to that of the temple sculptures, but also to point out that not all new developments of the style were due to foreign influence, some were conditioned by local tastes. Foreign influences seem largely to have derived from Roman Syria. An eastern contribution, however, was the tucked up tunic (*LinzerForsch* 1987, 43.5), a fashion known only in the art of Palmyra and Hellenistic Nemrud Dagh in Commagene, northern neighbour to Syria (COLLEDGE 1967, pl. 30). Otherwise the temple reliefs and other Palmyrene art of 1st cent. A.D. show nothing but Achaemenian and Semitic subjects the hairstyle of Baalshamin being an exception. In a relief from Dura (PERKINS 1973, pl. 30) and a relief of Baalshamin's triad (*LinzerForsch* 1987, 42.4) the hairstyle is that of the Parthian kings as portrayed on their coins (op.cit. 166-167.1-2). Very likely then, it was via the coins that this hairstyle, never adopted by Palmyrene mortals, entered the religious art of Palmyra. As to the art of Parthian Dura in 1st cent. A.D. it seems to have been the recipient of Palmyrene artistic impulses rather than the conveyor of eastern influences onto the art of Palmyra.

The most important finds of the 2nd cent. A.D. from Dura are again the frescoes. From Palmyra it is the funerary sculptures, the busts in particular. The funerary bust is a Roman invention known for sure in Palmyra from mid 1st cent. A.D. Being a most popular type of monument it was also an obvious object of artistic experiments, especially in 2nd cent. A.D. The artists did not only invent new kinds of folds, they also carried on with the older types, applying them, however, differently from what was customary. For instance groups of small semicircular or arrow-head shaped folds appear on 1st century reliefs with full-length figures, usually over the legs in the female tunic (*LinzerForsch* 1987, 315.39); no cases of their presence on busts from that time is observed, but in the 1st half of 2nd cent. A.D. they are characteristic of busts, on these placed on the shoulder or just below (INGHOLT 1928, 26-31, 55-59, pls. 1.3, 2, 10.2-3). In Artaban's funerary monument, *plate* 14a, A.D. 125-150, these folds are present on the shoulders and elsewhere on the sarcophagus sculptures, on the busts above, however, a different arrangement of folds are to be seen. Small semicircular folds from shoulder down are frequently seen on the Hatra sculptures, however, only appearing on statues in Late Parthian style, late 2nd-early 3rd cent. A.D. (HOMES-FREDERICQ 1963, pl. 2.2). Being an earlier sculpture, the statuette of a Hatra princess (COLLEDGE 1967, pl. 53), dated A.D. 137, therefore does not have the small semicircular folds; the style of the statuette displays, however, some likeness to the contemporary style of Artaban and his wife: the large semicircular folds covering chest and abdomen and the arrangement of the lower part of her tunic. These are stylistics already developed within the Palmyrene art of 1st cent. A.D. (*LinzerForsch* 1987, 314.36, 315.39).

As said above Palmyrene art of 1st cent. A.D. was largely unaffected by the contemporaneous art of the East. From about A.D. 125, however, representations of Parthian jewellery and of Parthian tunics and trousers with ornamental borders appear in the funerary sculpture of Palmyra. Very likely it was these 2nd century sculptures Seyrig had in mind when writing that the Palmyrenes copied Parthian noblemens' dresses. However, he made his statement in connection with the sculptures of 1st cent. B.C. and the plain tunics of these early riders reflect nothing but an ordinary, nomadic dress widespread in the Near East long before the opening of our era. It may not be mere coincidence that true Parthian elements are included in the repertoire of Palmyrene artists at a time when at least one Hatra sculpture, exhibits stylistics similar to those of Palmyrene sculpture. It looks as if the relationship between Palmyra and the Parthians, Hatra in particular, was intensified in this period. The remains of frescoes from Dura contribute further to this assumption.

One group of paintings found in the Zeus temple of Dura dates within 1st half of 2nd cent. A.D. (*Dura* 1939, 180-217, PERKINS 1973, 49). Although the paintings are very fragmentary, enough remains to demonstrate that all figures apart from horses and victories were en face, in marked contrast to the figures of the Durene fresco dated about A.D. 80, *supra* 135. Men are wearing Parthian dresses with borders, women exhibit Parthian jewellery. On account of the fragmentary state of the paintings the drapery style cannot be compared with that of contemporary Palmyrene frescoes (COLLEDGE 1976, 84, pl. 114), however, the Durene artists' entire adoption of frontality indicate influence from Palmyra. Another group of frescoes depicts the priest Konon and his family casting incense, *plate* 14b. It was found together with the fresco dated about A.D. 80, in the naos of the Durene Bel temple, a provenience resulting in a date of A.D. 80 for the Konon paintings too (CUMONT 1926, 41-72, 140-142, 296-298, pls. 31-41, HOPKINS 1979, 15-17). The Konon frieze, comprising exclusively frontal figures, has therefore been held to prove that frontality prevailed in Parthian Dura already in 1st cent. A.D. (GALL 1970, 316-317). The early date of the Konon frieze is now disputed by A. Perkins (1973, 40-41). In arguing a date about A.D. 180, she points to the advanced drapery style of the women and to their jewellery, and also suggests a new interpretation of the genealogical evidence. My own studies on Palmyrene drapery style and on jewellery agree with the views of Perkins. For instance the veil of Konon's wife and daughter held well away from the temples by the turban is a feature met with in Palmyrene busts of A.D. 175-220 (INGHOLT 1928, 75-81, pls. 14-15.1) and also appearing in Palmyrene frescoes of A.D. 180-200 (COLLEDGE 1976, 84-87, pls. 116-117). Moreover the figures on the frescoes of Dura and Palmyra look alike in the voluminous dresses and their noticeably long limbs bring to mind the Late Parthian sculptures of Hatra (HOMES-FREDERICQ 1963, pls. 6.1-2, 7.1).

Palmyra, a community which was never part of the Parthian empire, was in my opinion the originator in late 1st cent. B.C. of a style amalgating Greek, Achaemenian and western Semitic elements. There is no indication of a similar style neither in contemporary Mesopotamian material nor in that of the 1st cent. A.D. However, nearby Parthian Dura knew the style from 2nd quarter of 1st cent. A.D. because sculptors from Palmyra worked for Dura. The principle of frontality, always said to be a significant ingredient in "Parthian" art, does not appear in true Durene works until late 1st cent. A.D. when it mixes with profile view in a fresco painting. Frontality is of western Semitic origin and spread via Palmyra to Dura, where it overruled profile view during 2nd cent. A.D. Mesopotamian sculpture in a linear style somewhat similar to that of Palmyra appears for the first time in 2nd quarter of 2nd cent. A.D. and on a locality not far from Dura: Hatra in Upper Mesopotamia. From the same time onwards true Parthian motifs begin to appear in Palmyrene art.

Late in the 2nd cent. A.D. a striking uniformity could be observed in the style of the Durene and Palmyrene frescoes; moreover the late Parthian sculptures, as instanced by the Hatra school and the Iranian monuments, display styles which share certain details with the Palmyrene sculptures of late 2nd and 3rd cent. A.D. Such phenomena may have occurred in connection with new contacts of the East with the Roman world (WHEELER 1965, 564, INGHOLT 1954, 5), which from A.D. 164 also included Dura. Palmyra belonged politically to Roman Syria since the opening of our era. As to the tem "Parthian" applied to the hybrid art of the Middle East it is better abolished, because it includes allusions, which are not in accord with the development of the different regional styles, for instance that of Palmyra.

Peter Bangsvej 133
DK-2000 Frederiksberg

BIBLIOGRAPHY

ANDRAE 1938	W. ANDRAE, *Das wiedererstandene Assur*. Leipzig.
Bilan et perspectives 1976	*Palmyre. Bilan et perspectives.* Colloque de Strasbourg. 18-20. oct. 1973.
COLLEDGE 1967	M. A. R. COLLEDGE, *The Parthians*. London
COLLEDGE 1976	M. A. R. COLLEDGE, *The Art of Palmyra*. London. Bibliography: 305-309.

EAST SYRIAN ART 1ST CENT. B.C. — 2ND CENT. A.D.

Congres classique 1965	8me congres internationale d'archéologie classique. Paris [1963].
CONTENSON 1962	H. de CONTENSON, Les monuments d'art syd-arabe découverts sur le site de Haoulti (Éthiope) en 1959, *Syria* 39, 64-87.
CUMONT 1926	F. CUMONT, *Fouilles de Doura-Europos (1922-1923).* Paris.
Dura 1939	M. I. ROSTOVTZEFF-F. E. BROWN-C. B. WELLES, Dura-Europos. *Preliminary Report of the Seventh and Eight Seasons of work 1933-1934 and 1934-1935.* New Haven.
FELLMANN 1970	R. FELLMANN, *Le sanctuaire de Baalshamin 5. Die Grabanlage.* Rome.
GALL 1970	H. v. GALL, Beobachtungen zum arsakidischen Diadem und zur parthischen Bildkunst, *IstMitt* 20, 299-318.
HOMÈS-FREDERICQ	D. HOMÈS-FREDERICQ, Hatra et ses sculptures parthes. Étude stylistique et iconographique. *Publications de l'institut historique et archéologique de Stamboul.* 15.
HOPKINS 1979	C. HOPKINS, *The Discovery of Dura-Europos.* New Haven and London.
INGHOLT 1928	H. INGHOLT, *Studier over Palmyrensk Skulptur.* Copenhagen.
INGHOLT 1954	H. INGHOLT, Palmyrene and Gandharan Sculpture. *Yale University Art Gallery.* Oct. 14-Nov. 14.
LinzerForsch	*Palmyra, Geschichte, Kunst und Kultur der syrischen Oasenstadt. Linzer archaeologische Forschungen 16.* Linz.
Nabatäer 1981	*Die Nabatäer. Erträge einer Ausstellung im Rheinischen Landesmuseum Bonn.* 24. Mai-9. Juli [1978].
PERKINS 1973	A. PERKINS, *The Art of Dura Europos.* Oxford.
PIRENNE 1960	J. PIRENNE, Notes d'archéologie syd-arabe, *Syria* 37, 326-347.
PIRENNE 1962	J. PIRENNE, Notes d'archéologie syd-arabe, *Syria* 39, 257-262.
PIRENNE 1965	J. PIRENNE, Les phases de l'hellenisation dans l'art syd-arabe. *Congres classique* 1965, 535-540.
ROSTOVTZEFF 1935	M. I. ROSTOVTZEFF, Dura and the Problem of Parthian Art, *YaleClSt* 5, 157-304.
ROSTOVTZEFF 1938	M. I. ROSTOVTZEFF, *Dura-Europos and Its Art.* Oxford.
SABEH 1953	J. SABEH, Sculptures palmyreniennes inédites du Musée de Damas, *AAS* 2, 17-26.
SCHLUMBERGER 1960	D. SCHLUMBERGER, Descendants non-méditerranéens de l'art grec, *Syria* 37, 131-166, 253-318.
SCHLUMBERGER 1970	D. SCHLUMBERGER, *L'orient hellénisé.* Paris.
SEYRIG 1939	H. SEYRIG, Stèle d'un grand-prêtre de Hierapolis, *Syria* 20, 183-188.
SEYRIG 1941	H. SEYRIG, Ornamenta Palmyrena antiquiora, *Syria* 22, 31-44.
SEYRIG 1950	H. SEYRIG, Palmyra and the East, *JRS* 40, 1-7.
WHEELER 1965	M. WHEELER, Gandharan art: A Note on the Present Position, *Congres classique* 1965, 555-565.
WILL 1962	E. WILL, L'art sassanide et ses prédécesseurs, *Syria* 39, 45-63.
WILL 1965	E. WILL, La Syrie romaine entre l'occident gréco-romain et l'orient parthe, *Congres classique* 1965, 511-526.
WILL 1975	H. SEYRIG-R. AMY-E. WILL, *Le temple de Bel. Bibliotheque archéologique et histoire.* 83. Paris.
WISEMANN 1958	D. J. WISEMANN, *Götter und Menschen im Rollsiegel Vestasiens.* Prague.

GRAECO-ROMAN INFLUENCE ON GANDHĀRA SCULPTURE
by BENTE KIILERICH

ABSTRACT
The chronology and origins of Gandhāra art are problematic. Gāndhara sculpture (c. 1st to 5th century A.D.) is Buddhist in content but combines the features of Indian art and various foreign influences.
This study is concerned with the Greek and Roman contribution to Gandhāra sculpture and deals primarily with the problem of tracing a survival of the Hellenistic tradition in Gandhāra sculpture.

Gandhāra, the region around Peshāwar in what is now the Northern part of Pakistan (*fig.* 1) has yielded several thousand sculptures from twenty or more different sites in the ancient province of Gandhāra and the neighbouring territories. But only a small part can be assigned to known sites. Gandhāra sculpture is Buddhist in content and belongs to a particular architectural context. The Buddhist monasteries with their *stūpas* were decorated with statues of Buddha and narrative reliefs showing Buddhist legends. This sculpture was made of the local greyish blue schist or modelled in stucco; originally it was painted and gilded.

The chronology of Gandhāra sculpture is highly problematic. Not one single monument can be dated securely. That the era of the few dated pieces is unknown – Seleucide, Old Śaka, Vikrama, New Śaka, Azes and Moga eras have been proposed – only adds to the confusion (DEYDIER 1950, 223-248). It has not been possible to establish the beginnings of Gandhāra sculpture and the evolution of the style(s) is difficult to establish, being based mainly on stylistic criteria, which are open to debate. It is likely that Gandhāra sculpture may have begun in the 1st century A.D. The invasion of the White Huns or Hephtalites in the 5th century with the destruction of the monasteries probably put an end to the artistic output.

The origins of the eclectic Gandhāra sculpture are obscure. Gandhāran art combined the features of Indian art and foreign influences. This mingling of manyfold influences resulted in an output that lacks homogeneity and it is difficult to speak of a particular Gandhāra style or "school". In Gandhāra sculpture various styles are evident and borrowings from many sources are numerous. Whether variation is due to chronological or local differences is often hard to say. Formally

Gandhāra sculpture is influenced by the art of the West and has therefore been termed "Graeco-Buddhist" or "Romano-Buddhist"; both definitions though are too narrow.

The possible affinities with Syrian Palmyrene art, Parthian art, and for the later Gandhāra sculpture the influence of the Sassanians, and perhaps of Early Christian art fall without the scope of this study, which is concerned with the Greek and Roman contribution to Gandhāra sculpture. The question raised here is, whether it is possible to distinguish between Western inspiration deriving from the Indo-Greek tradition and inspiration deriving from commercial relations with the Roman empire. We shall here deal with the problem of tracing a survival – or revival – of the Hellenistic tradition in Gandhāra sculpture.

A lost Hellenistic tradition?

There is a time gap between the arrival of Alexander in Gandhāra and the emergence of Gandhāra sculpture with a belated florescence of Hellenistic art forms. There may have existed a Hellenistic art in the Indus regions conquered by Alexander in 326 and in the 2nd and part of the 1st centuries B.C. ruled by princes from various Graeco-Bactrian dynasties for longer or shorter periods, but the evidence from this period is meagre save for numismatic finds.

A pictorial tradition in the Indus valley in the late 4th century is hinted at by Quintus Curtius (*Vit. Alex.* 7.14.11), who informs us that a picture of "Heracles" – perhaps Shiva or Krishna? – was carried in front of the army of Porus, as he advanced on Alexander. Philostratus claims (*Vit. Apoll.* 2.20) that Porus after the death of Alexander dedicated in the temple at Taxila bronze tablets on which were engraved the exploits of Porus and Alexander, and the pattern was wrought with orichalcus, silver and gold. He also mentions various golden statues of Alexander erected in the neighbourhood of Taxila (2.24; 2.42). Philostratus is not the most reliable authority, but modern research has proved him right on some points, and there might be a kernel of truth in his stories.

The earliest Indian stone sculpture belongs to the reign of Aśoka (c. 273-236), who started his career as the viceroy of Taxila only fifty years after the arrival of Alexander at a time when the memory of the Greek conqueror must still have been vivid. A Greek contingent were still living at Taxila and one might speculate on the possible existence of a

Fig. 1. Map showing sites in Gandhāra and Bactria. (Drawing Poul Christensen).

Hellenistic artistic *milieu*. Aśoka, himself a quarter Greek, his grandmother being the daughter of Seleucos, included *Yavanas* (Greeks) among his officials. He used the Ionic order in his capital city Pataliputra and some of the ornaments found in Mauryan art such as honeysuckle and acanthus leaf are Greek in origin. One of Aśoka's Buddhist edicts was written in bilingual Greek and Aramaic and he also sent envoys to preach the *Dharma* (the Law of Buddha) in Egypt, Macedonia, Epirus and Cyrene *(13th Major Rock Edict)*.[1]

In Indian epic of the 3rd and 2nd centuries B.C. several words for image or picture are known: *daivatā, pratimā, pratikṛti, mūrti*, and *devatā-pratimā*. It is likely that the images mentioned were made of perishable materials such as clay or wood. Gandhāra was known for its teak-wood, which was an article of export. Some of the Gandhāra reliefs are stylistically close to woodcarving and appear to originate in a woodworking technique. It does not seem unlikely, that there may have existed a pre-Gandhāra sculpture in wood.

Hellenistic tradition in architecture

A Hellenistic tradition in Gandhāra can be followed most easily through architectural details and decorative elements. Common to Gandhāra sculpture is the enclosing of the relief fields within Corinthian columns or pilasters (the enframing columns is a device used also in Palmyrene sculpture). Corinthian capitals of a related type were in use in the 3rd century B.C. in the Hellenistic city Ai Khanum in Bactria.[2] Corinthian capitals were used in Gandhāran architecture of the Śaka-Parthian period in the 1st century B.C. and the 1st century A.D. The shrine of the Double-headed eagle in Sirkap (Taxila) from the 1st century A.D. shows an amalgamation of Indian, Parthian and Greek elements: Corinthian pilasters, triple architrave, modillions, and ashlar masonry belong to the Greek architectural tradition (WOODCOCK 1966, figs. 4-5). The Ionic order following Greek prototypes has been used in the partly Iranian temple at Jandial near Taxila from the Śaka

---

1. WOODCOCK 1966, 47-61; Ionic architecture: ROWLAND 1935; Aśoka columns: BACHHOFER 1929, I, 7-10; inscriptions: BENVENISTE 1964.
2. SCHLUMBERGER 1970, fig. on p. 30; BERNARD 1968. The site of Ai Khanum was discovered in 1964; excavation report by SCHLUMBERGER and BERNARD 1965.

period.[3] In the Gandhāra reliefs Greek mouldings such as bead-and-reel and egg-and-dart are used frequently, and the vine scroll is one of several Hellenistic ornamental motifs.[4]

One might of course claim that these architectural ornaments can be found in architecture and sculpture of the Roman period and that these traits in Gandhāran art are evidence of cultural contact with the Roman world. But the existence of Ionic and Corinthian elements in the local architecture of Taxila prior to the Gandhāra reliefs could indicate the survival of a local Hellenistic tradition; a tradition carried on from the Indo-Greek rulers of the 2nd and 1st centuries B.C. via the Śakas and the philhellenic Parthians into Gandhāra sculpture of the Kushan period.

Missing links in Bactria

The contribution of Bactria in the formation of Gandhāran art was pointed out by J. Hackin (HACKIN 1937), but the importance of Bactria remained uncertain until later excavations disclosed more substantial remains of a monumental Graeco-Iranian art in Bactria.

Gandhāra stucco heads display great variety. Most were made from moulds, but some stucco figures of lesser divinities, demons and donors were modelled freehand. The individualized realism in some of these heads – most of the bodies have perished – are related to the style known from Hellenistic terracottas and derive ultimately from Greek art (*plate* 15a). Most of the stuccos have been found in regions where stone is rare or absent such as Hadda and Taxila. The Hadda stuccos belong to a period between the 1st and the 5th centuries A.D., but the heads found in the apsidal temple of Sirkap (Taxila) are pre-Kushan, belonging to the Parthian phase c. 30-60 A.D. at a time, when the Hellenistic influence apparently was still strong (MARSHALL 1960, figs. 32-39).

In Central Asia stucco was used for a 3rd century B.C. cult statue in Ai Khanum in Bactria. In the Bactrian Khalchayan the walls of a small palace were decorated with painted clay figures in a Graeco-Iranian

---

3. KAHN 1978, fig. on p. 41; MARSHALL 1960, 100-108, pls. XVI-XVII; ROWLAND 1935, 493-496.
4. Mouldings: MARSHALL 1960, fig. 81; vine scroll: MARSHALL 1960, figs. 78, 80.

style. Among the figures are the Greek deities Athena and Nike. These clay figures display stylistic affinities with the stuccos from Taxila (PUGACHENKOVA 1965). If the Khalchayan figures can be dated to the 1st century B.C. – dependent on whether one of the heads is a portrait of the ruler Heraeus and if so, whether Heraeus belongs to this century or later – they provide a possible Graeco-Bactrian forerunner of the Taxila stuccos.

The stone sculpture, too, has its possible forerunners in Bactria. Fragments of musicians from a frieze from a temple at Airtam near Termez by the Oxus river belong to the 1st century B.C.-1st century A.D. (ROWLAND 1970, 47, 49-50; fig. 19). The style is close to some Gandhāra reliefs, and gold jewellery of the type worn by the Airtam figures have been found at Taxila. In the frieze busts are growing from acanthus leaves. At Chamquala near Surkh Kotal in the Qunduz valley have been found figural capitals of a Hellenistic type, dating perhaps to the 1st century B.C. (DAGENS 1964, pl. XXIV, I; ROWLAND 1970, 226, fig. 10). Related types of capitals with a small Buddha in the centre are known from Gandhāra (FOUCHER 1905, 235, fig. 112; MARSHALL 1960, fig. 147).

Though the examples of Graeco-Bactrian art known to date are not numerous, and though there appears to be some uncertainty concerning Bactrian chronology, it is nevertheless possible to point to a certain affinity between Bactria and Gandhāra, with certain Bactrian sculptures forming a missing link between the late Hellenistic and the Gandhāra sculpture.

The Kushans

Gandhāra sculpture flourish during the Scyto-Iranian Kushans c. 2nd and 3rd centuries A.D. Their vast empire reached from the Oxus in Afghanistan to the Ganges in India. One of the centres of the empire was at Gandhāra, the winter capital being settled near Peshāwar.

The adoption of Buddhism by the Kushans was an important factor in the development of Gandhāran art. Buddhism had been introduced to Gandhāra by Aśoka and some Greek kings, notably Menander (c. 155-130 B.C.), known from the *Milindapanha* or *Questions of Menander,* also showed an interest in Buddhism (WOODCOCK 1966, 94-114; RHYS DAVIDS 1890). The Kushan king Kanishka was a patron of the Buddhist faith for political as much as religious reasons, and the syncretic nature of Kushan religion still left amble room for representation of Greek and Iranian gods.

Unfortunately the chronology of Kanishka is very uncertain. His accession has been placed in A.D. 78, A.D. 110-115, A.D. 128, A.D. 144 and A.D. 232.[5] This question is far from settled, and I should prefer to go no further than assuming a 2nd century A.D. date for Kanishka.

Though Kanishka adopted the Buddhist faith, he built a temple of fire on the summit of Surkh Kotal in Bactria. Fragments of stone sculpture, dynastic portraits of the royal princes wearing their national trousered garments are Iranian in style, but Greek elements can be found in Corinthian pilasters, Greek architectural mouldings and fragments of painted stucco figures, which were placed in niches within the peribolos wall. These stucco figures belong stylistically to a Hellenistic convention (SCHLUMBERGER 1975; ROSENFIELD 1967, 154-163).

Not without interest are various inscriptions in Kharosthi using the Greek alphabet. Mentioned in one inscription is a certain Palamedes, probably the name of a Greek architect (CURIEL 1954). Gandhāran and Kushan art – and it is perhaps wise to make a distinction between the Buddhist art of Gandhāra under the Kushans and the dynastic Kushan art known from Surkh Kotal and Mathurā in India – like most ancient art are mostly anonymous, but yet another name of an artist could perhaps be Greek. A bronze reliquiary in the shape of a pyxis from a *stūpa* near Peshāwar, bearing the name of Kanishka (I, II or III?), is inscribed as the work of the slave Agesilas (Agisala) (ROSENFIELD 1967, fig. 60; KONOW 1929, 136).

The Buddha image

One of Kanishka's coins has a standing Buddha on the reverse with the legend BODDO in Greek (*fig.* 2). The coin depicts a statue of the Gandhāra type.

In the beginning the Buddha was aniconic, represented through symbols such as his footprints or empty throne. But for a religion that wanted to spread to regions, where the old religions had pictures of

---

5. For a summary of the discussion see ROSENFIELD 1967, 253-258; for a c. 232-260 A.D. date of Kanishka's reign see GÖBL 1984.

their gods, it was necessary to portray the object of worship in human form. The origin of the Buddha image is controversial.[6] The Buddha is represented either as a standing or a seated draped figure. It is likely that the anthropomorphic Buddha image was created in Gandhāra (perhaps almost simultaneously at Mathurā?), the question is, when it happened.

The freestanding Gandhāra Buddha of the type depicted on the Kushan coin does not seem to represent a formative, early stage; it seems to belong to a more advanced and already stereotyped phase. The existence of more primitive images of the standing Buddha therefore seems probable. The Buddha cult image in the round, standing or seated, probably preceded the representation of Buddha in narrative art. A group of early reliefs from Butkara with a seated Buddha (*plate 15b*) are dated on excavational evidence between the late 1st century B.C. and the early 1st century A.D. (FACCENNA 1974, 174). Therefore, one can assume the existence of seated cult images of Buddha around the late 1st century B.C. It is not unlikely that the seated Buddha type antecedes the standing Buddha.

Contact with the Western world presumably influenced the iconography to a certain extent. But the seated position must be of Indian origin: it is the position of the Indian *yogi.* (*plate* 15c). The dress is neither a Greek *himation,* nor a Roman *toga,* but the Indian monk's cloak, *sanghāti.* In the formal treatment of the drapery a Western influence is often apparent, as it is in the Classical regular facial features and the treatment of the hair. The religious texts are of importance to the image. The 32 signs of Buddha's predestination are described in the Indian texts; in the iconography two of these, the *ushnisha,* the cranial protuberance or top knot, and the *urna,* the circle of hair between the eyebrows, are shown. The *ushnisha* sometimes looks a little like a Greek *krobylos,* and in this version the hairstyle might be inspired by Greek deities, chiefly Apollo. A few Buddhas have the snailshell curls, a detail adopted from either Parthian or Bactrian art, deriving ultimately from Achamenian and Assyrian traditions.

The Buddha image was conventional, and it did not change much, as

---

6. LOHUIZEN-de LEEUW 1981; PLAESCHKE 1974, 68-101; DEYDIER 1950, 46-60, summary of discussion with earlier bibliography.

Fig. 2. Gold coin of Kanishka: Buddha with inscription in Greek letters. British Museum, London. (Drawing B.K.).

the same formulas were repeated over and over again. The idea of an anthropomorphic representation and some of the iconographic traits were determined by contact with the West.

Roman influence

The Roman influence in the art of Gandhāra cannot be denied. During the Kushans diplomatic and commercial relations with the Roman empire were frequent. Motifs may be absorbed from anywhere, and it is sometimes difficult to tell, whether a certain motif is derived from one source or another. Take the garland-bearing putti. This motif is well known from for example Hadrianic and Antonine sarcophagi, but it can be found also in the Graeco-Bactrian art of Khalchayan from the 1st century B.C.-1st century A.D. and it might have entered into Gandhāran art without Roman intrusion.

The Roman component is perhaps primarily found in the minor arts? The motifs on the so-called toilet-trays have their parallels in Roman art (BUCHTHAL 1945, figs. 1-16). Some of these are made of the local schist stone, others perhaps imported from Alexandria. The mythical subjects, Dionysian, erotic and others, are used in Gandhāra strictly as genre. The function and character of this private art is quite different from the official Buddhist art.

Gandhāra sculpture has not been romanized and it hardly deserves to be called a provincial Roman sculpture. The parts of the Roman empire with which Gandhāra during Kushan reign had contact were primarily old Hellenistic centres like Alexandria and cities in Syria. In the earliest Buddhist art of Gandhāra the Indian, the Hellenistic Greek and the Iranian elements are the main ingredients.

Gudenåvej 5
DK-2720 Vanløse

BIBLIOGRAPHY

AHRENS 1961	A. AHRENS, *Die römischen Grundlagen der Gandhāra Kunst.* Münster.
BACHHOFER 1929	L. BACHHOFER, *Frühindische Plastik.* Munich.
BARTOUX 1930	J. BARTOUX, *Les Fouilles de Hadda.* Paris.
BENVENISTE 1964	E. BENVENISTE, Edits d'Asoka en traduction grecque, *JA* 1964, 137-157.
BERNARD 1968	P. BERNARD, Chapiteaux corinthiens hellénistiques d'Asie centrale decouverts à Ai Khanoum, *Syria* 45, 111-151.
BUCHTAHL 1945	H. BUCHTAHL, The Western Aspects of Gandhāra Sculpture, *Proceedings of the British Academy* 31.
Central Asia I-II	*Central Asia in the Kushan Period I*, 1974, *II*, 1975 (*Proceedings of the Internat. Congress of the History, Archaeology and Culture of Central Asia in the Kushan Period*, 1968). Moscow.
COOMARASWAMY 1927	A. K. COOMARASWAMY, *History of Indian and Indonisian Art.* New Delhi.
CURIEL 1954	R. CURIEL, Inscriptions de Surkh Kotal, *JA* 1954, 189-205, esp. 194-197.
DAGENS 1964	J. DAGENS e.a., *Monuments préislamiques d'Afghanistan*, MDAFA XIX.
DEYDIER 1950	H. DEYDIER, *Contribution à l'etude de l'art du Gandhāra. Essai de bibliographie analytique et critique des ouvrages parus de 1922 à 1950.* Paris.
FACCENNA 1974	D. FACCENNA, Excavations of the Italian Archaeological Mission in Pakistan: Some Problems of Gandhāran Art and Architecture, in *Central Asia I*, 126-176.
FOUCHER 1905-51	A. FOUCHER, *L'art greco-bouddhique du Gandhāra, I-IV.* Paris.
GÖBL 1984	R. GÖBL, *Münzprägung des Kushanreiches.* Vienna.
HACKIN 1937	J. HACKIN, *L'art bouddhique de la Bactriane et les origines de l'art greco-bouddhique* (*Bull. Archeol. publié par la section historique de l'Académie Afghane*, fasc. 1).

HALLADE 1968	M. HALLADE, *The Gandhāra Style and the evolution of Buddhist Art*. London.
INGHOLT 1957	H. INGHOLT, I. LYONS, *Gandhāran Art in Pakistan*. New York.
KHAN c. 1978	A. N. KHAN, *Buddhist Art and Architecture in Pakistan*. Islamabad.
KONOW 1929	S. KONOW, *Corpus Inscriptionum Indicarum*, vol. II, part I, *Kharosthi Inscriptions*. Calcutta.
LOHUIZEN-de LEEUW 1981	J. E. van LOHUIZEN-de LEEUW, New Evidence with regard to the Origin of the Buddha Image, in H. HÄRTEL, ed., *South Asian Archaeology 1979*. (Papers of the 5th Internat. Conf. Assoc. South Asian Archaeologists ... Museum für Indische Kunst, Berlin). Berlin (1981).
MARSHALL 1951	J. H. MARSHALL, *Taxila*. 3. vols. Cambridge.
MARSHALL 1960	J. H. MARSHALL, *The Buddhist Art of Gandhāra*. Cambridge.
NARAIN 1957	A. K. NARAIN, *The Indo-Greeks*. Oxford.
PLAESCHKE 1974	H. PLAESCHKE, Buddhistische Kunst. Vienna.
PUGACHENKOVA 1965	G. A. PUGACHENKOVA, La sculpture de Khaltschajan, *IrAnt* 5, 116-127.
PUGACHENKOVA 1982	*Iskusstvo Gandhāri*, Moscow.
RHYS DAVIDS 1890	T. W. RHYS DAVIDS, *Sacred Books of the East*, vols. XXXV-XXXVI. Oxford 1890-1894.
ROSENFIELD 1967	J. ROSENFIELD, *The Dynastic Arts of the Kushans*. Berkeley and Los Angeles.
ROWLAND 1935	B. ROWLAND, Notes on a Ionic architecture in the East, *AJA* 39, 489-496.
ROWLAND 1942	B. ROWLAND, Gandhāra and Late Antique Art: The Buddha-image, *AJA* 46, 223-236.
ROWLAND 1945	B. ROWLAND, Gandhāra and Early Christian Art: Buddha Pallatius, *AJA* 49, 445-448.
ROWLAND 1960	B. ROWLAND, *Gandhāra sculpture from Pakistan museums*. New York.
ROWLAND 1970	B. ROWLAND, *Zentralasien*. Baden-Baden.
SCHLUMBERGER 1961	D. SCHLUMBERGER, Art Parthe, Art Greco-bouddhique, Art Greco-romain, *Atti 7th congr. archeol. class*. Ankara, III, 9-16.
SCHLUMBERGER 1965	D. SCHLUMBERGER & P. BERNARD, Ai Khanoum, *BCH* 86, 590-657.
SCHLUMBERGER 1970	D. SCHLUMBERGER, *Der hellenisierte Orient*. Baden-Baden.
SCHLUMBERGER 1975	Sur la nature des temples de Surkh Kotal, in *Central Asia II*, 97-102.
SOPER 1951	A. SOPER, The Roman Style in Gandhāra, *AJA* 55, 310-319.
WOODCOCK 1966	G. WOODCOCK, *The Greeks in India*. London.

WESTERN FEATURES IN THE KUSHAN COINAGE
by ANNE KROMANN

After the death of Alexander the Great the province of Bactria was part of the Seleucid kingdom until c. 250 B.C., when it became independent under Diodot. In their days of glory the Bactrian kings (*plate* 16.1)[1] ruled an area including the present Afghanistan and part of Pakistan. But in the course of the second century B.C. the kingdom was split up between local Greek petty kings and various tribes from Central Asia. The coinage was still Greek (*plate* 16.2) but with bilingual inscriptions in Greek and Indian.

Among the invading tribes were the *Sakas*, the *Pahlevas* and the so-called *Yuëh-chih*. According to Chinese sources[2] the Kabul area was occupied by five Yuëh-chih tribes, and there is a possibility that one of their leaders, Kujula Kadphises, formed a sort of joint rule with the last Greek king Hermaeus, since there exists an issue inscribed with the names of both (*plate* 16.3). Another explanation may be that part of Hermaeus' coinage was posthumous and still current in Kabul on Kadphises' arrival.[3] Kadphises also had another issue with an Augustus-like portrait on the obverse and an Indian clad male figure seated on a sort of Roman sella curulis on the reverse (*plate* 16.4) (MACDOWALL 1960, 144).

Vima Kadphises
Some time after the reign of Kujula Kadphises the five Yuëh-chih tribes were united under the *Kushan* tribe, and among the earliest kings was Vima Kadphises.[4] He extended the empire at least as fas as Mathura on

---

1. For a more detailed description of types and legends of the illustrated coins please use the references.
2. On Chinese sources and their translations cf. ROSENFIELD 1967 ch. I note 12 and GÖBL 1984, 7, note 1.
3. Hermaeus probably reigned in the beginning of the first century A.D. but his dates are uncertain. Cf. GÖBL 1978, 101-102 with bibliography.
4. Cf. GÖBL 1984, 61 with note 108. As it appears from the coins Vima must be the nearest predecessor of Kanishka (232-260) cf. note 17 and 18. Owing to a Chinese source Göbl dates the termination of Vimas reign to 230 and implies an interregnum of two years. His date of accession is uncertain – as are those of his predecessors. Göbl puts him after the aenigmatic Soter Megas and counts on an accession date of c. 166, which seems a bit early, even if is true that Vima had a longaevous father.

the Ganges river and started a regular coinage in bronze and gold.

Vima himself appeared on the obverses in various attitudes – e.g. standing (*plate* 16.7), driving a triumphal biga (*plate* 16.5), seated cross-legged on a cushion (*plate* 16.6) or emerging from a wall of rocks (*plate* 16.8). He is a typical eastern potentate with a long, wildgrowing beard, boots, trousers and caftan. On his head are various forms of hat-like crowns or helmets. But in spite of the king's oriental appearance there is still a Greek inscription on the obverse. The reverse type is the god Siva standing either alone or together with a humped bull (*plate* 16.5-8). The same Siva figure is used again by later Kushan kings, here with the legend Oesho, another name of Siva (ROSENFIELD 1967, 72). The humped bull has its prototypes in Indo-Greek coinage, and the Saka king Maues issued a rare coin with a standing male figure, which may have given inspiration to the Kushan Siva (ROSENFIELD 1967, 125 with n. 14).

Kanishka and Huvishka

Vima's successors continued the coinage after similar principles, but soon the bilingual inscriptions were replaced by Bactrian legends written in Greek characters (GÖBL 1984, 61 with n. 2. CHI 1983, 1031 with n. 20. CHATTOPADHYAY 1967, 216). The obverse portraits were confined to a few main types, but the variants were numerous especially under Huvishka, and there was quite an explosion of new reverse types representing deities from the Graeco-Roman, Indian and Iranian pantheons (*plate* 16.9-11, 17.12-15). Few of them can be recognized in the sculpture, presumably because most of the religious sculpture in the empire was Buddhistic, whereas the Iranian deities were dominating on the coins. What really was the religion of Kanishka and his successors is somewhat enigmatical. The coin types indicate some form of Mazdaism, but there are other signs hinting that the kings were sympathetic to Buddhism too (ROSENFIELD 1967, 72. CHI 1983, 204) – in fact one of the earliest Buddha images appears on a coin of Kanishka (GÖBL 1984, pl. VIII, 66). All in all there can be no doubt that many different religious influences were prevailing in the Kushan realm.

The later Kushans

After the multitude of types[5] in the coinage of Kanishka I and Huvish-

---

5. But even if the costum of transforming coins into jewellery and of hoarding metal is very old as suggested by Lloyd, there is no reason to believe that the procedure was more widespread in North India than in South India.

ka there was a drastic anticlimax under the later Kushans, where the enthroned Ardoxsho – goddess of Abundance – and Siva with the bull were the only reverse motives in a still deteriorating style (*plate 17.16-17*). After Vasudeva I, the successor of Huvishka, the empire seems to have been harrassed by inner conflicts which led to attacks from without and eventually the north-western part was occupied by the Sasanian king Shapur II (309-79) (GÖBL 1984, 75-77). The Sasanian conquerors issued coins for local use and the fact that this coinage is closely related to the last issues of the Kushan king Vasishka (GÖBL 1984, 77-86) is one of the pillars for the establishment of a new chronology of the Kushan kings.

The chronology of the Kushan kings
"The date of Kanishka" i.e. the problem of the Kushan era has occupied the minds of scholars for years and formed the subject of several conferences. No less than 150 dated inscriptions are extant from the Kushan period (ROSENFIELD 1967, 263-73). The dates allude to an era beginning with the accession of Kanishka I, but as the year of that event was unknown, the dates hitherto have been of no use except for establishing an internal chronology of the kings. And even that was difficult, because the Kushans seemed to have more than one era, and some of the kings who according to other criteria were supposed to be the latest, apparently had early dates in the inscriptions. But recently the Dutch scholar Louise van Lohuizen de Leeuw (GÖBL 1984, 58 with n. 96) has proved that there is not more than one Kushan era, which, however, had the peculiarity that it never went beyond a hundred but started over again whenever it reached the end of a century with the consequence that some incidents dated e.g. year 22 in fact took place in 122.

Apart from the inscriptions Chinese historical texts appear to be the only written sources we have got on the Kushans. And it is not always easy to percieve which kings the texts are alluding to, because the names are quite unrecognizable in Chinese. For these reasons it has been very difficult to find the exact date of Kanishka I, and the theories have fluctuated between 78 A.D. and 238 A.D. (ROSENFIELD 1967, 253-62). But now the problem seems to have found its solution thanks to the Austrian numismatist Robert Göbl, who has succeeded in establishing the evolution of the Kushan and the Kushano-Sasanian coinages by means of modern numismatic methods including die comparison combined with the study of typology, style and organization of the coinage (GÖBL 1984, 78-79). To fix the date of Kanishka Göbl starts with the Sasanian occupation which marked the end of the Kushan king Vasishka's reign. According to the dated inscriptions the six kings from Kanishka I to Vasishka between them reigned ca. 120-128 years. Thus, if the Sasanian occupation occured c. 337 A.D., Kanishka ought to have come into power c. 229-37 A.D. (GÖBL 1984, 78-79). This theory is further supported by a ninth century bilingual inscription from Tochi in Afghanistan, from which it appears that there must have existed a Bactrian era starting in 232 A.D. (HUMBACH 1960, 127. GÖBL 1984, 89). The result of Göbl's work is the following list of kings:

Vima Kadphises	166-230
Kanishka I	232-260
Huvishka	260-292
Vasudeva I	292-312?
Vasudeva II	312?-c. 332/50
Kanishka II	332-350
Vasishka	350-360.

Even if the new date of Kanishka has not – or not yet – been accepted by all, it seems extremely convincing, and it must have consequenses for our views on the relations between Roman and Kushan coinage.

At the Kanishka conference in London 1960, when Robert Göbl had not yet worked through the immense corpus of Kushan and Kushano-Sasanian coins, be believed in a Kanishka date of c. 114 A.D. and saw a parallel of Kushan types with contemporary or somewhat earlier Roman prototypes – thus Vima was corresponding to Trajan, Kanishka to Hadrian and Huvishka to Antonius Pius. He ascribed the phenomenon either to Alexandrian artisans working at the Kushan mints and bringing pattern books from which to choose the coin types, or to a more direct influence from the Roman aurei which were brought into Kushan India by trade (GÖBL 1960, 103-13). Today, when Göbl himself has moved the date of Kanishka almost a hundred years forward, he finds that many features of the Kushan coinage have parallels in the Roman coinage of the third century – and actually many coin types from the first and second century were reused in the third century – (cf. *plate* 17.18-19), but he also thinks that the basis of the Kushan gold coinage

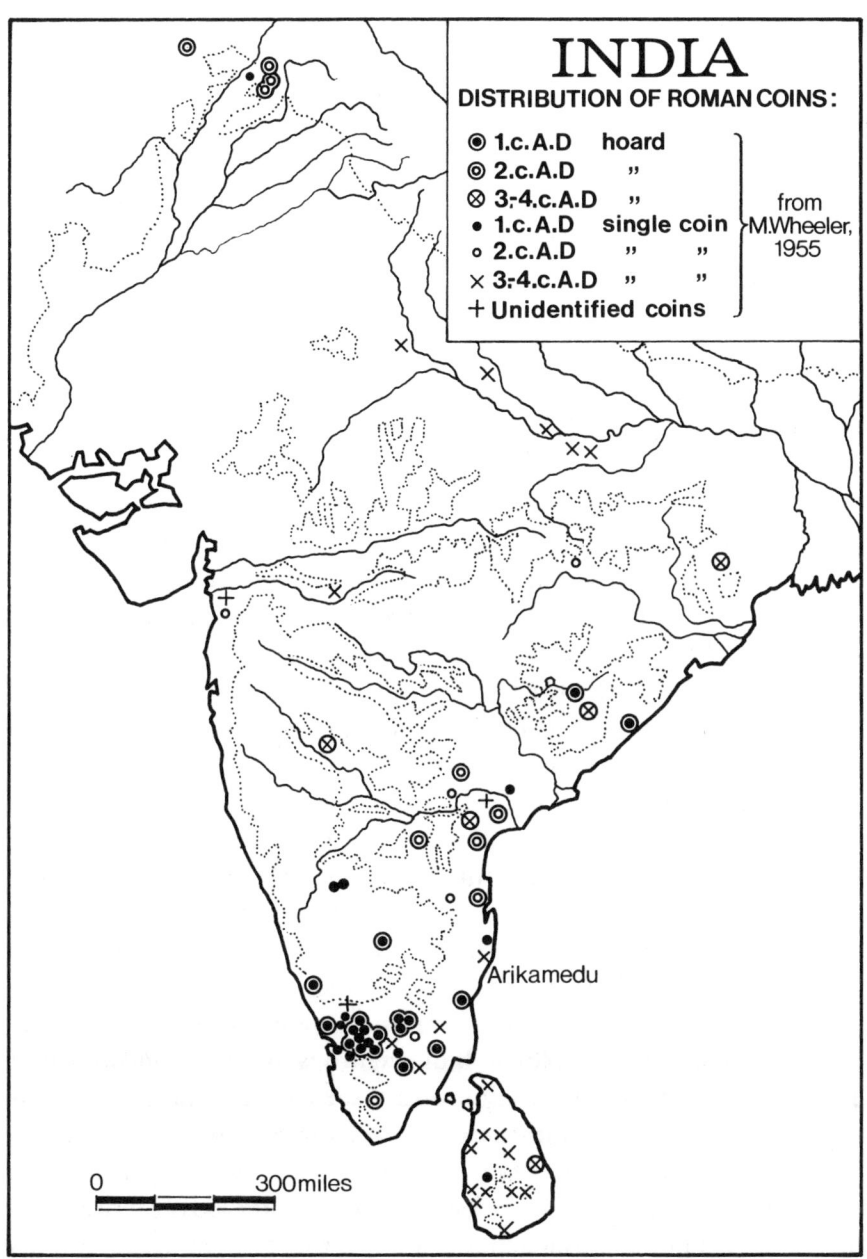

was great masses of Roman aurei, which Vima met, as he invaded India.

Rome and India

The connection between Rome and India is certified by several written sources mentioning embassies or trade routes and marvelling at the millions of sesterii which were spent on Indian luxuries by the Roman upper class (GÖBL 1984, 58-59) in the first and second centuries A.D. The statements of the sources were confirmed by thousands of gold and silver coins, of which the great majority was found in the area south of Coimbatore in Madras. Less numerous and somewhat later hoards were dug up further north along the Coromandel coast (ADHYA 1966, 130-31), but in the old Kushan domain Roman coin finds are restricted to a few second century aurei deposited in Buddhist stupas and some coins from the third to fourth century found around the river Ganges (WHEELER 1965, 141-48. ADHYA 1966, 132-36).

Robert Göbls theory that Vima and his sucessors caused this scarcity by using the imported aurei as raw material for their own coins, is shared by other scholars, also because it otherwise has been difficult to explain, from where the Kushans got their gold reserves (GÖBL 1984, 59 n. 99. ADHYA 1966, 180 n. 7). But if it is true that North India in the first to second century A.D. partook in the gold import in the same scale as South India, it is indeed strange that so few coins are exstant (GÖBL 1984, 59. LLOYD 1936, 427-38).[5] One might have expected that at least some hoards had found their way into the earth, before Vima started his extensive melting down scheme. Besides it can hardly be doubted that the major part of the Roman trade was concentrated to the south, which owned most of the commodities favoured by the western world, and where e.g. the beryl mines of Coimbatore were situated (ADHYA 1966, 135). In North India which was little endowed with articles of luxury and much afflicted by warfare, the trade is likely to have been less prolific and the import of foreign coins consequently smaller. If however Vimas coins quite evidently were influenced by early Roman aurei, we should have to consider the possibility that he had met them in India. But actually it is not so. His flamboyant obverse portraits with their attributes of divine and saecular power are closer to the aurei from the third century than to the earlier ones (cf. *plate* 16.5 and *plate* 17.19). And as Göbl points out (GÖBL 1984, pl. 74,12), Vima quite obviously, imitates Caracalla, when he issues gold coins in three denominations.⁶ As to his reverse types they are hardly Roman at all but rather following Graeco-Bactrian and Saka traditions – e.g. the standing Siva, the humped bull and the cross legged king (ROSENFIELD 1967, 125, pl. XIV, 27). The same is not true of his successors Kanishka and Huvishka, whose multitude of reverse types incessantly put the gods and allegories of Roman coins in mind (cf. *plate* 17.20-25). In spite of their varying identity and attitude the gods on the Kushan coins have rather a uniform appearance, which is more in accordance with the stagnation of Roman coin types in the third century than with the freshness and ingenuity of the first and second; but we cannot deny that some of their prototypes only occur on the earlier Roman coins (*plate* 17.15 and 25).

In my opinion there was no constant stream of Roman coins into the areas north of Ganges before the Kushan period, but as Roman coins seem to have found their way all over the antique world in larger or smaller quantities, they are not likely to have been totally absent from the Kushan domain. Thus having created an empire which might compare to the Roman, Vima set out to create a corresponding coinage⁷ inspired by the Roman but still owing much in style and types to the local coinage. The question of the Kushan gold reserves is not part of this contribution, but G. L. Adhya's theory of a Kushan gold supply from Ural through Oxus (ADHYA 1966, 180) seems not improbable – at least Vima may have used that source for a start. The Roman coin finds from North India are not very numerous, even if the later periods are better represented than the earlier ones. And we cannot tell for certain, if there was ever any regular import to the Kushan impire. The Roman influence on the Kushan coinage may have come from relatively few aurei. On the other hand, there may also have been favourable conditions for an import. The establishment of the Kushan empire was followed by a fairly long period of peace involving diplomatic and commercial connections with other peoples. Thus the import of Roman coins – new as well as older – to the Kushan domain may have been

---

6. For a survey of the Roman prototypes cf. GÖBL 1984, 46-48 and plates 173-76.
7. The weight of the Kushan gold coins is somewhat higher than that of the aureus in the third century, but the two coin sorts were probably not meant to circulate together. Thus ADHYA 1966, 185 may be right in suggesting that the weight of Vima's gold coins depended on the relation of value between gold and silver current under the Kushan regime.

considerably increased after Vima and caused a stronger Roman influence on the coin types of Kanishka I and Huvishka. It is possible that these coins were melted down to make new Kushan issues, but there seems to be no reason for implying lots of Roman aurei in North India before Vimas arrival.

The National Museum of Denmark
The Royal Collection of Coins and Medals
Frederiksholms Kanal 12
DK-1220 Copenhagen K

BIBLIOGRAPHY

ADHYA 1966	G. L. ADHYA, *Early Indian Coinage*, London.
BM	British Museum
BMC	*Catalogue of Indian Coins in the British Museum*, London 1896.
CHATTOPADHYAY 1967	B. CHATTOPADHYAY, *The Age of the Kushanas*, Calcutta.
CHI 1983	*The Cambridge History of Iran*, vol. 3, Cambridge.
Cop.	The Royal Collection of Coins and Medals, Danish National Museum, Copenhagen.
GÖBL 1960	R. GÖBL, Numismatic Evidence Relating to the date of Kanishka, *Kanishka Papers*, 1968, 103-13.
GÖBL 1978	R. GÖBL, *Antike Numismatik*, München.
GÖBL 1984	R. GÖBL, *Münzprägung des Kushanreiches*, Wien.
HUMBACH 1960	H. HUMBACH, The Kanishka Inscription from Surkh Kotal discovered by Dr. Maricqo, *Kanishka Papers* 1968.
Kanishka Papers	Papers on the Date of Kanishka 1960, (ed. A. L. Basham), Leiden 1968.
LLOYD 1936	A. H. LLOYD, Hoarding of Precious Metal in India, *Transactions of the International Numismatic Congress*, London 1938.
MACDOWALL 1960	D. MACDOWALL, Numismatic Evidence for the Date of Kanishka, *Kanishka Papers*, 134-49.
MITCHINER 1975	M. MITCHINER *Indo-Greek and Indo-Scytian Coinage*, London, vol. 3.
RIC	*The Roman Imperial Coinage*, vol. I, II, IV.1, IV.2 and V.2. London 1923-33.
ROSENFIELD 1967	J. M. ROSENFIELD, *The Dynastic arts of the Kushans*, Berkeley and Los Angeles.
SNG	*Sylloge Nummorum Graecorum*, Copenhagen, vol. 39 1965.
WHEELER 1965	M. WHEELER, *Der Fernhandel des Römischen Reiches in Europa, Afrika und Asien*, München-Wien. (A translation of *Rome beyond the Imperial Frontiers*, London 1955).

MONS CLAUDIANUS
ROMAN GRANITE-QUARRY AND STATION ON THE ROAD TO THE RED SEA
by ADAM BÜLOW-JACOBSEN

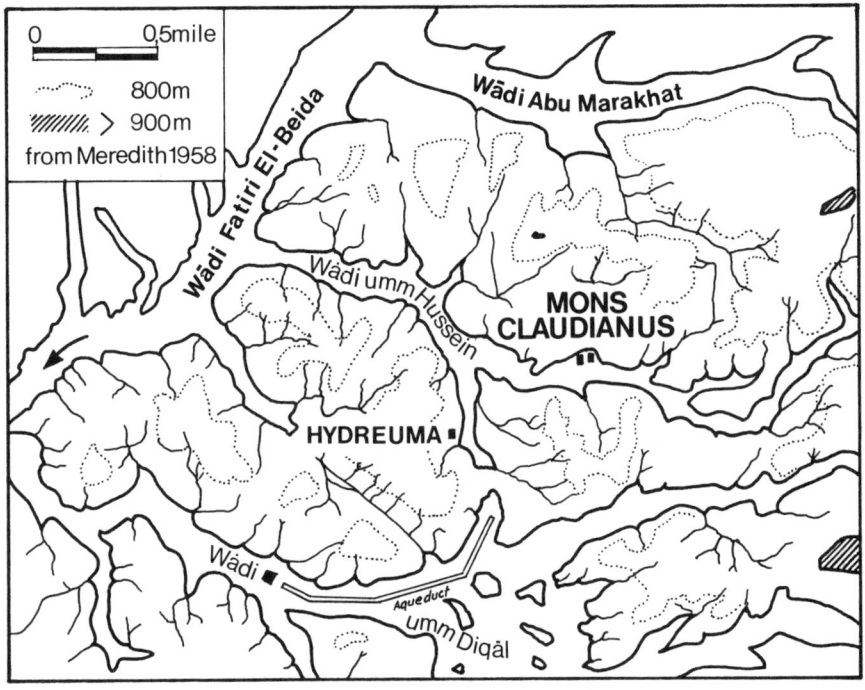

Fig. 1. Plan of the whole complex normally referred to as 'Mons Claudianus'. (Drawn by Poul Christensen. From MERIDITH 1958, 8).

It is well known that the Roman trade-route to Arabia and India went via Egypt: From Alexandria one sailed down the Nile to 'The Qena-Bend' whence a system of roads led to the harbours on The Red Sea, Myos Hormos, Philoteras, Leukos Limen and Berenice.[1] Besides the

---

1. See most recently SIDEBOTHAM, 1986. The roads have been studied MEREDITH, 1952 and 1953.

long-distance trading, this system of roads, which is largely intact today with its walled stations and wells that are now dry, also served the various quarries in the Eastern Desert. Since the Pharaonic period emeralds had been quarried at Σμάραγδος ὄρος near Berenice. The Romans quarried the 'Imperial' porphyry at Mons Porphyrites and granite at Mons Claudianus (FITZLER 1910).

By 'Mons Claudianus' one commonly understands the whole complex of buildings in the area of Wadi Fatirah as seen on *fig.* 1. It is situated in the mountains of the Eastern Desert, at an altitude of 6-700 m, 62 km from the town of Safaga on the Red Sea coast and ca. 140 km from Qena in the Nile valley.

It was to this place that I had a chance to go in February 1983 in the company of Guy Wagner (IFAO, Cairo) and Wilfried Van Rengen (VUB, Brussels). The short visit was an extraordinary experience for all three of us and we immediately began to think in terms of an excavation of the site, although we all considered such plans totally unrealistic, because of finance and logistis, not least the question of water supply. The area is now quite dry except for a beduin-well in the neighbourhood, so water for a team of escavators and workers would have to be brought from the nearest pipeline.

Although the site was untouched by archaeologists at that time, it was not unknown. The extraordinary state of preservation and, perhaps, the sheer beauty of the place, has always attracted travellers and has, even more important, been the object of two surveys by members of the German Archaeological Institute in Cairo.[2] Only the difficult access had so far protected Mons Claudianus from illicit excavation. But by the time I was first there, access had become much easier, since a modern military road had been opened to the public.

But, unrealistic or no, the plans for an excavation came to fruition in February 1987. Guy Wagner was unfortunately not able to participate, but his successor at the Institut français d'archéologie orientale in Cairo, Hélène Cuvigny, was eager to join the project and the IFAO

---

2. A complete list of all the travellers from the 19th and 20th century who have visited and written about Mons Claudianus would be long. The earliest testimony known to me is WILKINSON 1832. The most important research are the reports of two short expeditions undertaken from the German Archaeological Institute in Cairo: KRAUS & RÖDER 1962 and KRAUS, RÖDER & MÜLLER-WIENER 1967.

kindly undertook all the practical arrangements. The team was an international one[3] and it would be fair to say that the composition of the team was somewhat heavy in papyrologists and epigraphists. In fact, since the three British archaeologists, Thompson, Peacock and Maxfield, were only present on the site for a short period, there was only one archaeologist, Bodil Mortensen, who took part in the whole season. But as it happened, the amount of written material found fully justified the number of philologists. Just this first season yielded the largest single find of Greek ostraca ever to come from Egypt!

The excavation was begun at two different places in the mound of refuse immediately south of the walled camp (see *fig.* 2, *plate* 18). This was chosen because it is known that clandestine excavations have been carried out there by tourists and we feared that the mound was in danger of being seriously disturbed. But what we had thought would be just a question of digging away a quantity of earth while securing the finds, turned out to be more complicated. In both trenches we very soon reached unsuspected walls of houses inside the mound (see *fig.* 3). The function of these houses is not yet understood, but it is certain that they represent an older stage in the building history of MC than was hitherto known to exist. It is still debatable whether the refuse found in and around the houses stems from the time when they were still in use or from the subsequent period when the derelict houses were filled with refuse from the camp.

The written ostraca are mostly undated, but the few dated ones all belong to the years 10-14 of Trajan's reign, i.e. A.D. 106-111. We already knew that the quarries were in use at this period.[4] Apart from

---

3. The International Committee consists of J. Bingen, Fondation Egyptologique Reine Elisabeth, Brussels, F. H. Thompson, Society of Antiquaries of London, H. Cuvigny and myself. The field director during the first campaign was J. Bingen and the rest of the team consisted of W. Van Rengen, Brussels, W. E. H. Cockle, London, D. P. S. Peacock, Southampton, and V. Macfield, Exeter. Two Danes apart from myself were able to participate: B. Mortensen and L. Rubinstein, both Copenhagen.

The funding was equally international: Money was provided by a grant to the IFAO from the French petrol-company ELF Aquitaine, from various Belgian sources, from the Foundation of Queen Margrethe and Prins Henrik, and from the Danish Research Council in Humanities. Further, General Motors Denmark placed at the disposal of the first campaign an ISUZU Trooper 4x4 Turbo Diesel.

4. The epigraphic evidence all points to the reign of Trajan during whose reign the temple was built. A single Greek papyrus, P. Oxy. 3243 from A.D. 214/15, mentions the quarry and also provides the latest dated reference to it, (CALDERINI, s.v. *Clavdianvs Mons*.)

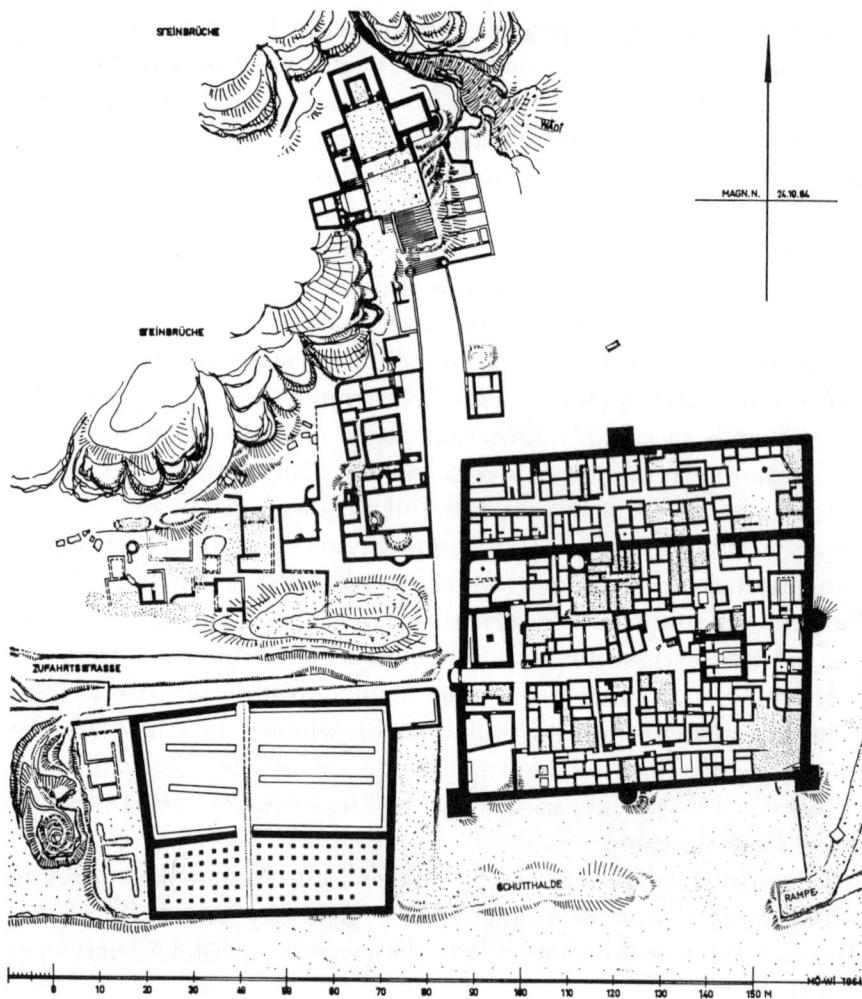

Fig. 2. The central camp with temple, exterior houses, stables and store-rooms. South of the square, fortified camp and marked 'Schutthalde' is the area in which excavation was begun in '87. (From KRAUS, RÖDER & MÜLLER-WIENER 1967, 115).

the written evidence our knowledge of the chronology of the camp and quarries stems from two sources: The architectural evidence of the fort and the evidence of use of the granite in dated buildings elsewhere. Both aspects are treated by the German team in *MDIK* 18 and 22. The fort shows an addition to the north which must be from the third or fourth century A.D. The granite is found in the Domus Aurea of Domitian, the forum of Trajan, in the Pantheon (Hadrian) and in the thermae of Caracalla. It is also found in the thermae of Diocletian and in his palace in Split. Whether the quarry functioned continously from Domitian to Diocletian, we do not yet know. It is quite possible to believe that it was opened only during periods of high building activity when the quarries at Assuan were not able to deliver enough granite. Future finds of Greek ostraca will hopefully enlighten us at this point.

Two types of finds were especially important: the ceramics and the Greek ostraca. The pottery was mostly coarse-ware from the Nile-valley which may prove of great interest, not least because of its well-dated context. It is hoped that it may form the basis of a highly desirable typology of Roman pottery from Egypt, but the work on the pottery is still at a very preliminary stage.

The Greek (and a few Latin) ostraca are, of course, far from ready for publication, but it will be attempted to publish them as soon as possible.[5] Ca. 900 were found during this season. Among them are private and official letters and small notices. Much of the material of course deals with supplies, whether of water, food or tools. Lists of names are plentiful and it is evident that the area was administrated by the Roman army.

So far there has been no evidence found of prisoners working in the quarries though one would have thought that Mons Claudianus, in spite of its natural beauty, would have been as nasty a place for *condemnatio ad metallas* as any, perhaps with the exception of the near-by Mons Porphyrites which is known to have been used as a penal camp at a later time.[6]

The mound has so far yielded little for archaeological treasure-hunters. The reason is easy to find in the fact that everything in the mound was thrown away in antiquity, mostly because it was broken. Apart from the coarse-ware, already mentioned, there were a fair number of oil-lamps, some press-moulded figurines, broken glass of high quality, sherds of fine-ware, some of it decorated, and a good deal of leather, some of it looking like body-armour. Not much iron was found – some

---

5. A few that were in private collections have already been published: PRÉAUX, 1951, GILLIAM, 1953, CUVIGNY-WAGNER, 1986, CUVIGNY, 1986, HANDLEY, 1987.
6. On this kind of punishment, see MILLAR, 1984 (esp. 137-43).

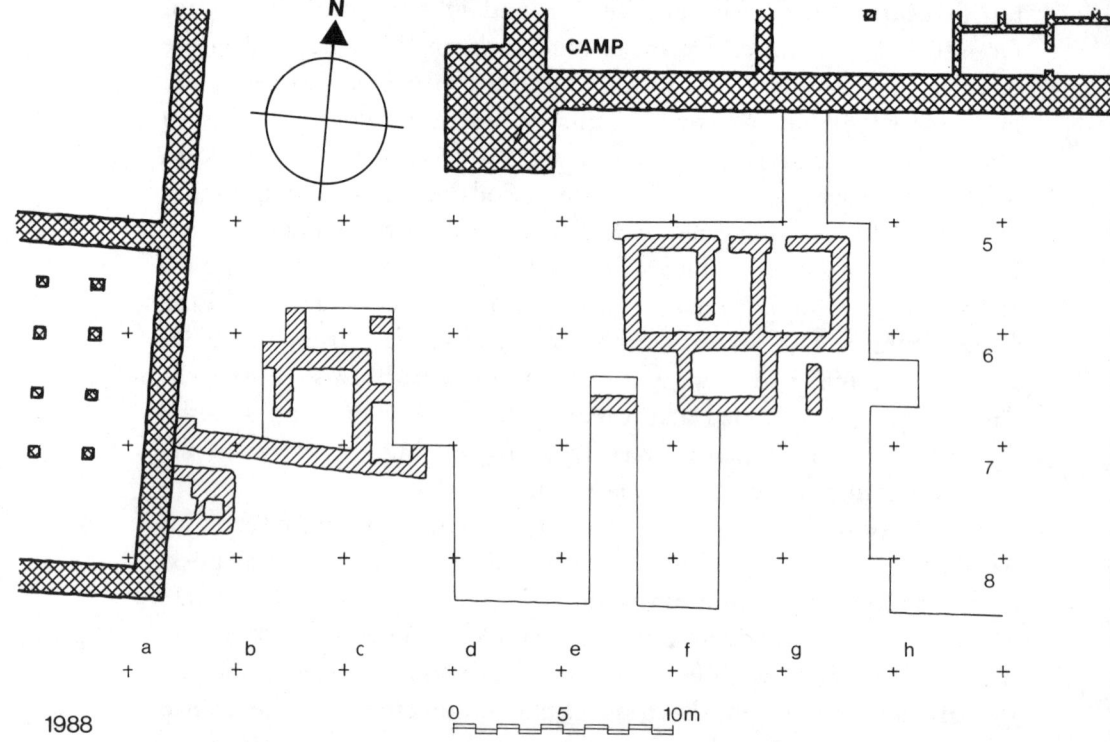

Fig. 3. Detailed plan of the trenches of the '88 campaign. The wall of the store-room (drawn in heavy black) to the west of trench I is built on the surface of the mound.

nails and a single, broken wedge of the many that must have been used in the quarry. The reasons for this scarcity are undoubtedly that iron was re-forged and that the conditions in the mound are unfavourable to iron. Bronze is represented by some fragments of fibulae, and some decorated pendants.

Other finds are awaiting study by specialists. A great deal of cloth, mostly wool, looks promising from a preliminary survey and a considerable quantity of bones (fish and mammal), date stones and even carbonized loaves of bread will undoubtedly give us much information about the ancient conditions of life in this remote and inhospitable place.

University of Copenhagen
Institute of Classical Philology
Njalsgade 94
DK-2300 Copenhagen S

BIBLIOGRAPHY

CALDERINI	A. CALDERINI, Dizionario dei nomi geografici e topografici dell' Egitto greco-romano. (Cairo) Milano, 1935-
CUVIGNY 1986	H. CUVIGNY, Nouveaux ostraca grecs du Mons Claudianus. *ChrEg* 61, fasc. 122, 271-276.
CUVIGNY & WAGNER 1986	H. CUVIGNY & G. WAGNER, Ostraca grecs du Mons Claudianus. *ZPE* 62, 63-73.
FITZLER 1910	K. FITZLER, *Steinbrüche und Bergwerke im ptolemäischen und römischen Ägypten.* Leipzig.
GILLIAM 1953	F. GILLIAM, The Ostracon from Mons Claudianus. *ChrEg* 28 fasc. 55, 144-146.
HANDLEY 1987	E. HANDLEY, O. Mons Claudianus 13, (*ZPE* 62, 71ff.) *ZPE* 68.
KRAUS & RÖDER 1962	Th. KRAUS & J. RÖDER, Mons Claudianus. Bericht über eine erste Erkennungsfahrt im März 1961, *MDIK* 18, 80-120.
KRAUS, RÖDER & MÜLLER-WIENER 1967	Th. KRAUS, J. RÖDER & W. MÜLLER-WIENER, Mons Claudianus – Mons Porphyrites. Bericht über die zweite Forschungsreise 1964, *MDIK* 22, 108-205.
MEREDITH 1952	D. MEREDITH, Roman Remains in the Eastern Desert of Egypt. *JEA* 38, 94-111.
MEREDITH 1953	D. MEREDITH, Roman Remains in the Eastern Desert of Egypt. *JEA* 39, 95-106.
MEREDITH 1958	*Tabula Imperii Romani, Sheet N.G. 36: Coptos.* Compiled by David Meredith. (Society of Antiquaries of London).
MILLAR 1984	Fergus MILLAR, Condemnation to Hard Labour in the Roman Empire. *BSR* 52, 124-147.
PRÉAUX 1951	Cl. PRÉAUX, Un ostracon grec du Mons Claudianus. *ChrEg* 26 fasc. 52, 354-363.
SIDEBOTHAM 1986	Steven E. SIDEBOTHAM, *Roman Economic Policy in the Erythra Thalassa.* Leiden.
WILKINSON 1832	J. G. Wilkinson, Notes on Part of the Eastern Desert of Upper Egypt. *Journal of the Royal Geographical Society.* Vol. 2. 53-57 concern Mons Claudianus.

ABBREVIATIONS

AA	Archäologischer Anzeiger
AAS	Annales archéologiques arabes syriennes
ActaArch	Acta Archeologica
AJA	American Journal of Archaeology
Africa	Africa. Institut national d'Archéologie et d'Art, Tunis.
ARID	Analecta Romana Instituti Danici
ANRW	Aufstieg und Niedergang der Römischen Welt
AntAfr	Antiquités africaines
AntK	Antike Kunst
ArchCl	Archeologia classica
AttiMGrecia	Atti e memorie della Società Magna Grecia
AW	Antike Welt
BCH	Bulletin de correspondance hellénique
Boreas	Boreas. Münstersche Beiträge zur Archäologie
BSA	The Annual of the British School at Athens
BSR	Papers of the British School at Rome
ChrEg	Chronique d'Égypte
DdA	Dialoghi di Archeologia
DenkschriftenWien	Österreichische Akademie der Wissenschaften. Philos.-Hist. Klasse. Denkschriften.
Expedition	Expedition. Bulletin of the University Museum of the University of Pennsylvania
HamBeitrA	Hamburger Beiträge zur Archaeologie
Hephaistos	Hephaistos. Kritische Zeitschrift zur Theorie und Praxis der Archäeologie und angrenzender Wissenschaften.
HUCA	Hebrew Union College Annual
IrAnt	Iranica Antiqua
Iraq	Iraq, published by the British School of Archaeology in Iraq.
IsrExplJ	Israel Exploration Journal
IstForsch	Istanbuler Forschungen
IstMitt	Istanbuler Mitteilungen
JA	Journal Asiatique
JANES	Journal of the Ancient Near Eastern Society of Columbia University
JARCE	Journal of the American Research Center in Egypt
JbzMusMainz	Jahrbuch des Römisch-Germanischen Zentralmuseums, Mainz
JdI	Jahrbuch des Deutschen Archäologischen Instituts
JEA	The Journal of Egyptian Archaeology
JHS	The Journal of Hellenic Studies
JNES	Journal of Near Eastern Studies
JRS	The Journal of Roman Studies
JSemSt	Journal of Semitic Studies
Karthago	Karthago. Revue d'archéologie africaine
Klio	Klio. Beiträge zur alten Geschichte
Kokalos	Κώκαλος. Studi pubblicati dall'Istituto di storia antica dell'Università di Palermo.
Latomus	Latomus. Revue d'études latines.
MAAR	Memoirs of the American Academy in Rome
MBeiträge	Madrider Beiträge

MDAFA	*Memoirs de la Delegation Archéologique Française en Afghanistan*
MDIK	*Mitteilungen des Deutschen Archäologischen Instituts, Abteilung Kairo*
MEFRA	*Mélanges de l'Ecole française de Rome. Antiquité*
MIO	*Mitteilungen des Instituts für Orientforschung*
MM	*Madrider Mitteilungen*
Muséon	*Le Muséon. Revue d'études orientales*
MusHelv	*Museum Helveticum*
MusTusc	*Museum Tusculanum*
MVAG	*Mitteilungen der Vorderasiatisch-aegyptischen Gesellschaft*
OA	*Oriens antiquus*
Öjh	*Jahreshefte des Österreichischen archäologischen Institutes in Wien*
OLP	*Orientalia Lovaniensia Periodica*
OpAth	*Opuscula Atheniensia*
OPUS	*OPUS. Rivista internazionale per la storia economica e sociale dell'antichità.*
OR	*Orientalia. Commentarii periodici Pontificii Instituti Biblici*
ProcPrHistSoc	*Proceedings of the Prehistoric Society*
PP	*La parola del passato*
QuadAEI	*Quaderni del centro di studio per l'archeologia etrusco-italica*
RA	*Revue archéologique*
RDAC	*Report of the Department of Antiquities, Cyprus*
REPPAL	*REPPAL (Tunis)*
RM	*Römische Mitteilungen*
RStFen	*Rivista di studi fenici*
SIMA	*Studies in Mediterranean Archeology*
StEtr	*Studi Etruschi*
SvInstSkrifter	*Svenska Institut i Rom. Skrifter (Opuscula Archaeologica)*
Syria	*Syria. Revue d'art oriental et d'archéologie*
WürzJbAltWiss	*Würzburger Jahrbücher für Altertumswissenschaft*
YaleClSt	*Yale Classical Studies*
ZA	*Zeitschrift für Assyriologie und vorderasiatische Archäeologie*
ZDPV	*Zeitschrift des Deutschen Palästina-Vereins*
ZPE	*Zeitschrift für Papyrologie und Epigraphik.*